PROTECTING MULTICULTURALISM

Protecting Multiculturalism

Muslims, Security, and Integration in Canada

JOHN S. McCOY

McGill-Queen's University Press

Montreal & Kingston • London • Chicago

© McGill-Queen's University Press 2018

ISBN 978-0-7735-5278-4 (cloth)
ISBN 978-0-7735-5279-1 (paper)
ISBN 978-0-7735-5416-0 (ePDF)
ISBN 978-0-7735-5417-7 (ePUB)

Legal deposit second quarter 2018
Bibliothèque nationale du Québec

Printed in Canada on acid-free paper that is 100% ancient forest free
(100% post-consumer recycled), processed chlorine free

Funded by the Financé par le   Canada   Canada Council   Conseil des arts
Government   gouvernement   for the Arts   du Canada
of Canada   du Canada

We acknowledge the support of the Canada Council for the Arts, which
last year invested $153 million to bring the arts to Canadians throughout
the country. Nous remercions le Conseil des arts du Canada de son soutien.
L'an dernier, le Conseil a investi 153 millions de dollars pour mettre de l'art
dans la vie des Canadiennes et des Canadiens de tout le pays.

Library and Archives Canada Cataloguing in Publication

McCoy, John S., 1976–, author
Protecting multiculturalism: Muslims, security, and integration
in Canada / John S. McCoy.

Includes bibliographical references and index.
Issued in print and electronic formats.
ISBN 978-0-7735-5278-4 (cloth). – ISBN 978-0-7735-5279-1 (paper). –
ISBN 978-0-7735-5416-0 (ePDF). – ISBN 978-0-7735-5417-7 (ePUB)

1. Multiculturalism – Canada. 2. Muslims – Cultural assimilation –
Canada. 3. Racism – Canada. 4. Social integration – Canada.
5. National security – Canada. 6. Canada – Race relations. I. Title.

FC105.M8M42 2018   305.6'970971   C2018-900501-7
                                             C2018-900502-5

This book was typeset by Marquis Interscript in 10.5/13 Sabon.

For my parents, Jane and David McCoy

Contents

Tables

Acknowledgments

The genesis of the book, in many ways, can be found in my first days as a graduate student and my thesis on social integration in Western Europe. I would, therefore, like to express my gratitude to my first supervisor, Gavin Cameron, and the faculty members at the Centre for Military, Security and Strategic Studies in Calgary, for it was in this early work that I first started exploring ideas and policies related to security and social identity.

If I trace the genesis of this book back even further, I can say that my interest in security and cultural relations is deeply rooted in my childhood and the time I spent in the birthplace of my parents: Northern Ireland. Growing up, in a way, in two worlds, in Canada and in the towns that my grandparents called home during the time of "the Troubles," taught me about how security for some often comes at the expense of others. In the summers of my childhood and youth spent in Ireland, I witnessed the ever-present shadow of the violent clashes of centuries past: obsessively remembered, annually and publicly celebrated by the right-wing unionists of the Orange Order, and bitterly deplored and denounced by the nationalists for whom the marching, banner waving, and drum banging remain a constant thorn in the flesh. History, poverty, and social identity were woven together to shape contemporary social relations in ways that created what was seemingly an irreconcilable conflict. In the late sixties, when the conflict in Northern Ireland began, Canada became a sanctuary for my parents, and so it remains today for many fleeing conflict, including many Canadian Muslims.

As a PhD candidate and now adjunct professor at the University of Alberta, I have been fortunate to develop a series of rewarding professional and personal relationships. First and foremost I have enjoyed a long friendship with my mentor and supervisor, Dr W. Andy Knight. I am eternally grateful for his guidance over the past years, his thoughtful comments on early chapters and drafts, and his meaningful support through the tough times.

I am thankful to the interdisciplinary partners with whom I have been involved during my doctoral research and academic work. In particular, Dr Anna Kirova has had a long-standing and resonant impact on my work and understanding of the experience of immigrants in Canada. Dr Bruce White, professor of cultural anthropology at Doshisha University and director of the Organization for Intra-Cultural Development, has been a long-time research partner and friend who, through his anthropological work, has helped me to better understand how social identities are constructed, both within and between communities.

Finally, I must also acknowledge the longest standing academic influence in my life, my mother, Jane McCoy: teacher and copy editor extraordinaire. This work simply would not have been possible if it had not been for her support and guidance.

PROTECTING MULTICULTURALISM

1

Introduction

The worldwide hegemony of Orientalism and all it stands for can now be challenged, if we can benefit properly from the general twentieth-century rise to political and historical awareness of so many of the earth's peoples.

Edward Said, 1979, *Orientalism*

Western Europe is being invaded again, this time through demographic warfare (mass Muslim immigration in combination with high Muslim birth-rates). The forces of Islam are flooding the European gates once more, the only difference – the gates are open. Aided and abetted by the cultural Marxist/multiculturalist elites of Western Europe ... The time for armed resistance has come.

Anders Breivik, 2011, "2083: A European Declaration of Independence"

This is a book about how Canadian multiculturalism and Canadian Muslims have fared in our highly securitized contemporary climate. It is a book about a form of institutionalized racism or "xenoracism" that, as its name suggests, targets those who are perceived as foreigners – most especially Muslims. Xenoracism today can be measured in the kind of demagoguery we see among the re-emboldened far right in Europe, the politicking of Donald Trump, and the failed 2015 re-election bid of former prime minister Stephen Harper. Xenoracism is intertwined with the seemingly endless global War on Terror and its attendant national security practices that have become deeply institutionalized in the years since the world-altering events of 11 September 2001. The fear of "Islamic terrorism" that the War on Terror has generated has helped to stimulate public concerns over visible diversity and immigration in Western societies and undermined support for multiculturalism.

Yet, with hope and optimism, this book argues that Canada, despite
its demonstrable susceptibility to xenoracism and anti-Islamic sentiment in some quarters, remains a viable multicultural state where
Canadian society is largely supportive of immigration and cultural
diversity and aware of the benefits they bring. Despite the experience
of a sizeable minority of Canadian Muslims with discrimination and
prejudice, these diverse communities exhibit resilience and a strong
sense of belonging to the Canadian state, thereby demonstrating a
high level of social integration. On the basis of this optimistic assessment, Canada, compared with other Western states from Australia to
Sweden, is an outlier that has maintained its multicultural appeal,
even if that appeal is somewhat tarnished after nearly a decade of
divisive governance under Stephen Harper's Conservatives and a
decade and a half of post-9/11 security.

Yet it would be naive not to recognize that Canada's unique multicultural success story is in jeopardy – that much was plainly evident
in the 2015 federal election campaign – even if the election heralded
the return of the party that introduced official multiculturalism to
Canada and elected as prime minister the eldest son of the man who
championed it. The fragility of public support for immigration and
multiculturalism is plainly evident in the vitriol we see around the
debate in the courts over the wearing of the niqab during citizenship
ceremonies and the debate over the admission of Syrian refugees. It
is manifested in the rhetoric of fringe Conservative politicians like
Kellie Leitch and in the comments expressed in social media posts.

It is also of no surprise, in a globalized world of hyper-connectivity
between peoples, information, and ideas, that Canada is not immune
to the ideologies that are undermining our collective security – those
of both the global militant Islamism of groups like al-Qaeda and
Daesh and their neo-conservative and neo-fascist dance partners.
Fears over radicalism and extremism in the Muslim community have
led to sometimes targeted national security practices resulting in differential treatment of Canadians on the basis of religious and ethnic
identity. This can undermine ideas of equity and equality that are
fundamental to multiculturalism. Furthermore, those same fears have
driven the growth of political and social movements that are vehe-
mently opposed to the presence of Muslims in the West.

Some of these issues have been explored elsewhere. There is a long
list of scholarly assessments of Canadian multiculturalism,[1] several
of which touch on the issue of religious identity and accommodation.

For example, Jack Jedwab's (2014) excellent edited volume on "the multicultural question" represents one of the more notable attempts. There is also at least one scholarly work, by Baljit Nagra (2011), that has focused on the experience of Canadian Muslims in the multicultural framework. What is unique about the present book is its focus on the impacts of security and integration policy on religious minorities and multiculturalism. Building on my established work and interests in security studies, the book strives to provide much-needed elucidation of how security practices are impacting Canadian Muslims and multiculturalism. Further, the book imports some of the theoretical and conceptual approaches that have been used in the European context to examine multiculturalism and its perceived failures – to explore how these concepts and ideas apply (or not) to the Canadian case.

Today, Muslims are exposed to xenoracism at the societal and state level. At the societal level, there is a growing social movement that is fixated on the perceived threat posed by multiculturalism and Muslims. This "anti-Islamic social movement" has grown in power in recent years. It is stimulating, and is stimulated by, the rise of the far right, and somewhat paradoxically, given its focus on the issue of "Islamic terrorism," it is generating its own brand of militancy. Indeed, it is argued here that a good starting point for the analysis to come, a good starting point for understanding contemporary xenoracism and opposition to multiculturalism, is gaining a better understanding of the more militant manifestations of the anti-Islamic social movement.

THE ANTI-ISLAMIC SOCIAL MOVEMENT
AND THE CRISIS OF MULTICULTURALISM

When the far-right terrorist Anders Breivik killed seventy-seven of his fellow country-women and men in two acts of terrorism in 2011, he did so in the fervent belief that he was protecting Europe from an invasion, a nefarious plot hatched by Islamists working with "multiculturalists" and "cultural Marxists" to establish "Eurabia" and "Islamize" Europeans. The immediate reaction to the tragedy, as we see in many cases where white citizens carry out terrorist attacks (take as a prime example the 2015 mass shooting by the white supremacist Dylann Roof in North Carolina in which nine black church parishioners were murdered in an attempt to spark a "race war") was to view the individual as mentally ill, a lone wolf, *not* a terrorist. But however mentally unstable Breivik was (in the end, court psychiatrists deemed him to be a narcissist with an anti-social personality disorder), his actions and the justifications he gave for his murderous acts were firmly planted in a commonly held set of political beliefs that are ingrained in the discourse of the established far right in Europe and elsewhere. Thus, Breivik is *not* a lone wolf. Rather, he is the representation of a wider radical and extremist milieu; he is the logical end point of the ideas and language of a social movement whose adherents see themselves locked in an existential struggle with Muslims and "multiculturalists" for the future of Europe and European culture – where, to quote Breivik, "the forces of Islam are flooding the gates once more."[2]

Recognizing the inadequacy of the lone wolf descriptor in the Breivik case, Berntzen and Sandberg identify how Breivik was not an individual with a wholly divergent world view. Rather, he was part of an anti-Islamic social movement composed of far-right anti-immigrant parties, such as Norway's Progress Party, a number of civil society and extremist groups, bloggers, academics, and everyday individuals who adhere to a broad continuum of anti-Islamic beliefs and offer a variety of strategies for addressing what is perceived uniformly as an invasion and a cultural conflict.[3] It is a startling revelation for some that Scandinavia, a region that has historically been lauded for its progressive social programs and viewed as largely welcoming to immigrants and refugees, has become a hotbed for anti-immigrant political parties and civil society groups. Yet, the Progress Party shared power in Norway after 2013, and the Danish People's Party is among the most popular political parties in the country. In one of the few remaining avowed multicultural states in Europe, the anti-immigration party, Sweden Democrats, garnered 13 per cent of the vote in 2014 and by the winter of 2016 was polling close to 25 per cent, a number that is close to five times the level of support they enjoyed in 2011.[4]

So unsurprisingly, in Breivik's rambling 1,500-page "manifesto" entitled "2083: A European Declaration of Independence," he doesn't paint himself as a loner. Rather, he sees himself as part of a band of patriots – the enlightened few who are aware of the imminent dangers facing Norway and the West. In his manifesto, he frequently cites popular anti-Islamic crusaders like the Americans Daniel Pipes, Bruce Bawer, and Robert Spencer and the Scandinavian blogger Peder

Nøstvold Jensen (pseudonym Fjorman). These are individuals who, taken together with a growing list of demagogues – Geert Wilders, Marine Le Pen, Donald Trump, and the like – have helped to shape a war-like narrative where Muslims are identified as dangerous fifth columns in Western states. Robert Spencer, the American founder and director of the controversial website "Jihad Watch," warns in his alarmist treatise *Stealth Jihad: How Radical Islam Is Subverting America without Guns or Bombs* that "Islam is unique among the major world religions in having a developed doctrine, theology, and legal system mandating warfare against and the subjugation of unbelievers ... it aims at nothing less than the transformation of American society and the imposition of Islamic law here, subjugating women and non-Muslims to the status of legal inferiors."[5]

Evoking similar themes of war and invasion, Marine Le Pen, the leader of the powerful French far-right party National Front, has compared Muslims praying in Lyon to the Nazi occupation of France during the Second World War: "I'm sorry, but for those who really like to talk about the Second World War, if we're talking about occupation, we can also talk about this while we're at it, because this is an occupation of territory ... It's an occupation of swaths of territory, of areas in which religious laws apply ... for sure, there are no tanks, no soldiers, but it's an occupation all the same and it weighs on people."[6] With these examples in mind, Breivik's manifesto, its language and ideas, are consistent with the writing and speeches of the wider anti-Islamic movement and its warlike tone. Moreover, as we see in Le Pen's comments, beyond the extremist fringes of the anti-Islamic social movement lies an increasingly mainstream popular anti-immigrant, anti-Muslim, and anti-European Union integration political movement. On this trend Liz Fekete comments, "Under the guises of patriotism, a wholesale anti-Islamic racism has been unleashed that itself threatens to destroy the fabric of multiculturalism."[7]

Yet beyond the increasingly powerful far right there is another political force, arguably more conservative in orientation, that is also playing a role in this drama. These more mainstream political parties overlap with the anti-Islamic social movement as they dip into the well of anti-immigrant and anti-Islamic popular sentiment for their own strategic purposes, namely the acquisition of or maintenance of political power. The "crisis" they espouse may be less existential and warlike in tone (although sometimes that language is used); rather, it is a crisis that is dressed in the language of the post-9/11 era: fears over terrorism, worries over the existence of "parallel communities,"[8] and cultural incompatibility between host cultures and immigrants, especially those who engender dangerous and "barbaric" cultural practices (here, read Muslims). Using strategies employed by conservatives since the late 1970s, they tie social and economic problems to issues with immigration and newcomer integration while incriminating the policies of the social democratic era.

We are told by these politicians that the born-in-Canada social and political experiment of the late twentieth century, multiculturalism, has failed. We are told this by some of the most powerful politicians in Europe. For example, in a speech on radicalization and extremism in Britain, the former prime minister of the United Kingdom, David Cameron, attacked "state multiculturalism," implicitly tying the policy to homegrown terrorism in Britain; Angela Merkel, the chancellor of Germany, despite her laudable support for Syrian asylum seekers, has publicly stated that multiculturalism has "failed utterly" in Germany; the Dutch vice-president of the Council of State, Piet Hein Donner, has stated, "The government shares the social dissatisfaction over the multicultural society model and plans to shift priority to the values of the Dutch people."[9] As we see in these statements, centrist and conservative political parties of Europe have rejected multiculturalism: they have blamed a social policy for violent extremism and social and economic ills, and in doing so they help to reinforce the narratives of the far right and the anti-Islamic social movement.

Cameron, Merkel, and other political leaders may not be as explicit as the far right in blaming immigrants and minorities for the "crisis" or "failure" of multiculturalism, but one does not need to dig very deep into their language to identify this message. To illustrate this point, we can look to some of the comments that Merkel made when she declared multiculturalism a failure: "We kidded ourselves a while, we said, 'They won't stay, sometime they will be gone.' But this isn't reality."[10] In Merkel's statements, "they" take the blame for the failure of multiculturalism, but who are the "they"? In short, in the context of the decade after 9/11, they are peoples who adhere to the diverse traditions of the religion of Islam. In Germany "they" could refer to Germans of Turkish ancestry, who have been particularly singled out by the anti-Islamic social movement in that country.[11] As observed by Lentin, what conservatives have presented is really quite a basic argument: "Immigration societies have been too tolerant of minority cultures. Minorities have been allowed too much leeway to practice their own traditions at the expense of integration with the wider community."[12]

Scholars from a variety of disciplinary backgrounds have sought to deconstruct and decode some of these trends. Alana Lentin and Gavin Titley (2011) have analyzed what they refer to as the crisis of multiculturalism; Phil Ryan (2010) has deconstructed what he calls multicultiphobia; Ben Pitcher (2009) and Geoffrey Levey and Tariq Modood (2009) have examined the role of racism in multicultural politics. Collectively their analyses have found that what lies behind the failure of the multiculturalism narrative cannot be taken at face value as it conceals, among other things, the inability of politicians to effectively manage both the economic and migratory effects of globalization and regionalization and a continuing "neoliberal" assault on the social democratic welfare state. As Ryan observes, the critics of multiculturalism believe the policy has endorsed illiberal practices among minority groups and opened a space for extremism in Western societies: it has promoted moral relativism and encouraged separateness.[13] Moreover, these scholars tell us that what is presented as rehabilitative action needed to fix the damage wrought by multiculturalism, such as the assimilation of migrant cultures, in effect contains ideologies of racism.[14]

Some of the recent successes of the far-right and more mainstream conservative political parties can be traced to their ability to harness latent xenophobia directed at growing numbers of immigrants and refugees who originate from the Global South.[15] In exploiting and fomenting these underlying fears, or "popular racism" as it has been referred to, they have institutionalized xenophobia: they have turned the fear of the foreign into a structured ideology, and, in this way, they have turned xenophobia into xenoracism. They have seized on this ideology as they struggle to engage an increasingly socially and economically alienated electorate that is drifting toward the demagogues in a sea of popular discontent.

In an early twenty-first century that has been framed by a Great Recession and a War on Terror, mainstream parties have failed to calm popular anxieties over immigration and increasing racial, religious, and ethnic diversity; they have failed to create prosperous and equitable economies in an era of mobile industry, labour, and capital. These fears and anxieties have driven dramatic political events, including the election of Donald Trump and Brexit. And in these contexts, the perceived failure to integrate the foreign "other" has been singled out as a threat to national security and to European cultures: multiculturalism is the policy that is said to have opened the door to that danger. In Breivik's words, "Multiculturalism, as you might know, is the root cause of the ongoing Islamisation of Europe which has resulted in the ongoing Islamic colonisation of Europe through demographic warfare."[16]

Related to security, two significant and mutually reinforcing trends have been taking place since the events of 9/11 that have arguably lent themselves to the construction of Muslims as the dangerous "other" in the West. First, military action abroad in the Muslim world within the War on Terror and a series of homegrown terrorist attacks in cities like Madrid, London, Amsterdam, Boston, Ottawa, Paris, and Brussels have been used to paint Muslims as externalized and internalized physical threats: both the enemy over there and the enemy within. Then there is the cultural and demographic threat constructed by the anti-Islamic social movement that focuses on "dangerous" values and ideas contained in Islam and "out of control" population growth among Muslim communities. The language used by anti-Islamic activists consistently draws out these fears. Take, for example, the anti-Islamic cheerleader Daniel Pipes's musings on Donald Trump's election campaign, "Trump has raised a critical and urgent issue that all Westerners must face, as symbolized by the recent tsunami of illegal immigration to Europe and the huge strains it has created. Simply put, Muslims present a disproportionately large source of problems."[17]

These narratives and ideas are not confined to Internet bloggers, far-right extremists, and contemporary demagogues: they have found their way into pseudo-academic literature. In scaremongering books like Christopher Caldwell's *Reflections on the Revolution in Europe: Immigration, Islam and the West,* or Jim Sciutto's *Against Us: The New Face of America's Enemies in the Muslim World,* these two insecurities are pulled together as Islam is presented as a homogenous hyper-identity whose values threaten "Western" values and whose militancy threatens public safety.[18]

Xenoracism has penetrated the political discourse in Europe and the United States, and while the levels of fear and hatred have not yet reached the same scale as that of the 1930s, where Jews rather than Muslims were the perceived fifth columns, there are echoes of our troubled past. José Manuel Barroso, head of the European Commission, alluded to this idea when he stated that "in Europe, not so many decades ago, we had very, very worrying developments of xenophobia and racism and intolerance."[19] For noted migration scholars Stephen Castles and Mark Miller, these trends are significant concerns for liberal democratic societies: "Racism is a threat, not only to immigrants themselves, but also to democratic institutions and social order. Analysis of the causes and effects of racism must therefore take a central place in any discussion of international migration and its effects on society."[20]

THE CANADIAN EXCEPTION?

Until recently, Canada, as the original multicultural state, seemingly stood largely apart from the troubles that plague Western Europe. In 2011 Canadians marked the fortieth anniversary of multiculturalism, and Canadian social scientists have frequently trumpeted the success of the official policy of multiculturalism. Biles, Burnstein, and Frideres write, "Canada has long been a world leader in welcoming and accepting immigrants, which in turn has contributed to Canada's growth and prosperity, as well as helping shape our current society."[21] Pollster and author Michael Adams, in his 2007 book *Unlikely Utopia: The Surprising Triumph of Canadian Pluralism*, notes the remarkable success Canada has had as a multicultural society: "There is ample empirical evidence to suggest that Canada *is* special, both in its social conditions and in the way its people (Canadians new and old) respond to those conditions."[22]

A series of Canadian scholars have also drawn positive conclusions on the efficacy of Canada's approach to newcomer integration, citizenship, and social cohesion: for example, Keith Banting, Thomas Courchene, and Leslie Seidle's (2007) analysis of shared citizenship and belonging, the work of sociologist Jeffrey Reitz and colleagues (2009) on discrimination and social cohesion, and the analysis of John Biles, Meyer Burnstein, and James Frieders (2008) on immigration and integration. Reitz (2014) identifies how popular support for Canadian multiculturalism has buttressed support for immigration and immigrants – the perception that immigrants are a net positive for Canadian society: "In short, findings from public opinion and other survey research suggests that for most Canadians, support for multiculturalism is an expression of support for the idea of Canada as a country committed to immigration and its benefits ... popular multiculturalism is a pro-immigration ideology."[23] Noting similar successes, Adams claims that multiculturalism has penetrated the very idea of the nation itself, forming an essential aspect of Canadian nationalism: "What is sometimes called the 'multiculturalism experiment' isn't an experiment at all. It's a national aspiration at the very core of Canadian idealism. It's the Canadian Dream."[24]

Furthermore, underlining the relative success of Canada's multicultural project is the fact that it is difficult to expose an explicit failure of multiculturalism narrative among politicians in Canada. The far right in Canada exists largely on the fringes of party politics and Canadian society: it is resigned to rantings on social media or in civil society and extremist groups. Therefore, there seems to be a considerable disconnect between what are the generally positive empirical findings among Canadian social scientists and what is increasingly becoming a shared, common-sense understanding globally that multiculturalism as state policy has been tried and failed. May we ask, then, whether Canada has "dodged the bullet"?

Unfortunately, the answer is no, at least not entirely. Even a cursory examination of scholarly work reveals some troubling signs for the official policy of multiculturalism and Canadian Muslims. Reitz has indicated that Canada has not escaped the issue that has surfaced in Europe: "The questions in Canada as elsewhere have focused on religion, whether certain religious minorities have values, beliefs or practices that are difficult to integrate into Canadian society because they clash with Canadian ideas about gender equality or secularism in public institutions."[25]

Additionally, there are findings from scholarship specifically focused on Muslims that indicate that Canadian Muslims have suffered significant xenoracism. For example, in *Diaspora by Design: Muslim Immigrants in Canada and Beyond*, scholars from York University have pointed to the fact that discrimination and securitization of Muslim populations in states like Canada have both driven the development of a more unified identity among Canadian Muslims and negatively affected integration.[26] Canadian Muslims, as in other states of the West, have also been subject to the securitized policies that emerged after 9/11, as exemplified by the experience of Canadian citizens like Omar Khadr.[27]

Moreover, under the former Conservative federal government of Prime Minister Stephen Harper, several political initiatives were launched that resemble some of the "rehabilitative" policies that have been employed in states where xenoracism and the crisis of multiculturalism are most apparent. These policies will be subject to a more rigorous analysis in the chapters to come. In brief, they include changes to citizenship legislation, examinations and guides (e.g., revoking the citizenship of dual citizens under Bill C-24) and a public emphasis on monoculturalism: one defined by British colonial history, the monarchy, and re-branded "royal" armed forces.[28] Additionally, starting in 2011, and further emphasized in the 2015 election campaign, specific wedge issues were used by the Harper Conservative government related to Canadian Muslims, such as the ban of the niqab at citizenship ceremonies and public musings among cabinet members on banning head coverings in government buildings.[29]

The 2015 election campaign outlined how vulnerable Canada was to some of the discourses of the anti-Islamic social movement – the fear mongering seen in Europe and the United States. There was the implicit equating of Syrian refugees with terrorism when the Conservatives expressed concerns over bringing in refugees from a "terrorist war zone." There was the more long-standing use of the niqab as a political wedge issue in Quebec and elsewhere, and the aforementioned bill that sought to revoke the citizenship of dual citizens convicted of terrorism-related charges. Many of these strategies reeked of desperation – a last-ditch effort to mobilize "old stock" Canadian conservatives against the "barbaric practices" of "undesirable" new stock Canadians. Of course, these strategies failed, insofar as the Conservatives were soundly defeated by the Liberals. But, as the *Toronto Star* writer Edward Keenan points out, the tactics the Conservatives used shared something in common, "to vilify some Muslim Canadians."[30] More recently, the failed fringe Conservative leadership candidate Kellie Leitch mobilized some of these ideas in her promise to institute a "Canadian values" test for newcomers.

Do these policies and trends represent a relatively short chapter in Canadian history? How resonant has the Harper Conservatives' nation-building campaign been in terms of shaping public attitudes? Here the jury will remain out for some time, but unsurprisingly the purposeful sowing of fear and divisiveness by the Conservative government in the Canadian public over its near decade in power has had some impacts on public attitudes toward newcomers, at least as indicated by polling data. According to EKOS in 2005, the year before the Conservatives came to power, 25 per cent of Canadians believed "there were too many immigrants" in the country. By 2015 that number had nearly doubled to 46 per cent.[31] These trends challenge the view that Canada is immune to xenoracism and the symptoms of the crisis of multiculturalism.

In an attempt to analyze and reconcile these seemingly divergent experiences between Canada the seemingly robust multicultural state and the more divided Canada of the Harper years, this book will go beyond the statistics and existing empirical studies to examine the experiences of those most prone to our contemporary xenoracist moment: Canadian Muslims. The book argues that the case study of Muslim minorities represents, to borrow a term from the contemporary economic climate, a stress test of multiculturalism. In other words, the true strength, or lack thereof, of Canadian multiculturalism can be discerned by its ability to accommodate those most prone to xenoracism.

It should be made clear at the outset that the book does not extend to Quebec or the experiences of Muslims in Quebec. As the book is focused on Canadian multiculturalism it cannot be extended to a province that has historically rejected multiculturalism as public policy. The rejection of state multiculturalism in Quebec will be briefly discussed in the section on the history of the policy (within the chapter on multiculturalism). In brief, as York University political scientist Kenneth McRoberts observes, Pierre Trudeau's adoption of multiculturalism as a policy framework, and as a tool for nation building, was aimed at shifting the Canadian state away from a bicultural vision of Canada. It was aimed at reducing the conflicts contained in the bicultural model by replacing it with a more individualistic and liberal rights-centred national model, while maintaining bilingualism as official policy.[32] In response, successive provincial governments in Quebec rightly viewed multiculturalism as a nation-building strategy that sought to undermine the bicultural vision of the state (a vision that some federalist elites and politicians in the province preferred) and as a policy that was potentially detrimental to the sovereignty movement.[33]

Alternatively, Quebec adopted interculturalism, a loose policy framework that is said to embody some elements of the multiculturalism adopted in English Canada. What critically differentiates the policy from multiculturalism is that interculturalism maintains a central cultural-identity core into which minority cultures are expected to integrate. In this sense interculturalism is not unlike the more assimilative approaches to diversity and social integration taken in some European states.[34] In the context of the 2013 debates over the

Quebec government's proposed Charter of Values, and prior episodes of xenoracism in the province culminating in the province's public debates on reasonable accommodation, the inadequacies of the intercultural framework have come to light. As recognized by Kymlicka, "the rhetoric of interculturalism may not provide an effective check on either xenophobia or assimilationism."[35] Of course, Quebec's woes, in terms of its approach to diversity, should not be viewed in isolation: these debates are now a regular feature across the Western world, and as seen in the 2015 election campaign, they are not absent in the rest of Canada.

The book is organized into three sections: xenoracism, multiculturalism, and security.

XENORACISM

The first section of the book offers an improved understanding of the term xenoracism. Chapter 2 will examine some of the existing literature on race and racism as a point of departure for the discussion of xenoracism. Rather than viewing racism as a misinformed set of prejudices and beliefs it is argued here that racism should be understood as an ideology. According to race and racism scholar Robert Miles, ideologies of racism contain ideas of a hierarchical relational order in which groups are assigned characteristics that are used to compare and contrast with other groups: in this sense, characteristics "refract and define each other."[36]

Chapter 3, on xenoracism, will expand on this idea by looking at how particular characteristics have been assigned to Muslim communities within the ideology of xenoracism and how this refracting of characteristics between groups can be used to establish a relational order. Ideas and ideologies of nationalism have been singled out for their role in supporting forms of racism. Scholars like Alana Lentin have pointed out that, while racism cannot be reduced to nationalism, the two ideologies aid and abet each other, especially when nationalism is structured around ideas of cultural exclusivity.[37] Since xenoracism targets those who are deemed to be foreign, ideologies of nationalism that assign ideas of cultural exclusivity may play a role in projecting understandings of belonging and exclusion, native and foreign.

The term xenoracism was first used by Ambalavaner Sivanandan, director of the London-based Institute of Race Relations, as a means of describing emergent forms of institutionalized racism that he observed at the turn of the twenty-first century in the European Union. Sivanandan sought to explain what he saw as institutionalized racism that targeted refugees and economic migrants irrespective of skin colour, a form of racism that "denigrates and reifies people before segregating and/or expelling them, it is a xenophobia that bears all the marks of the old racism. It is racism in substance but 'xeno' in form."[38] In the wake of 9/11 and the 2005 London transit ("7/7") attacks, Liz Fekete, Sivanandan's colleague at the Institute of Race Relations, sought to explain the prejudicial targeting of Muslim minority communities. For Fekete, Muslim populations in Europe, even those who have resided in Western Europe for multiple generations, had been caught up in the expanding "loop of xenoracism," targeted with structured and institutionalized racism.[39] On this form of xenoracism Sivanandan notes that "the racism directed at Muslims on the basis of religion, signified this time not just by race or immigration status (refugee, asylum-seeker, and so on), but by dress and appearance as well – combining the characteristics of both asylum seeker and terrorist, [reflects] the combined 'war' on asylum and on terror."[40]

What is noteworthy about the previous usages of the term xenoracism by members of the Institute of Race Relations is that it was used to explain contemporary manifestations of racism. There is little attention given to genealogy, to historical legacies and influences on the ideology, and this represents a shortcoming. Decoding xenoracism today requires an approach that can capture not only the immediate influences and manifestations but also the historical and ideational roots of the phenomenon. It is these historically established narratives that allow certain communities to be constructed as distinctly foreign (e.g., in reference to a particular national community). Therefore, a key task for the first section of the book is exploring how social relations are shaped by historical knowledge of the "other."

In part, the historical aspects of xenoracism that targets Muslim communities have been captured by the literary and cultural critic Edward Said in his influential 1979 work *Orientalism,* which traces centuries of Western discourse on the "other." Said presents a critical understanding of how the West has historically defined the Orient, and most especially Islam, as the *foreign* other. As Said notes in *Orientalism,* Muslims, and specifically Arabs, have tended to be represented (to borrow a term from the eminent sociologist Max Weber) as an ideal type – a static image of a historically declining civilization (when compared with the European civilization) that has a propensity for conflict.[41] Undoubtedly, these historical narratives have a powerful influence on xenoracism that targets Muslims. Understanding xenoracism today requires an understanding of the roots of the phenomenon – the ways in which the other, specifically the Muslim other, has been historically constructed through Western literature, media, and scholarship.

Outside of his analysis of representations of the Orient in Western literature, Said was also a cultural critic, a Palestinian exile and refugee living in the United States who experienced first hand what he termed "the web of racism, cultural stereotyping, political imperialism, [and] dehumanizing ideology."[42] Said's work, and the works of those who have followed – those who have experienced racism first hand – offer a great deal to this study. As seen in one of the epigraphs of this chapter, despite his sometimes troubled experience, Said saw great possibilities in the collective knowledge and experiences of culturally plural societies – the potential to benefit from our shared histories and experiences.

MULTICULTURALISM

The term multiculturalism is marked by multiple meanings. At its most basic level, multiculturalism is about thinking and talking about each other's identities and how those identities are contained within the social and political relations at a given place and time.[43] However, multiculturalism can also describe, among other things, a government policy aimed at managing culturally diverse societies, an ideology, or even a critical discourse of resistance.[44] For many it is simply a fact of life, a reality on the streets of Sydney, London, Singapore, New York, Istanbul, or Vancouver.

Driving this contemporary multicultural "lived" reality is the endlessly debated and amorphous concept of globalization. As *New York Times* journalist Thomas Friedman has described it, today's globalization enables us to "reach around the world farther, faster, deeper and cheaper than ever before."[45] Through the greater exchange of goods, peoples, and ideas, globalization has created interdependence between economies, states, and societies.[46] The rapid and diffuse movement of peoples, especially from the societies of the Global South to the North, has been one of the primary engines of globalization, and these "sojourners of globalization" bring with them new ideas, values and practices, and transnational identities.[47]

This "lived" multiculturalism can be differentiated from multiculturalism as public policy or state multiculturalism, which is the focus of chapter 5. The section on multiculturalism will examine the historical development of the policy and some of the scholarly arguments that have been made for and against it. As a policy, state multiculturalism recognizes the disadvantages that newcomers face during and after their settlement process and the right of newcomers to retain their cultural identities. It is based on the understanding that disadvantages related to racial, cultural, ethnic, or religious identity can deny newcomers and minority communities upward mobility in core institutions and social integration into the host society.[48]

As Kymlicka illustrates, these policies are intended "to contest inherited ethnic and racial hierarchies through the recognition and accommodation of ethnocultural diversity, inspired and constrained by norms of human rights and civil rights liberalism. As such, they fit together with other policies aimed at contesting status hierarchies, such as gender and sexual orientation, as part of a larger package of liberal-democratic reforms."[49] But more than this, state multiculturalism can represent a form of nation building. In the words of Fleras and Kunz, it seeks to create "a new symbolic order, along with a corresponding mythology," for a state, one that "help[s] to paper over any inconsistencies at odds with present realties."[50] In other words, multiculturalism is not only the public management of diversity, it is the re-imagination of national identity in a way that is less tied to a uni- or bi-cultural image of the state and less tied to exclusivist ideologies of nationalism.[51]

Starting in 1971, under the stewardship of Prime Minister Pierre Elliott Trudeau, Canada was the first country to embrace this policy. In the Canadian context, multiculturalism as public policy took on the form of a mandated approach to cultural diversity that aimed to allow newcomers and members of ethnic minorities to maintain their cultural identity and participate equitably in Canadian society while adhering to the legal and normative standards of the state. And for a short period, in the late twentieth century, this policy was a popular Canadian export, one that the Australians, Dutch, Swedes, and British were eager to consume, in their own culturally and historically determined manner.

But like many social policies born during the "golden era" of social democracy and the welfare state, in the neoliberal era, state multiculturalism has been attacked by neo-conservative politicians, together with critics in academia and the media, and as of late declared an abject failure by some of the world's most powerful leaders, resulting in the "crisis of multiculturalism." Speaking from decades of work on issues of race and racism in Europe, Fekete registers some surprise in relation to these trends, writing that she "could not have predicted … that the extreme-Right's call for an exclusive national preference and cultural identity would come to fruition … For a variant of the extreme-Right's call for national preference is today written into government social programmes that demand compulsory integration (i.e., assimilation) of minority ethnic communities into superior British, German, French (etc.) 'values.'"[52]

Building on Fekete's observation, the second half of the section on multiculturalism will focus on what has been presented as a policy response to the perceived crisis of multiculturalism: a repackaged form of "integration."[53] This rehabilitative approach contains a common set of programs and priorities – new citizenship laws, compulsory civics and language tests, codes of conduct for religious leaders, and in some cases guidelines for style of dress in public spaces – such as the banning of head coverings.[54] According to Asad, in the case of Muslims these policies have operated on the perception that Muslim communities' attachment to faith commits Muslims to values that are "an affront to the modern secular state."[55] Arguably, religion rather than ethnicity has become the centre of attention in the politics of diversity, the focal point in immigration and social integration policy.[56] Whereas in the past diversity was conceived in terms of ethnicity or race, increasingly religion is being invoked in the public sphere as a meaningful (and problematic) form of difference.

There are multiple approaches to and understandings of integration when it comes to newcomers. For example, integration may operate within a multicultural paradigm where identity groups can maintain cultural boundaries while enjoying state-mandated equality in public and private arenas. In Canada, newcomer integration has been described as a two-way-street marked by expectations for inclusion in the social, economic, and civic life of the state and expectations that newcomers will actively seek to acquire citizenship, learn one of the official languages, and engage in the political life of the country. As observed by Wilkinson, "integration is a reciprocal process where newcomers are incorporated into a new society. During the process, both the newcomer and host society change as a result of interaction with one another … the immigrant makes alterations to their behaviour to 'fit in,' while the host society changes as a result of the incorporation of newcomers."[57]

By comparison, assimilative approaches to "integration" are intended to incorporate migrants through a one-sided process in which they give up their language, culture, and other characteristics to become largely undifferentiated from the majority of the population.[58] As states and state leaders, particularly in Western Europe, respond to the perceived crisis of multiculturalism, they call on newcomers to adhere to the values of the host culture while shifting the balance of newcomer integration to this assimilative paradigm. In large part this has been driven by fears over the existence of separate, unintegrated "parallel communities" in multicultural societies – communities that may harbour "barbaric" or even extremist ideas and ideologies that can breed criminality, violence, and terrorism.

Therefore, in some instances, integration has become another conduit for national security – following on the logic that social marginalization is a root cause of extremism and domestic terrorism. As demonstrated in chapter 6, newcomer integration in some Western states has been securitized, since integration is increasingly seen as a means of addressing extremism and preventing terrorism – most especially in Muslim communities. In this sense, newcomer integration can be seen as part of a wider approach to policing Muslim communities in the West. But do these trends extend to Canada? According to Canadian social scientists, they do not. Newcomer integration is said to remain wedded to the two-way-street model. Yet, as was seen during the Harper years, at the very least the *language* of assimilation has entered the Canadian political discourse, in particular around debates over citizenship and national identity.

SECURITY

The third section of the book will focus on security and how security practices can impact multiculturalism and Muslims. It will examine how security legislation, practices, and language have shaped the portrayal of Muslim communities in the West and how security concerns have been invoked in the crisis of multiculturalism. The section on security will explore the premise that security policy, much like integration policy, may provide an additional avenue for xenoracism that targets Muslims. The anti-Islamic social movement and the crisis of multiculturalism exhibit ideas and narratives related to "societal security": concern that Muslims possess values and ideas that pose a potentially existential threat to the integrity of national values and national identity. In addition to this perceived societal threat, there are fears over physical or national security, framed by concerns over radicalization, extremism, and homegrown terrorism in Western Muslim communities.

To illuminate societal security, the book will use a constructivist approach attributed to a group of scholars who are collectively known as the Copenhagen School. According to these theorists, security is not an objective condition or process but rather contains a significant subjective element.[59] Here, security is understood as a particular set of discourses and practices, carried out by actors, that rests upon shared understandings. As one of the Copenhagen theorists, Ole Waever, contends, "What is essential [to a case of securitization] is the designation of an existential threat ... and the acceptance of that designation by a significant audience."[60] Such an understanding of security opens up the traditionally understood "referent object" of security (i.e., national-military security) to a host of potential objects, which, when portrayed as threatened, can lead to extraordinary security measures; for example, in the case of societal securitization, a politician may make reference to a national community being threatened by newcomers with cultural traditions that are "dangerous" or opposed to the norms, values, and laws of the community.

Indeed, returning to the ideas and narratives of the anti-Islamic social movement, we frequently see reference to existential threats. Here the referent object is national identity, and the security threat is minorities and the values and demographics (i.e., high birth rates) they are said to exhibit. The language of security, particularly in the post-9/11 era, has been used to justify extraordinary actions in the pursuit of national security. As Van Munster notes, "References to security invoke some sort of pre-political priority ('if we don't act now, it will be too late!'), the invocation of security in policy discourses often works as a rhetorical device through which the legitimacy and political support for political action is legitimized."[61]

A key point raised by scholars like Van Munster is that over the past decade security concerns have been institutionalized and bureaucratized into immigration and social policy, arguably in ways previously unseen. The language and priority of security is becoming normalized and integrated into the everyday workings of governments and their approach to national security, diversity and immigration.[62]

In particular, according to Fekete, the assimilationist approach to integration is an adjunct to national security measures contained in anti-terrorism law. Simply put, it "is impossible to divorce the current debate on the 'limits of cultural diversity' from the war on terror."[63]

Governments and security organizations across the West, including Canada and its Canadian Security Intelligence Service in its annual reports, have designated "militant Islam" as the primary threat to national security since the early 2000s.[64] In the West, political Islam or Islamism has often been viewed as a homogenous entity from which extremism and terrorism have emerged.[65] The issue of homegrown terrorism has played a significant role in constructing the perception of Muslims as internal threats (i.e., threat of domestic terrorism) and externalized enemies (i.e., within the larger War on Terror), thereby blurring ideas of belonging.[66]

Movements like al-Qaeda, and offshoots like Daesh, through their ability to carry out catastrophic mass-casualty terrorist attacks in the West, have fomented public fears over radicalization and extremism among Muslims. By successfully drawing attention to their cause through violence and instilling fear in a target audience, the wider al-Qaeda social movement has established itself as the primary security threat for many Western states. The oft-spoken concern among politicians and security personnel in the West is that this social movement could take hold in non-integrated parallel communities, thereby producing domestic terrorists.[67] In this narrative an equivalency is drawn between a small extremist minority group and the larger peaceful Muslim community living in the West. From these understandings and fears the logical response has been to focus law enforcement and intelligence resources more widely onto Muslim communities.

Given the events of late October 2014 in Ottawa and Quebec, these concerns have become even more pronounced. In two separate terrorist attacks that occurred two days apart, the idea that Canada was relatively insulated from the phenomenon of homegrown terrorism was shattered. In the more publicized and dramatic attack, Michael Zehaf-Bibeau, a 32-year-old Canadian citizen with a record of petty crime, shot and killed a Canadian Armed Forces reservist, Corporal Nathan Cirillo, who was standing on ceremonial sentry duty at the National War Memorial in the nation's capital, Ottawa. Shortly thereafter, Zehaf-Bibeau entered the Centre Block building on Parliament Hill on an apparent suicide mission. The attack on the ramparts of an open-to-the-public seat of government has led to questions in the media and among politicians and the Canadian public about how to respond to the emergent security threat of "lone wolf" terrorism without sacrificing Canadian values.

Canada has also been targeted in several failed terrorist plots, such as the Toronto 18 plot in 2006, the liquid explosives plot originating in Britain that same year, and a plan to attack passenger trains in Southern Ontario in 2013. In response, the Canadian government has passed and reinforced security legislation that resembles security measures seen elsewhere, for example, the Anti-terrorism Act and Bills c-36 and c-51. Despite reassurances that the Anti-terrorism Act and its amendments are neutral legislation that does not target Canadians on the basis of their ethnic or religious identity, Canadian Muslims have expressed concerns that such legislation has resulted in the targeting of Muslims to the detriment of their civil liberties. Two regularly cited cases that illustrate the potential pitfalls of Canadian government security practices are those of Maher Arar, a Canadian citizen unlawfully detained, deported to Syria, and tortured on the basis of information-sharing activities between American and Canadian security officials, and Omar Khadr, a child soldier abandoned by the Canadian government and allowed to reside in the extra-legal environment of Guantanamo Bay as a juvenile.

The danger in these security practices is that the thin divide that exists between treating communities as suspects and treating them as partners in a community policing paradigm can be breached, creating alienation and marginalization. These dangers, and the fears that security practices cause among diverse Muslim communities in the West, are highly evident today. For example, as indicated by the opinions of the interviewees used for this study, experiences with no-fly lists, surveillance practices, and fears over detention are disturbingly common among Canadian Muslims. Scholars focused on migration studies and multiculturalism have overlooked these developments to their detriment, as security increasingly shapes state approaches to immigration, integration, and diversity. Ultimately, these are complex and multi-faceted arguments that require further analysis in the pages to come.

METHODOLOGY

The book rests on an interdisciplinary approach to academic scholarship. Sivanandan and Fekete's conceptual development of xenoracism;

Said's work on Orientalism; Ryan, Lentin, and Titley's work on the crisis of multiculturalism; and the Copenhagen School's securitization theory are employed in the three primary sections of the book. These are the lenses that filter the substantial body of research employed in the wider analysis. In terms of its methodological approach (methods, procedures, etc.) the book will employ what are seen as multiple complementary methods.[68] The book focuses on a single case, Canada (outside of Quebec), while drawing on comparative elements in examining, for instance, various states' experiences with xenoracism and the crisis of multiculturalism. Much of the existing work on xenoracism and the most vocal opponents of state multiculturalism originate in Europe and increasingly the United States. Canada is marked by differing social, economic, political, and historical experiences that shape experiences with xenoracism and multiculturalism. This book argues that these local particularities can only be understood within an in-depth case study.

As Peters points out, the real problem for social scientists is making convincing statements about the causation of political phenomena.[69] Ultimately, for many academics this realization leads to the smaller contextualized narratives that small-N studies offer.[70] Small-N studies do not lend themselves to extensive generalization beyond the case(s) at hand. Rather, they are intended to act as intensive qualitative analyses that perhaps can later be included in larger studies with similar studies from other localities.[71]

To demonstrate connections between xenoracism, multiculturalism, and security, the book relies on a narrative style that seeks to contextualize research findings.[72] In addition, the book employs a combination of quantitative and qualitative sources of data. Having admitted the limitations and possibilities offered by these approaches used in isolation, a growing body of academics has been advocating for increased methodological fusion.[73] Here the combination of both quantitative and qualitative approaches is aimed at strengthening an understanding of social phenomena.[74] In this approach, methods operate in a complementary fashion with the ultimate intention of converging research methods on the issue(s) being studied.[75]

With this in mind, the book will employ an extensive literature review related to the three key themes of xenoracism, multiculturalism, and security. It will also make use of empirical data in the form of Statistics Canada's Ethnic Diversity Survey (EDS), publicly released in 2003, and Environics' 2016 Survey of Muslims in Canada (SMC).

The S M C is a follow-up to another Environics survey (Focus Canada: The Pulse of Canadian Public Opinion), which examined the attitudes and opinions of Canadian Muslims, for example, related to experiences with discrimination and a sense of belonging to Canada. The 2016 survey provides a comparison of the 2006 and 2016 data, offering two snapshots of attitudes and opinions in Canada's diverse Muslim communities.

By comparison, the E D S is a rich but dated source of data. As such, it does not fully reflect issues related to multiculturalism, security, and integration that have emerged over the past decade and more.[76] However, importantly for this analysis, the E D S offers a unique and substantive picture of public attitudes at a critical juncture for Canadian Muslims – shortly after 9/11. When combined, the E D S and the S M C provide basic summaries of statistical data related to social integration and experiences with discrimination among Canadian Muslim communities over a 15-year period. Moreover, the E D S and S M C provide a portrait of attitudes and opinions during some heightened periods of anxiety for Canadian Muslims. For example, the E D S was conducted in 2002, shortly after the 9/11 terrorist attacks; the 2006 S M C data were collected around the time of the Shari'a law debate in Ontario and Canada's escalating combat mission in Afghanistan in 2006; and the 2016 S M C data were collected after a particularly divisive period of Canadian politics for Muslim communities (the 2015 federal election and its accompanying polarizing debates on the niqab and the admission of Syrian refugees).

The E D S has already been subject to established academic study and applied to subject matters such as multiculturalism. For instance, the Reitz et al. (2009) edited work *Multiculturalism and Social Cohesion: Potentials and Challenges of Diversity* heavily employed the study in its analysis. Critically, considering the focus in the present book on xenoracism in the Muslim community, the E D S provides indicators of experiences of discrimination and social, economic, and political integrative indicators and represents a comprehensive examination of attitudes among Canadian religious groups. While the E D S has been the subject of past studies, few have focused specifically on religious communities, and to date its findings have not been compared with those of the more recent S M C.

In addition to the quantitative data provided by the E D S, S M C, and other publicly available surveys, the book will employ qualitative data from semi-structured interviews. The interviews were conducted between spring 2010 and summer 2017 with two sample groups. Together with the ED S snapshot data, the interviews provide more updated, nuanced, and contextualized evidence of the potential presence (or not) of xenoracism, its manifestations, and its effects. The first group of interviewees is an "elite" level sample of twenty-three leaders in the Canadian Muslim community. The sample provides a diverse group of individuals in terms of profession, religious affiliation (sect) or religiosity, and ethnic background. It includes Imams, politicians, academics, lawyers, business people, heads of women's advocacy groups, and senior members of cultural-religious associations. Interviewees came from Sunni, Shi'a, and Ismaili religious interpretations; some defined themselves as religiously conservative while others expressed more secular leanings. Interviewees were first- and second-generation Canadians from a variety of ethnic and national backgrounds including Pakistan, Lebanon, Egypt, Palestine, India, Uganda, Somalia, and Kenya. Muslim leaders ("elites") were selected as interviewees on the basis of their ability to provide community-level insight into research areas, such as experiences with xenoracism and perceptions of multiculturalism in Canada.[77]

The use of semi-structured interviews and elite-level sampling offers some distinct advantages related to the book as a whole. Semi-structured interviews allow a more reflexive interview style that seeks to understand the complexities and uniqueness of individual experience.[78] In comparison, standardized interviews with closed-ended questions assume the interviewer is (mostly) fully informed about the subject matter he or she seeks to examine. The issue here, especially in ethnographic research, is omission, in that by failing to account for the reflections of the interviewee, the interviewer may ask the wrong question or fail to critically examine his or her own preconceived notions and existing knowledge.[79]

Semi-structured interviews allow the interviewer to be partly informed by the interviewee, allowing the interviewee to frame, in his or her own words, how the question and/or problem the interviewer is seeking to examine is understood.[80] As suggested by Leech, the middle ground between structured and unstructured approaches offers some advantages, "one that can provide detail, depth, and an insider's perspective, while at the same time allowing hypothesis testing and the quantitative analysis of interview response."[81] Certainly this offers advantages in a critically framed study seeking to understand the experiences of Canadian Muslims.

Elite-level samples offer both advantages and disadvantages in terms of generating rigorous academic findings. One issue is random error, which occurs when we extrapolate, from a small sample group, estimations of a larger population's experiences. As elite-level interviews are by definition conducted with a smaller number of people, these extrapolations are certainly prone to this issue.[82] In this type of sample the researcher selects members on the basis of his or her own assumption of key traits with the research population.[83] Thus, sampling is based on the researcher's subjective interpretation of social stratification and who should be designated as an elite. Indeed, this form of data collection is, by its nature, an exercise in eliciting subjective opinion and perception rather than seeking objective truth. As Walford argues, "At best, interviewees will only give what they are prepared to reveal about their subjective perceptions of events and opinions ... It can be argued that identity is created rather than revealed through narrative."[84] Recognizing this limitation brings us back to the preference for multiple research methods.

It should be noted that the interviewees included in this study were almost all what Moore defines as "good informants" in the opinion of the author: they demonstrated the knowledge and experience necessary to meaningfully reflect on the subject matters of the book.[85] With this in mind, the use of an elite-level sample provided significant qualitative depth in terms of knowledge and insights, while lacking width (size).[86]

The second interview group is a policy-level sample composed of policy officials from a variety of governmental bodies engaged with state multiculturalism, including current and former employees of Citizenship and Immigration Canada (renamed Immigration, Refugees and Citizenship Canada by the Liberal government) and the Multiculturalism Program, non-governmental organizations, community and settlement agencies, and anti-racism and cultural advocacy groups. All of these individuals have been engaged with state multiculturalism, either directly as a civil servant or as an advocate for community and minority rights. Thirteen people were interviewed in this group; therefore, the total number of semi-structured interviews conducted for the book is thirty-six. In the policy-level group, questions focused primarily on the current state of affairs in official Canadian multiculturalism, integration, security, and the role of religious minorities in the multicultural framework. This sample provides another window into state multiculturalism in Canada and its inner workings.

A NORMATIVE COMMITMENT

In the spirit of full disclosure, this book contains a normative commitment – one that seeks to provide social scientific research less encumbered by the legacies of the past. As Said points out, "Orientalism's failure" is a human one as much as it is an intellectual one. He writes, "for in having to take up a position of irreducible opposition to a region of the world it considered alien to its own, Orientalism failed to identify with human experience, failed also to see it as human experience."[87] This quote draws out the priority of this book: a commitment to improving intercultural relations by seeking out human experience and drawing lessons from those experiences.

In a world of migrants, diasporas, and sojourners, to borrow descriptions from Knight, successful plural societies are essential for the development of more peaceful global relations.[88] Globalization is shrinking time and space: through modern technology and communications, human beings are more interconnected than ever. Cultural difference can enrich; shared experience and intercultural exchange can be the basis of successful nation-states and international communities. However, even a brief review of the last century of human history, of global wars and genocides, reveals that conflict is in many ways tied to the ways in which peoples divide each other – racially, religiously, ethnically, and so on. What explains this dichotomy? What is the difference between a successful plural society and one that tears itself apart? This is a philosophical question at the heart of this book. It is hoped that it can provide some answers on how to address what can be argued as significant threat to multicultural systems throughout the Western world: xenoracism and the divides that it erects between Canadian Muslims and the host culture.

2

Race and Racism

This chapter will first unpack some of the key terms used in the book, commencing with an examination of the controversial topics of race and racism. Put simply, debates over racism, its nature, and its effects have been contentious and even acrimonious; certainly, the subject of racism can provoke an emotional reaction, especially for those who feel its ill effects. For many people, the topic of racism is something that produces uncomfortable and awkward exchanges; they view it as a subject best avoided in polite conversation. As one interviewee, Charlene Hay, executive director of the Centre for Race and Culture, observed, "Very rarely are people willing to acknowledge that there is a problem. If you can acknowledge the problem then you can start talking about solving the problem." As she recognized, racism has become a taboo subject, even if it is acknowledged, begrudgingly or not, as a serious social issue. As the noted social theorist Alana Lentin observes, "When probed further, racism provokes a 'don't go there' attitude that reveals that it is something we are both deeply familiar with and profoundly troubled by."[1]

There have been many notable, scholarly explorations of race and racism, and sometimes they offer very different answers to how race should be framed and racism understood.[2] The debate over race and racism rests in a vast body of literature, and as a result a comprehensive review is simply beyond the scope of this book. Instead, this chapter will examine race and racism as a point of departure for a large analysis on xenoracism, focusing on the idea of race as a socially constructed concept and racism as an ideology.

Understanding racism as an ideology challenges the common perception of racism as a set of knee-jerk and misinformed understandings or prejudices. If racism is associated with political programs such as nation building, colonialism, imperialism, and war, racist ideologies are intimately connected with power and the institutions of the state. If politics is about, to borrow Lasswell's famous phrase, "who gets what, when and how" then the ideology of racism presents a potential answer, a justification, to why power is distributed in the way it is.[3]

As this chapter seeks to unravel some of the meanings of race and racism, it will briefly discuss some of the definitional debates on race and racism before moving into a consideration of how racism may be understood as an ideology that is structured both by institutional and societal factors and how nationalism has acted as a powerful influence on the development of racism.

DECODING RACE AND RACISM

The term "race" has origins in the Romance languages, in the old French term "rasse" but also in the Italian term "razza" from roughly the 1500s. However, it is generally recognized that our contemporary understanding of race emerged in the late eighteenth century as anthropologists and biologists sought to understand the significance of human variation and European empires sought to justify colonial projects.[4] Today, as several scholars have recognized, race, although understood by many to be biologically defined, is first and foremost a social construct.[5] Shih et al. simply state that "race does not exist outside of our social world."[6] This observation lends a cautionary note to social scientists who study race. To illustrate this point, a 2002 study by Harris and Sim on multiracial identity in the United States used census data to show the opaque, multiracial character of many Americans' identity and cautioned that "analysts must think critically about what they mean by race."[7]

Modern concepts of race and racism also have their roots in nineteenth century European romanticism, which helped give birth to ideologies of nationalism and a preference for Darwinian scientific classification.[8] As Europeans "discovered" those whom they deemed culturally and biologically inferior, they used the concept of race as a means of giving meaning to these differences while justifying violent colonial subjugation. Emerging European states used ideas of culture and racial difference to assign unique identities to "nations." When conceived of in culturally exclusive terms, these ideas of the nation

lent themselves to the development of notions of belonging and otherness – superiority and inferiority.

Racism in particular is a concept that is subject to numerous definitions and interpretations. Etymologically, the term racism is quite
modern, with origins in the early twentieth century. While human
beings have long suffered discrimination, prejudice, subjugation, and
violence on the basis of in-group membership, the term racism has
much more contemporary origins. Specifically, it can be traced to the
French word "racisme," which was initially used to critique German
nationalism in the 1920s.[9]

Today, our understanding of racism is shaped by contemporary and
recent historical experience: South African apartheid, segregation and
the Jim Crow American South, Nazi anti-Semitism, and the genocides
in Turkey, the Balkans, and Rwanda. The Second World War in particular highlighted the potential destructiveness of ideas born during
the European Romantic and Enlightenment periods, as fascism helped
to produce humanity's most self-destructive wars. Nazism came to
represent the most dangerous political outcome of biological ideas of
race and nation, although imperial projects in Japan produced similarly murderous results. It was during this period that the potential
consequences of biological racism (where human beings are placed
in distinct self-reproducing and biologically defined groups) became
painfully clear. From eugenics and phrenology tests to racial purity
examinations to the racially framed genocide of European Jews,
biological racism divided humanity into seemingly separate species
and provided justification for the murder of millions.

Biological ideas of race dominated scientific and popular understandings in the nineteenth and early twentieth centuries until what
Duffield refers to as the "cataclysm of the second World War" demonstrated the horrifying consequences of modern racism.[10] By 1966
the international community had, in its United Nations International
Convention of the Elimination of All Forms of Racial Discrimination,
called for the rejection of racism and ideas of biologically superior
races. Reflecting these concerns UNESCO offered its definition of
racism as "antisocial beliefs and acts which are based on the fallacy
that discriminatory intergroup relations are justifiable on biological
grounds."[11] Thus, as the international community attempted to prevent genocide and another cataclysmic war, modern racism was singled
out and identified as a threat to global peace and security.

In the mid to late twentieth century, biological racism was also attacked on purely scientific grounds. As Miles and Brown summarize, "It was generally concluded after the Second World War that the scientific conception of 'race,' grounded in the idea of fixed typologies and based upon phenotypical features, did not have any scientific utility. Moreover, the evidence showed no causal relationship between physical or genetic characteristics and cultural characteristics. Genetics demonstrated that 'race,' as defined by scientists from the late eighteenth century, had no scientifically verifiable referent."[12] Therefore, not surprisingly, today one can see highly differing approaches to race among scholars, ranging from those who believe the racial idiom should be wholly rejected (e.g., Michael Banton) to those (such as Robert Miles, Malcolm Brown, and David Goldberg) who recognize that, while it is not a scientifically grounded concept, the socially constructed idea of race can have pernicious social impacts that cannot be ignored. Goldberg, for instance, has been particularly critical of theorists such as Banton for attempting to reject the racial idiom.[13]

In short, Banton believes that race in particular has been "securely established in the practical language," in other words in everyday use that cannot be easily dispelled. For Banton, challenging racism involves "superseding 'race' in the theoretical language of social science ... [and] the development of a better theory of group formation and dissolution."[14] Racial categories for Banton are distinctly tied to the biological and are created to "exclude persons from equal relations."[15] He points out that unlike categories such as nation or class, race creates a "hard boundary" for individuals seeking social mobility.[16]

Banton's suggestion that we reframe difference away from the ideas of race has produced some sharp reactions from his peers. Goldberg has responded by stating, "No race here. No imagination of the racial because the terms are deadened, taken away. And so no conceivable recognition of the marks of its effects, let alone of the effects themselves. Buried. But buried alive."[17] Elaborating on this point, Dei has stated, "I find it hard to believe that one can take a stand that denies race and simultaneously can challenge racism effectively. Denying race is both theoretically and politically suspect."[18] According to scholars like Goldberg and Dei, ignoring race means neglecting its continuing social resonance as a category of human difference and potentially very negative social effects.

As race and racism theorists Michael Omi and Howard Winant point out, there are two temptations for those who seek to understand

and employ race in social analyses. One is to view race as an essence, something that is fixed and objective; the other is to view it as merely an illusion. They state, "It is necessary to challenge both these positions, to disrupt and reframe the rigid and bipolar manner in which they are posed and debated, and to transcend the presumably irreconcilable relationship between them."[19] Omi and Winant have called for race to be viewed as an element of social structure: "as a dimension of human representation rather than an illusion."[20] To this end they have used the concept of racial formation to describe the sociohistorical process through which ideas of race are created and transformed.[21] Following on this premise, race should be viewed as a term with both static and dynamic qualities: static in that it is constructed as a timeless and rigid social category of identity but dynamic in that, as shown by scholars like Omi and Winant, ideas of race are constructed within particular social structures and change over time. Thus, racist ideologies may connote a timeless hierarchy of social relations even if in reality race and racial hierarchies are dynamic – they are constructed in a specific place and time and shift because of changing norms, ideas, and material relations. For example, the Irish, particularly in American society, were viewed in the nineteenth century as racially inferior, whereas today they are very much part of mainstream society.

Even with the realization that race is a problematic category, for a variety of reasons, to ignore it, to "bury it alive" as Goldberg so artfully puts it, is to eschew an understanding of a highly destructive social force in our world. Social scientists may recognize the socially constructed nature of racial categories but this should not result in our ignoring its potentially pernicious effects.[22] With this understanding of race in mind, how then should we understand racism? How is it manifested? If scientific racism was relegated to the margins of society by the horrors of the Second World War, what has replaced it?

Balibar and Wallerstein take a holistic view of racism, viewing it as a "total social phenomenon" that inscribes itself through practices, discourses, and representations articulated around "stigmata of otherness" such as cultural or religious practices, skin colour, or name.[23] From this perspective, racism contains both evaluative and descriptive elements. In the descriptive process, often referred to in the literature as racialization, people are distinguished by what Balibar and Wallerstein refer to as the stigmata of otherness whether that otherness is defined by skin colour, ethnic identity, cultural affiliation, language, or religious belief. When the descriptive element is combined with the evaluative discourses and representations of the "other" in a discriminatory, exclusionary, or prejudicial manner that ascribes ideas of inferiority and superiority, we encounter racism.

Racist ideologies provide readily understandable explanations for social relations and a popular or common-sense account of the stratification of societies. Barker was one of the first theorists to clearly explain how racism (he was speaking of a particular kind of racism that he termed new racism) can be viewed as an ideology: "It is not a simple set of attitudes or prejudices, nor bodies of misinformation (though it can use all these). It is a structure of concepts which organize typical experiences, classify them for their importance, for their acceptability or unacceptability and which make policy formation possible. In this way, the ideology of the new racism can appear to be very like a science, because it is a worked-out theory."[24]

According to Memmi, the ideology of racism, or what he calls the philosophy of racism, postulates the existence of "pure" identities that are superior to others on the basis of social and cultural characteristics. It is these "superiorities" that explain and legitimize the exercise of power and economic and social stratification within a society.[25] Generalizable characteristics and qualities may be visible features and/or cultural behavioural tendencies that other groups are said not to share.[26]

Miles has long identified racism as a form of ideology. In his work, he has shown how ideas of race exist within a hierarchal system of signification and representation where racism has established a relational order.[27] Within a relational order, the racist ideology assigns various group characteristics that are used to compare and contrast with others, leading to claims of superiority. As Miles surmises, these "characteristics refract and so define each other."[28] Miles and Brown claim that "defining racism, as we do, as ideology rather than a doctrine includes within its scope relatively unstructured, incoherent and unsupported assertions, stereotypical ascriptions and symbolic representations."[29] In this way racism is an ideology that can be uncritically accepted by some, becoming a taken-for-granted or common-sense frame of reference for day-to-day social relations.

A popular understanding of racism is that it is a set of irrational beliefs and misunderstandings founded on ignorance and prejudice.[30] Balibar and Wallerstein outline how popular racist discourses provide "immediate interpretive keys not only to what individuals are

experiencing but to what they *are* in the social world."[31] Essed
describes this as "everyday racism" and describes how it can provide
a foundation for more institutionally grounded forms of racism: "It
links ideological dimensions of racism with daily attitudes and inter-
prets the reproduction of racism in terms of the experience of it in
everyday life."[32] Recognizing this interconnection, we can begin to
understand how racism becomes a comprehensive ideology that can
structure social relations and understandings. Political forces can tap
into the well of popular or everyday racism as a means of cementing
power and justifying political projects, such as anti-immigration and
border control policies, anti-crime and terrorism measures, and welfare reform.

Miles and Brown borrow Gramsci's understanding of common
sense to illuminate how this base-level understanding can be part of
a larger political project – what Gramsci referred to as hegemony.[33]
For Gramsci, common sense is an embedded and somewhat incoherent form of knowledge that helped to reinforce hegemony through
generating consent. In other words, it helped to make the status quo
(which is favourable to elites) seem natural and thus prevent social,
economic, and political change.[34] For hegemony to be adequately
challenged, for the elusive "revolution" to emerge, Gramsci believed
that, importantly, certain intellectuals would have to challenge these
forms of knowledge or "world view."[35] Omi and Winant, echoing
Gramsci's understanding of common sense, state that "in order to
consolidate their hegemony, ruling groups must elaborate and maintain a popular system of ideas and practices – through education, the
media, religion, folk wisdom etc. – which he [Gramsci] called 'common
sense.' It is through its production and its adherence to this 'common
sense,' this ideology (in the broadest sense of the term), that a society
gives its consent to the way in which it is ruled."[36] Within this social
formation, hierarchies are established that define inter-group relations
and avenues for political action. Put simply, if unstructured prejudices
were not rooted to underlying power structures – both political and
economic – they would not persist.

Thus, while today the language of scientific or biological race and
racism is taboo, as domestic and international norms largely disallow
its mobilization in the political sphere, these ideas may linger in the
realm of popular racism only to be re-articulated and reframed by
politicians and demagogues in ways that mask appeals to established
ideologies and "common sense." As shown in the introduction of this

book, new forms of racism have emerged, with the ideologies surrounding the anti-Islamic movement regularly used by political elites in the West today.

CULTURAL RACISM

Some race and racism scholars argue we have witnessed a shift in the descriptive element of racism: a shift from biological to cultural or ethnic forms of racism. According to Balibar and Wallerstein, racism can be presented in both biological and cultural terms, with the latter often imbued with the qualities of the former: "What we see here is that biological or genetic naturalism is not the only means of naturalizing human behaviour and social affinities ... *culture can also function like a nature*, and it can in particular function as a way of locking individuals and groups a priori into a genealogy, into a determination that is immutable and intangible in origin."[37] In other words, ideas of cultural difference can be construed as a natural aspect of human difference, and in this sense cultural racism can reflect ideas similar to biological racism; it can retain negative evaluations of difference, of superiority and inferiority, but alter the descriptive element of the ideology. Cultural racism shifts from positing racial superiority or inferiority to defending "superior cultural values" versus "barbaric cultural values" and in doing so indicates the supposed negative difference or intractability of some cultures.[38]

As highlighted by theorists such as Modood, this form of racism adds a new layer to existing racist discourses by positing a less overtly racist (as understood in biological expressions of racism) preference for one's own culturally defined background.[39] Barker, in his prominent 1981 work *The New Racism: Conservatives and the Ideology of the Tribe*, was one of the first race and racism scholars to highlight this understanding of racism. According to Barker, the new racism "is a pseudo-scientific theory, which is being articulated ... within 'commonsense' political arguments."[40] Importantly, what Barker identified was the highly political nature of this form of racism. Using the example of Margaret Thatcher's Britain, the discourse of racism was altered by political elites to sanitize the language of racism – to make racism palatable to a public weary of the language of biological racism.

By avoiding the language of biological racism, by altering the discourse and instead using the language of culture and ethnicity, immigrant and native, British Conservative politicians were able to shroud policies that, if dressed in the language of biological race, would have drawn outrage. Barker viewed the British Conservatives as particularly adept at concealing this form of new racism by concealing an ideology of racism "inside apparently innocent language. Its concealment enables it to provide form and structure to people's experiences and reactions, without displaying itself as a whole theory with big and dangerous implications."[41] A particularly salient observation for this book is that so-called new or cultural racism was employed by state actors within an anti-immigrant discourse. The "intractability of cultural difference" was used by conservative movements in the late twentieth century as justification for immigration controls and limits on the access of newcomers to the social democratic welfare state (which anti-Keynesian conservatives sought to at least partially dismantle).[42] Once these ideas were accepted publicly, according to Barker, "the danger from immigration is that the alien-ness of the outsiders cracks the homogeneity of the insiders."[43]

Importantly, for scholars like Barker, conservatives sought to use new racism as part of a populist strategy and as a means of obscuring other forms of identity division – for example, related to class. Thus, during the latter part of the twentieth century race and racism theorists saw the coming together of political forces that shifted the patterns of conflict and contestation among identity groups. This took place during a period of political upheaval and economic reorganization as many national economies went through a period of crisis known as stagflation.

Immanuel Wallerstein views the 1970s as the watershed moment when the dismantling of the welfare state and economic malaise in the West fueled renewed nationalism and stimulated the emergence of new political ideologies with a racist bent.[44] Arguably, the emergence of the (neo) conservative agenda was to have a lasting effect on patterns of racism in the decades to come, and it was in this moment in time that race and racism scholars began re-evaluating their understandings of racism.

Moreover, the post-war shift in discourses in racist ideology – from the biological to the cultural – corresponded with a change in how academics and bureaucrats conceptualized human difference and identity. The word "ethnicity" came to replace racial descriptions of difference. This change was driven by a new sociological scholarly work and the emergence of ethnicity theory. According to Omi and

Winant, within this approach "race was but one of a number of determinants of ethnic group identity or ethnicity. Ethnicity itself was understood as the result of a group formation process based on culture and descent."[45] The concern for some scholars, such as Chanock, was that labels like "culture" and "ethnicity" are misunderstood as homogenized identities. As he points out, "Cultures are very complex conversations within any social formation."[46] The concern was that academics were constructing fixed and essentialized images of human identity with little bearing on the locally and historically formed social relations that actually gave meaning to people's lives.[47] For policy-makers the concept of ethnicity allowed the homogenization of complex differences into a single category, potentially allowing the concealment of class- and race-based inequalities.[48]

In addition, the ethnicity discourse was harnessed by policy-makers in the West as a means of framing policies related to newcomer integration. Ethnicity and culture became the categories through which governments framed societal difference and the social "engineering" policies, including multiculturalism, which they employed as a means of managing growing diversity in the wake of post-war migration.[49] The concept of ethnicity came to displace other labels of identity as the chosen description of difference for policy-makers and bureaucrats.[50]

It is at this point in the analysis that we begin to approach an understanding of xenoracism – a form of racism that approximates cultural racism and can be differentiated from earlier biological forms. As Miles observes, racism experienced by Muslims cannot be neatly placed in the old black-and-white descriptions of race and racism: "The attempt to generalize the 'black' struggle to all those whose lives are influenced by racism therefore disavows the specific cultural and historical origins of non-African peoples. Thus, so the argument continues, the idea of 'black' has been of little or no significance in the mobilization of Muslims."[51]

Indeed, anti-Muslim racism is only one of multiple forms of racism that cannot be neatly placed in colour-coded descriptions and therefore cannot be contained in a binary-like, black-and-white understanding of race. Early twenty-first century Japanese imperialism and the discriminatory targeting of Chinese and other Asian peoples, Turkish genocide perpetrated against the Armenians, and the Nazi holocaust of the Jews are some examples of particularly murderous forms of racism that have taken place within phenotypically similar groups.

As we will see in the next chapter, xenoracism was one attempt by race and racism theorists to capture this non-colour-coded form of racism. As Omi and Winant recognize, "there can be no timeless and absolute standard for what constitutes racism, for social structures change and discourses are subject to re-articulation."[52]

NATIONALISM AND RACISM

Recognizing that historical social relations shape our contemporary understandings of race and racism today, the book now turns to examine a particularly influential ideology, one that has been consistently implicated in stimulating racism (and vice versa). Balibar and Wallerstein contend that "without the existence of an overt or latent racism, nationalism would itself be historically impossible."[53] Similarly, Lentin observes that "racism cannot be reduced to nationalism, or vice versa, yet each aids and abets each other. By the mid-nineteenth century, nationalism had emerged as the dominant political ideology and led to the construction of territorial and cultural nation-states. Therefore, it is the nation-state that is the main political vehicle for racism."[54]

The idea of the nation, much like the idea of race, is a socially constructed conception of human identity that is presented to the outside world as natural, relatively timeless, and immutable. Yet, building on the work of Benedict Anderson, the nation is perhaps best thought of as the "imagined community." Anderson viewed national communities, the idea of the nation as imagined, as "inherently limited and sovereign" where "the members of even the smallest nation will never know most of their fellow-members, meet them, or even hear of them." A nation is a finite construct, a "deep, horizontal comradeship," no nation has viewed itself as a political entity with global aspirations, and nations are bordered by other nations that contrast their uniqueness and distinctiveness.[55] A nation is imagined through the stories, myths, and legends that define its foundational character and place in the modern "family of nations." In this sense a national identity is not unlike other socially constructed categories like race. As Said writes, "The very idea of identity itself involves fantasy, manipulation, invention, construction,"[56] and as Goldberg observes, "Underlying racialism, not unlike nationalism, is an abstract presumption of familialism."[57]

The idea of the nation is often grounded in the mythos of an idealized past containing seminal peoples who share a language, high culture, and values. As with ethnic or racial identity, national identities are relational in nature – the nation only exists insofar as it is contrasted with other nations and peoples.[58] In this sense not only does nationalism act as a form of political representation on a global stage, but also, as Hall notes, the idea of the nation is "something which produced meanings – a *system of cultural representation*."[59] In particular, since the emergence of the nation-state in the context of European modernity it has been national cultures that have produced distinct notions of cultural superiority and belonging and otherness.[60]

From these observations it follows that how peoples define themselves and others, how they construct the nation, is important in terms of establishing the relational structure not only within but also between nations. According to Anderson, to understand ideas of nationhood, "We need to consider carefully how they have come into historical being, in what ways their meanings have changed over time, and why, today, they command such profound emotional legitimacy."[61] Noted cultural anthropologist Ernest Gellner, who was raised in Czechoslovakia (where he was later forced to flee Nazi annexation) developed a lifelong fascination with the subject of nationalism. In his early observances of the development of Czech nationalism and the emergence of fascist Nazi Germany, Gellner, similar to Anderson, identified what he believed to be the highly contingent and socially constructed nature of nationalism. He concluded that nations are not the natural and given political constructs they are portrayed as, but rather they are constructs of individual agents – authors, poets, political leaders, and generals who present sometimes competing versions of nationalism within a state.[62]

Gellner viewed nationalism, much like ideas of race, as a by-product of the Enlightenment and Romantic periods in Europe marked by the social development of a mobile anonymous mass of peoples with a shared high culture linked to a political unit, territory, or "state."[63] From philosophers like Herder emerged the idea that it was not the universalism of the Enlightenment that mattered but rather the diversity and specificity of European cultures. Therefore, for Gellner it was ultimately culture, which he defined as a shared set of traits, values, norms, and traditions that are transmitted from generation to generation, together with emerging forms of social organization (post-feudal) that represented the building blocks of national identities.[64]

When the idea of the nation was blended with the observations of Darwin it created a potentially explosive combination: communities were now not merely culturally distinctive but also biologically differentiated. These ideas gained currency during a period of socio-economic reorganization, caused by mass industrialization, which led to a groundswell of nativist ideas that sought to return to an idealized history: the "agrarian values" of seminal peoples. Building on the ideas of Darwinian classification of human difference and that certain peoples shared a high culture, ideas of extreme or ultra-nationalism emerged. This is a highly exclusivist form of nationalism where similarity of cultural, racial, and linguistic identity becomes a *precondition* for national membership and belonging.

As briefly discussed above, this form of nationalism has had particular consequences historically – for example, in helping to give rise to the ideas of European inter-war fascists and their calls for "racially pure" nation-states. Moreover, as Gellner notes, ultra-nationalism had particular consequences in plural state-societies. In these societies Gellner believed that either more extreme nationalists altered their views, accepting plural societies where the host culture adopted a "de-fetishisation" of the land (a de-linking of the idea that a culture has sole right to possession of a country) or ethnic conflict was inevitable.[65] Following on the same general observation, contemporary security theorists have focused on societal security, highlighting the connection between exclusivist conceptions of nationalism and ethnic cleansing. Take, for example, the work of Buzan and Segal, who acknowledge nationalism's penchant for creating conflict, "where its very definition of self presupposes exclusive groups, each bound together by deeply rooted cultural tradition and historical perceptions: things that automatically and strongly differentiate insiders from outsiders, us from them."[66]

Thus, the idea of the nation and the idea of race are similar in that they are imagined, or socially constructed, categories containing prescriptive ideas of inclusion and exclusion that demarcate boundaries between peoples, defining those who belong (members of the nation) and those who do not (foreigners).[67] Of importance for this book is the observation that the myth of exclusivity contained in certain forms of nationalism may lead to the social construction (within a national discourse) of newcomers, and those deemed culturally alien to the national ideal, as foreign (xeno) to the national identity.[68] This sort of ideal may wax and wane in terms of popularity (e.g., during periods of economic stress and prosperity) but can remain part of the historical narrative of a state.

Historically, nationalism was a contingent social construct built on the philosophical and scientific ideas of the time, founded during the socio-economic stress of the industrial transformation of agrarian societies. In the post-war era, when migrants entered the Western world in greater numbers, national projects that were based on exclusivist ideas of culture or ethno-racial identity have proven an unwelcoming environment for those who do not fit the national ideal. This is especially true in the context of globalization and neoliberal economic policy, with its associated periods of economic crisis, for example, as we experience today during the ongoing fallout from the Great Recession. If history is guide, we should be unsurprised over the re-emergence of a rejuvenated ultra-nationalist far right.

By comparison, there are nations, like Canada, that have historically been constructed as plural nations – for example, under the vision of biculturalism and state multiculturalism. Canada may provide an example of a form of nationalism that is constructed in a manner that is more amenable to cultural difference and less prone to institutionalized racism. Building on this idea, Anderson holds that, while ontologically similar to racism, nationalism may be evaluated in positive terms, while racism has been typically associated with negative emotions.[69] While this last observation will be unpacked further in the chapters to come it should be noted that a "thinner" and less exclusivist idea of Canadian nationhood (at least outside of the province of Quebec) helps to explain why Canada has avoided trends seen elsewhere – for example, the empowerment of more mainstream far-right political parties and overtly racist political discourse.

CONCLUDING REMARKS

Thus far the book has examined some of the key debates within race and racism studies and identified how racism is best understood as an ideology that can only be fully elucidated when contextualized within local and historical settings. It has shown how the concept of race has both static and fluid characteristics. Hierarchical social relations between identity groups may seem, on some levels, stable and immutable, but upon further examination ideas of race can also shift, resulting in new sets of social relations. On one level the realization that racial identity is a fluid concept may bring us some hope. Indeed, Lentin observes that "the fact that racialization and racism are repeated, affecting different groups over time, does not mean that racism is inevitable." She goes on to write, "Our political systems, our social and cultural infrastructure, and our discourse – the very way in which language is used – need to change if racism in Western societies is to be overcome."[70]

Colonialism, the development of nation-states, and periods of economic stress and reorganization were historical trends that helped to establish ideas of racial classification situated in biological difference. Philosophical and scientific ideas drawn from the Enlightenment and Romantic periods, most especially social Darwinism and ultranationalism, were essential in the development of modern racist ideologies. Yet, today scientists have shown that the concept of biological race has little scientific validity, even if, as observed by social scientists, this demonstration may do little to limit its ongoing popular resonance and negative effects. The legacy of biological racism remains, and even when descriptively repackaged in its cultural form it retains a seemingly timeless quality. In short, racism is deeply situated in social relations and continually (re)shaped by political power.

Acknowledging the influence of political projects on the development of racism, one must recognize that racism is not merely prejudice or unstructured beliefs – the purview of the uneducated and misinformed. Racism is linked to political priority – to the priorities of power, whether these are the exploitation of colonized people, enslavement for material gain, or the identification of undesirable immigrants. Ideologies of racism are framed and shaped by historically resonant narratives like nationalism that provide simplistic and easily understandable "common-sense" ideas of social relations.

Today, particularly in Europe, ideologies of racism are reinforced by political elites originating from both the far right and the conservative centre. In the face of globalization and heightened migration these political forces have called for a more homogenous and exclusive vision of nationhood and the assimilation (or even deportation) of those deemed to be alien, "barbaric," or foreign to that national vision. Some have called for a return to a mythical chimera – the monocultural state. These social and political forces, as in prior periods of socio-economic reorganization and crisis, call for a return to an idealized past – even if that image bears little resemblance to reality – both past and present.

The next piece of the puzzle in this book will be developing an understanding of xenoracism and how it may apply to Canadian Muslims. Recognizing that identities are relational and that social relations are situated in particular historical structures means that any analysis of a racist ideology must elucidate these structures. It is important to understand how identities are framed and how they are socially constructed, whether those identities are national, racial, or cultural in nature. As Miles has stated, when it comes to the construction of human identities, "characteristics refract and so define each other" and thereby lead to claims of superiority.[71] Thus, this book argues that racism, however it is structured, can only be adequately understood through the lens of history and locality. Given these observations, the primary question for the next chapter is as follows: does the concept of xenoracism best capture the racism being experienced by Canadian Muslims?

3

Xenoracism and Orientalism

Xenoracism today is most easily detected in the narratives and actions of a growing anti-Islamic social movement. Inflated fears over violence, dangerous and "barbaric" cultural values, and uncontrolled population growth among Muslims in the West have been exploited by right-wing extremists, bloggers, academics, and politicians of various stripes. Since 9/11, fears over homegrown violent extremism and terrorism have driven states to adopt a series of security practices. Some of these practices were necessary to protect public safety, but others have resulted in forms of profiling, surveillance, and detention that are detrimental to the civil liberties of Muslim populations living in the West. In this sense, xenoracism is a form of racism that can be (intentionally or unintentionally) generated through security, immigration, and citizenship policies.

As shown in the preceding chapter, racism is an ideology that posits a hierarchical social order. Racist ideologies are shaped by and dependent on locality, political priorities, and historical knowledge or "discourse" vis-à-vis the other. Ideas of social identity and how identity is constructed in a particular context are central to a racist ideology. Identity is relational: the values and characteristics that are said to belong to one community highlight, or "refract," to use Miles' description, different characteristics of other identity groups. Thus, identities related to race or culture are not constructed in isolation. Racism places social identities in a hierarchical order and posits ideas of superiority and inferiority. Combined with underlying political and economic structures, these ideas help to shape social relations in a particular time and place: material relations and ideational forces combine to create a "common-sense" framework or structure of social relations.

If a nation-state or community defines itself in exclusivist terms, tied to an idea of cultural or racial uniformity or purity, everything outside of that identity is the xeno, the foreign. In a project of nation building, or a period of crisis and conflict, the foreign "other," especially those defined as the enemy, may be identified as an existential threat to a nation, its values, and its existence as a homogenous, territorially defined socio-political unit. This kind of perceived existential threat is what security theorists have referred to as societal insecurity.[1] The perception of threat from alien outsiders to a monocultural nation-state was a critical component of what Barker and Lentin have described as "new" or cultural racism – a discourse that builds a case for the intractability of cultural difference and why some immigrants simply do not belong in the West.

According to Mac an Ghaill, today we experience "highly contested national arenas in which questions about immigration and what constitutes the nation-state are major debates."[2] Globalization, post-colonial migration, and multicultural societies have challenged established understandings of nationhood and belonging. Over the past decade and a half, debates over immigration and what constitutes the nation-state have become increasing acrimonious. The looming threat of terrorism and extremism has worked its way to the centre of this debate, over what is safe and desirable cultural diversity and what is dangerous and undesirable diversity. According to Lentin, this securitized discourse "is based on creating a separation between insiders and outsiders with only those who are within the nation protected."[3] Fekete has described some of these outsiders as the "suitable enemy," an apt description that highlights how some outsiders – especially Muslims – have been heavily securitized in debates over immigration and diversity.[4] The narrative of us versus them has not solely been the purview of far-right politicians or their ideological supporters in the media; it has been adopted by "intellectuals" as well. A good example of this can be found in Jim Sciutto's 2008 book *Against Us: The New Face of America's Enemies in the Muslim World*: "Just after 9/11, President Bush declared nations around the world 'with us or against us' in the war on terror. Now, those in the Muslim world are against us in greater numbers than ever before – and they have a new face. A remarkable variety of people – normal people – believe the United States intentionally obstructs rather than promotes progress. Al-Qaeda may be losing the military campaign, but, in considerable ways, it is winning the ideological war."[5]

The message from Sciutto is clear. We are at war: not just with al-Qaeda but with much of the Muslim world, with everyday "normal" Muslims, the kind you see on the bus on the way to work or in the supermarket, the ones in the taqiyas, hijabs, and niqabs. "They" are uniformly against "us." They oppose our cultural values. They reject progress and hate our freedom. In fact, they possess "barbaric" and dangerous values, which if not regulated, controlled, or stamped out will destroy who we are. In short, this is the narrative of the anti-Islamic social movement and it is the narrative that was mobilized by a re-emboldened neo-conservative movement in the United States in 2001 (under the leadership of George W. Bush) that eagerly pursued a militarized agenda against the "suitable enemy" – suitable in that it conveniently replaced the Soviet Union as the existential threat for the American people and allowed for the pursuit of the neo-conservative agenda, namely the extension of American power.

Xenoracism is both the result and the foundation of these narratives and strategies. Ultimately it is Muslims who feel the negative effects of xenoracism in their day-to-day lives. As Fekete writes on this subject, "Since Islam now represents 'threat' to Europe, its Muslim residents, even though they are citizens, even though they may be European-born, are caught up in the ever-expanding loop of xenoracism. They do not merely threaten Europe as the 'enemy within' in the war on terror, their adherence to Islamic norms and values threatens the notion of European-ness itself."[6] In this ideology, Islam is as a threat to national and societal security: the threat of the suicide bomber is juxtaposed with the cultural threat of the veiled woman and the demographic bomb.

This chapter will elaborate on the concept of xenoracism by first looking at how it has been employed historically in race and racism literature and by reviewing some of the debates over its usage. It will then examine what can be described as the historical roots of the ideology: the relationship between "the West" and Islam, between the Occident and the Orient, that has structured contemporary xenoracism. Finally, the chapter will deconstruct this relational identity through the theory of Orientalism, as conceived by the social and literary theorist Edward Said.

CONCEPTUALIZING XENORACISM

It was during the 1980s and 1990s that race and racism theorists began questioning long-standing assumptions on the nature of racism.

As Sajid observes, during this period "many sociologists and cultural analysts observed a shift in racist ideas from those based on skin color to those based on notions of cultural superiority and otherness."[7] On this point Miles acknowledges that racism can be colour-coded or non-colour-coded: "One can conclude that those who cannot be seen by virtue of their existing phenotypical features are equally vulnerable to being racialised: their 'non-visibility' can be constructed by the racist imagination as the proof of their 'real' and 'essential' (but 'concealed') difference, which is then signified by a socially imposed mark."[8]

As the term suggests xenoracism, or more accurately xenoracists, target their victims on the basis of a perception of foreignness. But the term xenoracism has most commonly been used to describe non-colour-coded racism; for example, it has been used to describe racism experienced by white economic migrants, such as Poles and Romanians, who relocated to Western European labour markets in the 1990s and 2000s. As the originators of the term, race and racism scholars Liz Fekete and Ambalavaner Sivanandan used xenoracism to describe a form of racism they believed they were witnessing in the European Union in the late twentieth century: racism toward asylum seekers and white migrants introduced into Western European labour markets through the supranational integration of the European community. Sivanandan conceptualized xenoracism as a form of racism that "denigrates and reifies people before segregating and/or deporting them, a xenophobia that bears all the marks of the old racism, except that it is not colour coded. It is racism in substance, though xeno in form."[9] For Sivanandan, this form of racism was tied to modern political and economic structures, "a feature of the Manichaean world of global capitalism, where there are only the rich and the poor – and poverty is the new Black."[10] Drawing these understandings, Lentin states, "Under this rubric, the poor of the ex-Soviet Union and its satellite states – Albanians, Poles, or Roma gypsies – are as alien as the African with whom they may find themselves sharing a dormitory in an Immigration Detention Centre awaiting deportation."[11]

To date xenoracism has been employed sparingly within Critical Race Theory literature, and in some cases its usage has sparked debate. Some race and racism theorists, such as Mike Cole, adopted the term as a means of describing class-based discrimination against white Eastern European economic migrants.[12] Lentin also favoured this understanding.[13] However, others, such as Critical Race Theory theorist Charles Mills, have been altogether dismissive of the term: "Recognizing the equal moral badness of the many different forms of discrimination should not cause us to conflate them with one another. We already have a term, 'xenophobia,' signifying fear and hatred of the foreigner. Why do we need 'xeno-racism?'"[14] What critics such as Mills fail to recognize is that xenoracism conceptualizes a form of racism that goes beyond an ahistorical/apolitical "fear of foreignness," as contained in the term xenophobia, to capture a politically and institutionally driven form of racism.[15]

Ultimately it has been Sivanandan's colleague Liz Fekete who has developed and expanded the usage of the term, using it as a means of describing racism that targets Muslim communities in the post-9/11 environment. Again, this usage has drawn some criticism from race and racism scholars. For example, Cole prefers to keep what he considers to be Islamophobia as a separate category of racism. Cole contends that Fekete's usage of the term xenoracism is "wide," views the term as more "region-specific," and prefers to use the term in regard to the marginalization of economic migrants in the European Union. Recognizing these criticisms, how can we judge Fekete's usage of the term that includes racism that targets religious communities, specifically Muslim populations?

Fekete notes that, as with asylum seekers and economic migrants, Muslims are being targeted as foreign outsiders, especially in the highly securitized post-9/11 environment in the West: "What appears to have happened post-September 11, though, is that the parameters of that institutionalised xeno-racism – anti-foreignness – have been expanded to include minority ethnic communities that have been settled in Europe for decades – simply because they are Muslim. Since Islam now represents 'threat' to Europe, its Muslim residents, even though they are citizens, even though they may be European born, are caught up in the ever-expanding loop of xeno-racism."[16]

This form of racism is not unlike anti-Semitism, which is a form of discrimination and prejudice with deep historical roots that targets individuals on the basis of religious and cultural difference – a perception of foreignness.[17] There are obvious similarities in racist ideologies that target Muslims and Jews. As Goldberg acknowledges, in Europe it has been Jews and Muslims who have "historically book-ended modern Europe's explicit historical anxieties" about the "other."[18]

On one hand, xenoracism is an appropriate term for describing discrimination against Muslim communities residing in the West because religious adherents to Islam are racially, ethnically, linguistically, and culturally highly diverse: in short, Islam is a global religion. Since Muslim communities are so diverse in their origins, for example, containing a number of white converts and European Muslims from Balkan states, a racist ideology cannot be readily constructed in colour-coded terms. Instead, Muslims are targeted on the basis of a perception of foreignness signified through visible cultural and religious symbols (such as the hijab) or fears over concealed sympathies for "barbaric" cultural values. Even critics of this wider usage of the term by Fekete (such as Cole) recognize that "Islamophobia, like other forms of racism, can be colour-coded: it can be biological (normally associated with skin colour). But it can also be cultural (not necessarily associated with skin colour), or it can be a mixture of both."[19]

The term Islamophobia, like the term xenophobia, refers to fear and anxiety; for example, Gottschalk and Greenberg define it simply as "a *social* anxiety toward Islam and Muslim cultures."[20] Sajid traces the term's original usage to the Runnymede Trust report, which defined it as "unfounded hostility towards Islam, and therefore fear or dislike of all or most Muslims."[21] In this sense Islamophobia, like xenophobia, refers to the sort of unstructured, or "unfounded" as Sajid puts it, ahistorical/apolitical form of societal prejudice. However, this understanding of racism ignores the often highly politicized and institutionalized nature of racist ideologies – it ignores how racist ideologies are imbued with political and economic power. For social theorists like Lentin the role of political institutions is critical in maintaining racist ideologies. In spite of the fact that most social scientists have recognized race as a social construct, racism persists: "It persists because of the political power of racism and the fact that, despite proclamations to the contrary, it has become institutionalized in the structures of our societies."[22]

In examining contemporary forms of racism in the European Union, with a specific focus on Britain, the members of the Institute of Race Relations laid bare the institutionalized nature of racism, especially within the context of the modern nation-state. On this Fekete comments that "it is racism in substance in that it bears all the hallmarks of demonisation and exclusion of the old racism – and the mechanisms that set foreignness in situ are legal and structural and institutional."[23] Sivanandan too ties xenoracism, its popular and institutional facets, back to the state. Using the example of Britain, he states, "To put it another way, institutional racism and popular racism are woven into state racism and it is only in unraveling it that you begin to unravel the fabric of racism."[24]

Barker's work on "new" racism identified how racism had been incorporated into the public narratives and policies of the British Conservatives in the late 1970s and early 1980s, as exemplified by the Thatcher conservatives.[25] For Fekete and Sivanandan, these political discourses were co-opted in the 1990s into the policies of the so-called Third Way, for example, as under Tony Blair's "new" Labour Party; in particular it could be detected in policies related to the management of asylum seekers.[26] Specifically this involved a shift from policies that were centred on the guiding principles of human rights to a policy that was geared toward security and an economically centred management of migration that aimed at deterring non-skilled migrants. According to Fekete, this political decision was to provide "the ideological space in which racism towards asylum seekers became culturally acceptable."[27]

A central argument in this book is that after the events of 9/11 these already-established patterns of xenoracism were expanded through another channel of public policy, namely national security, and immigration and integration policy. Scholars have pointed out how the securitization of immigration and integration, for instance, the portrayal of some minority groups as a threat to the security of the nation, can rest on the construction of a quality of "dangerous foreignness." For example, according to Abu-Laban and Dhamoon, "'foreignness' and especially the construction of 'internal dangerous foreigners' seem to coincide with discourses of nation-building, security, and race-thinking."[28]

In their Canadian-based study, Abu-Laban and Dhamoon examined linkages between conflict, nation building, and the targeting of "internal dangerous foreigners" by examining a series of case studies, such as the internment of Japanese-Canadians during the Second World War. They concluded that in these case studies foreignness was "produced and regulated in historically specific ways with consequences for how 'the nation' is viewed."[29] They found that "while foreignness is a constant and long-standing marker of racialized Otherness," this quality is "not static but is, instead, historically changeable according to the security threats deemed most significant to those [who are in power]."[30]

In the case studies used by Abu-Laban and Dhamoon, the idea of the dangerous foreigner challenges our ideas of belonging in the context of the nation-state; it challenges our understanding of who is a legitimate citizen, of what is desirable and safe diversity, and of what is undesirable and dangerous diversity. As in previous periods of profound conflict and instability, within the so-called War on Terror a dangerous foreigner has been identified: a global religion with more than one and a half billion adherents. As one interviewee in the present study, Ahmed Shoker, director at the Canadian Islamic Congress, noted, "The problem of it in my judgement is that since September 11th the Muslim communities have been on the spot to really, if I may say, answer to the larger community to prove their innocence ... [it] puts us on a sort of indictment chair."

Importantly, Abu-Laban and Dhamoon point out that discourses on security are critical in defining notions of foreignness and belonging to a nation. Today, security is not only a discourse but rather is also a reality for people in their day-to-day lives. This reality has been experienced through mass casualty terrorism in New York, Madrid, London, Paris, and elsewhere, through the terrible imagery it produces, endlessly repeated on twenty-four-hour news services (much to the perpetrators' delight). It is experienced through counterterrorism measures that states impose as a means of preventing future attacks, through no-fly lists and biometric security. But in those preventive measures, especially the legislative response to 9/11 and subsequent attacks, we may find another potential institutional channel for xenoracism. According to Fekete, "What finally set the seal on xenoracism" was the way in which counterterrorism was pursued in the early twenty-first century.[31]

The War on Terror became a war that was fought not only on the ground and in the air in Somalia, Afghanistan, Iraq, Libya, Yemen, and Syria but also at "home" in the context of the sometimes very real fears over "homegrown" "radicalization," violent extremism, and terrorism. Fekete notes the connection between local and global factors in constructing a xenoracist narrative. She writes, "Western interventions in Muslim countries provide yet more opportunities for the media to demonise particular groups, even nations, serving to weave general public opinion into a global warfare against Muslims."[32] In short, securitized integration and citizenship laws go beyond the "social anxiety"or "unfounded fear" contained in a term such as Islamophobia – rather it is here where we encounter xenoracism.[33]

Therefore, in this book the term xenoracism is used to describe racism that emerged in the post-9/11 environment and has been felt most acutely by Muslims. As an ideology, xenoracism's descriptive element is distinctly tied to ideas, or a quality, of foreignness (as denoted in its xeno prefix). As illustrated above, what is viewed as foreign in a particular local context can vary and is dynamic. It doesn't necessarily have to be based on appearance or skin colour – rather it is based on historically framed social, economic, and political relations. In particular, ideas of foreignness, rooted in perceptions of belonging and exclusion, are influenced by conflict, and those who are designated as dangerous or the enemy in a particular social context are most prone to this form of racism. Further, while situated in the contemporary, xenoracism that targets Muslims is also tied to historical knowledge of the "other." The term itself may be a recent invention, but there are historically established patterns of discrimination and prejudice aimed at Muslims, a phenomenon that is partially captured in the work of Said.

ORIENTALISM AND HISTORICAL REPRESENTATIONS OF ISLAM

So far the chapter has explored some of the previous usages of the term xenoracism and how it was originally conceptualized by members of the Institute of Race Relations. At the end of the twentieth century Fekete and Sivanandan were trying to capture manifestations of racism they were witnessing in Western Europe. They spoke of a political campaign against asylum seekers and economic migrants that after the events of 9/11 became a campaign against terrorism and religious communities. Yet, to fully understand xenoracism that targets Muslims one must look to deeper, more complex, and established historical social relations between Islam and the West.

Indeed, central to the historical construction of the West, historically conceived of as the European and Christian world, was a relationship with Islam. Returning to Goldberg's observation that religious minorities, such as Jews, have historically "book-ended" Europe's historical anxieties over religious difference, Miles and Brown note that within the historical narratives of Europe, the Muslim, Moor, Saracen, or Turk became the identity that marked the boundaries of Europe territorially and ideationally: "Thus, not only did Europeans create a discourse of an imagined Other at the edge of European civilization, but they created a discourse of a real Other represented as a result of conflicting material and political interests with a population which came to mark the boundary of Europe, spatially and in consciousness."[34] As Miles and Brown point out, "contemporary representations are always the product of historical legacy and active transformation in the context of prevailing circumstances."[35]

With these points in mind, an ideology of racism, like xenoracism, is situated in both contemporary social relations and historical knowledge, even if that history is as reconstructed and re-imagined to carry resonant meaning in contemporary times. Arguably, Said has carried out the most effective deconstruction of the modern representations of the Orient and the Occident. Through deconstructing the ways in which the West has portrayed the Orient, especially the Islamic world, Said reveals the preconceptions and biases that have long shaped how the West views Islam. According to Said, historical representations of Islam contain a number of biases or dichotomies that led to a representation of the Islamic world within a reductive and oppositional discourse. Within eighteenth- and nineteenth-century European literature, Islam came to represent atavism, a reactive counter-response to an enlightened Europe – an anti-modern and anti-democratic identity that was a threat to the West.[36]

Said focused much of his work on the literature of Western Orientalists, scholars whose subject is the Orient – those who produce Western knowledge of the "other." Said's 1979 work *Orientalism* has been the subject of numerous scholarly works, critiques, and expansions. The term Orientalism in and of itself does not necessarily refer to discriminatory representations of the Orient; rather it is a field of study that focuses on the languages, culture, and society of the wider Orient.[37] Orientalism must be viewed in the context of the historical relations between the Occidental and the Islamic world, especially their historical legacy of exchange, conflict, and colonization.

A key underlying theme of Said's work is that "Orientalism is the affiliation of knowledge with power."[38] Orientalism, for Said, became a "Western style for dominating, restructuring, and having authority over the Orient."[39] Thus, paralleling an understanding of racism as an ideology, Said demonstrated how ideas of human difference structure social and political relations and are grounded in underlying power structures, both ideational and material.

In particular, Said's work draws on that of Michel Foucault, who believed that knowledge was inseparable from power. Said specifically used Foucault's notion of discourse from *The Archaeology of Knowledge* to understand Orientalism as Western knowledge that is used "to manage – and even produce – the orient politically, sociologically, militarily, ideologically, scientifically, and imaginatively during the post-enlightenment period."[40] As observed by Elgamri, this defines not only what can be said and thought about the Orient but also who has the authority to speak. It was this discourse, this form of knowledge, that justified European nation building and projects of imperialism and colonialism.[41] Indeed, historically European imperialism required the development of "ideological formations" built on notions of superiority that ultimately lead to the justification of military and economic domination.[42]

Within historical texts, Muslims were represented through a set of specific stereotypes: as fanatical, violent, lustful, and irrational, an "idea [that] has persisted because it's based very deeply in religious roots where Islam is thought of as a kind of competitor of Christianity. Islam arises out of the same soil as Christianity, the religion of Abraham: first in Judaism, then Christianity, then in Islam."[43] This generalized and stereotypical imagery of the other created a position of "irreducible opposition to a region of the world it considered alien to its own."[44] With respect to xenoracism that targets Muslims in the West, discourses on relations between the Islamic world and the West reinforce the seemingly natural and timeless nature of social relations between these two essentialized identities.

However, these narratives and stereotypes are not static: Orientalism is dynamic in character. In studying post-Enlightenment writings on the Middle East, Said noted not only the stereotyping of Muslims as atavistic, fanatical, and potentially violent but also a considerable tendency toward exoticization and sexualization. As with other Orientalist stereotypes, this idea was constructed through juxtaposition of the image of a powerful masculine West and a weaker effeminate East, the latter being irrational and depraved when contrasted with the rational, sexually conservative, and virtuous West.[45] Today, some elements of these ideas and representations seem quite opposed to contemporary thought. For instance, the sexualized image of the Islamic world, something to which Said paid considerable attention in his work (he even used the nineteenth-century Jean-Léon Gérôme painting "The Snake Charmer" for the cover of *Orientalism*, which features a nude, rather androgynous figure wrapped in a serpent), seems somewhat foreign to the current image of Islam in the West, for example as portrayed in the media. Today, the sexualized images of North African and the Middle Eastern men and women so associated with nineteenth-century Western imagery have been replaced with a new form of fetishization: that of the desexualized female. It is far more likely that public representations of Muslim women in the West today rest on the hijab, the niqab, and the burka rather than the sexual imagery seen on *Orientalism*'s cover.

What has remained as a relatively unchanging element of Orientalist representation of Islam is the view of a static and monolithic religion that is reactive, violent, intolerant of pluralism, and, at its core, anti-modern.[46] This essentialized view of Islamic identity has deep roots in established Western scholarship. In particular, these ideas were shaped by the writings of sociologists like Max Weber, who evaluated the Orient on the basis of his understanding of the West, its culture, its history, and its approach to modernization. From this perspective the Orient, most especially the Islamic world, lacked rational law and a modern-European-style state that Weber believed were essential for successful modernization.[47]

This Weberian understanding has been particularly influential in the works of prominent Orientalists like Bernard Lewis. Undoubtedly Said launched his most scathing and convincing critiques for individuals like Lewis, who in his work *What Went Wrong? The Clash between Islam and Modernity in the Middle East* attempted to analyze what he saw as the long-standing decline in Islamic civilization, a popular theme in contemporary Orientalist works. Lewis's ultimate answer, derived from a comparison of European and Middle Eastern history, is that Islam *is* the problem, that religion and an inability to adopt aspects of modernity and secularism have prevented the Islamic world from embracing essential values and aspects of modernization, such as Western ideals of freedom of speech and religion. The consequence of this failure is said to be the historical decline of a great "civilization" relative to the West, which, according to Lewis, results in regions like the Middle East being increasingly beset by violent and reactive social movements best represented by the image of the suicide bomber.[48]

For Said, the work of Lewis and other contemporary Orientalists is evidence of the repetition of the same discourse, the same stereotypes, as in the nineteenth century. He maintains that "all of Lewis's emphases in his work are to portray the whole of Islam as basically *outside* the known, familiar, acceptable world that 'we' inhabit [author's italics]."[49] On these understandings, Said states that "most of this is unacceptable generalization of the most irresponsible sort, and could never be used for any other religious, cultural, or demographic group on earth."[50]

In our highly globalized era, contemporary Orientalism, like other forms of knowledge, is now disseminated more widely than ever before. Present-day xenoracists such as Daniel Pipes and Robert Spencer now have online mediums through which they can spread their toxic message. As in prior iterations, that narrative rests on opposition to Islam and "Islamic values" that are seen as antithetical to European modernity, progress, and success. These narratives are coloured and influenced by historical texts, and it is these historical representations that give greater legitimacy to the orators of contemporary xenoracism. The legacy of Orientalism layers the ideology of xenoracism with contextualization and resonance, which in turn gives the construction of Muslims as the dangerous "foreign other" greater salience. Thus, Said's *Orientalism* leads us to the conclusion that xenoracism is imbued with power and that intellectual knowledge of the other can be a significant source of power; power is, of course, essential to the construction of a racist ideology.

Despite the fact that the world is an increasingly interconnected place marked by diffuse patters of migration, cosmopolitanism, and intercultural exchange, the stereotypical understanding of Islam in the West has persisted. The stereotypes have been re-articulated and recontextualized within the politicized and publicized events of the twentieth century. For example, in *Orientalism,* Said wrote of three factors involved in the politicization of Islam in the later twentieth century. First was the historical anti-Islamic prejudice in the West, which was a major focus of Orientalism. Second was the ongoing Arab-Israeli conflict, and third was an absence of a neutral "cultural position" that would allow for a dispassionate discussion of the Islamic world in the West.[51]

Said was forthright in his view that Orientalism was first and foremost tied to a "political vision of reality."[52] The often fractious political reality of the post-war era and the later part of the twentieth century, especially the 1960s and 1970s, which witnessed the emergence of "post-material values" and social movements around the world, had a meaningful impact on Western perceptions of the "Islamic world." Notably, the Iranian revolution was to have a lasting effect on the perception of the Muslim world in the West; however, this was only one of a number of events that was to shape contemporary views. The civil war in Algeria, the Soviet invasion of Afghanistan, the protracted violence of the Arab-Israeli conflict, the condemnation of and controversy over Salman Rushdie's work *The Satanic Verses*, the first Gulf War, the failed American intervention in Somalia, and the emergence of militant groups such as the Taliban, Hamas, Hezbollah, and al-Qaeda were the events that shaped the modern Western image of the Islamic world.

One interviewee, Baha Abu-Laban, a professor of sociology at the University of Alberta, views anti-Muslim sentiment as being expressly driven by global geopolitical events: "The 1967 Arab-Israeli war was one of those events ... [the] 1973 war was similar with the oil embargoes ... Lebanon in 82, the First Gulf War ... all of it is event-based, to a large degree, but after a few years ... it goes back to normal. Like today the situation is different to that which followed 11th September."

Pnina Werbner, a British scholar who focuses on the South Asian and Muslim communities in Britain, singles out the Salman Rushdie affair as a key event in altering the Western-Islamic dynamic, particularly in Western Europe. What Werbner described as the "moral panic" created by the book in some Muslim communities and the later revulsion of some over Rushdie's "death sentence" unearthed many of the underlying misconceptions that Said had highlighted in *Orientalism*.[53] As in the past, Muslims were again being portrayed, for example in the media, as atavistic and as monolithically extreme; they were said to have rejected Western conceptions of free speech and "secularism" and to have distinctly violent reactions when faced with "Western values." Not surprisingly, then, by the late 1990s Said was again sounding the alarm over anti-Islamic sentiments in the West, especially as contained in the media: "Sensationalism, crude xenophobia, and insensitive belligerence are the order of the day, with results on both sides of the imaginary line between 'us' and 'them' that are extremely unedifying."[54]

Thus, not surprisingly given the political and social context of the preceding decades, for some the events of 9/11 acted as a powerful confirmation of Orientalist messages – a point when pre-existing notions were combined with contemporary reality. This kind of reaction was perhaps best exemplified by the statements of former Italian prime minister Silvio Berlusconi after the 9/11 attacks when he stated, "We should be confident of the superiority of our civilization because of the religious and human rights generated – something that does not exist in Islamic countries."[55]

The post-9/11 period heralded an arguably unparalleled wave of Orientalist writings: books, scholarly studies, media articles, and online publications. A significant volume of this material was focused on the threat of "Islamic terrorism" and political Islam or Islamism, which had previously gained attention in the West with the Iranian revolution and the emergence of the Taliban in Afghanistan. But after 9/11, as Mohammed Ayoob has highlighted, Islamism became "fetishized" as a social and political Islamic movement in the West. Reflecting the legacy of Orientalism, understandings of Islamism became grounded in the old dichotomous comparisons and reifications: first, political Islam, like Islam itself, is monolithic, second, political Islam is an inherently violent movement, and third, the non-secular intermingling of religion and politics is unique to Islam.[56] The reality was of course quite different: Islamism, much like Islam itself, is a heterogeneous, broad-based political movement that is shaped by local and historical conditions.

Moreover, opposed to the violent image of political Islam, a majority of political Islamic advocacy is pursued through peaceful means.[57] The reality, which quickly becomes evident to an informed observer, is that the extremist or militant element of political Islam represents the minority, even if that minority is highly vocal and effective at using mainstream and online media to distribute its message.[58] Unfortunately, for some there is not only an association with militant Islamism and Islamism but also with militancy and the religion as a whole. Not surprisingly this has had particularly negative results for Muslims communities in the West. Fekete has noted that Muslim community groups have actively lobbied governments to not exaggerate the influence of the extremist minority in the Muslim community, which has led to the stigmatizing of Muslims. On this subject Fekete writes, "The views of a few rabble-rousing anti-western imams are presented as symptomatic of the whole Islamic community. 'Honour killings,' genital mutilation of African girls, North African youths who carry out gang rapes are, it would seem, all part of one Islamic cultural continuum."[59]

Today, for the re-emergent far right and the anti-Islamic social movement, historical grievances represent a rallying call, a tool for mobilizing opposition to what is seen as a contemporary "Islamic invasion." In the narratives of the anti-Islamic social movement, current events, especially examples of violent extremism associated with Muslims, are juxtaposed with battles that are centuries old. Individuals like Anders Breivik frequently used references to the crusades and past battles at the "Gates of Vienna" as examples of the kinds of actions that were needed to halt the "Islamic invasion" – entering the realm of the absurd, Breivik even identified himself as a born-again member of the Knights Templar.

These views are not held solely by the extremist fringes of the far right – they extend into a number of civil society and extremist movements. Take, for example, growing vigilante anti-immigrant movements like the Soldiers of Odin, which was formed in Finland to "protect" Europeans from immigrants, most especially Muslims, or the Patriotic Europeans against the Islamisation of the West, which has drawn tens of thousands to anti-Muslim rallies across Europe; these movements are energized by similar ideas and grievances.[60] The stories, myths, and legends born in the texts of the early Orientalists continue to resonate for those who see the Islamic world as an oppositional force. Whether it is the fringes of the anti-Islamic social movement drawing on crusade references or the more mainstream conservatives using the contemporary language of the War on Terror, they all draw on the same dichotomies that Said described nearly 40 years ago. For those who buy into that discourse, those representations, xenoracism has an almost natural and timeless quality.

The brief review of Orientalism offered above, of how Islam has been constructed through forms of historical knowledge in the West, demonstrates a great deal of continuity in portrayals of Muslims from the nineteenth century to the twenty-first century. However, it should be noted in brief that although Said's work was efficacious in deconstructing ideas of identity, his ideas are not without detractors. One criticism is that there is a degree of hypocrisy in Said's work, that much as Weber built an ideal type of the Orient, Said created an ideal type of the Occident. Also, it is hard to deny that the tone of his work is pessimistic, at times perhaps overly so. However, in Said's defence, while Weber sought to identify the ideal type of the West to explain its success, Said sought to deconstruct the Western ideal type as a means of challenging its validity.[61] It was a deconstructive mission that aimed to elucidate the fallacies and misrepresentations within the literature and undoubtedly such a task requires a commitment to a set of generalizations. It should also be recognized that while Said was undeniably pessimistic in his assessment of social relations he still held to the possibility of the creation of a more neutral standpoint and knowledge that could be the foundation of a relationship founded on respect and dignity.

CONCLUDING REMARKS

Ultimately, Orientalism was formed during an age of Western economic growth, military superiority, and imperialism. As Western states and societies encountered and dominated peoples who were clearly different – in dress, culture, religion, and race – they attempted to give meaning to those differences and justify the pursuit of power. A descriptive and racialized hierarchy of social relations was required for the development of these initiatives. As European society defined the other, and simultaneously defined itself, it developed a body of knowledge that was imbued with coercive power.

What these understandings of the other reveal, whether contained in an ideology of xenoracism or in Orientalism, is a highly generalized and stereotypical understanding of identity that does not reflect the complex and multi-layered nature of human identities. As Said argues, the conception of the Orient as a "constituted entity" where inhabitants "can be defined on the basis of some religion, culture, or racial essence proper to that geographical space is ... a highly debatable idea."[62] Said set out to deconstruct this knowledge with a hope that it can be replaced with a far more nuanced and sympathetic understanding. He asked, "How does one *represent* other cultures? What is *another* culture? Is the notion of a distinct culture (or race, or religion, or civilization) a useful one, or does it always get involved either in self-congratulation (where one discusses one's own) or hostility and aggression (when one discusses the 'other')?"[63] Additionally, as Said points out, historical intercultural and inter-religious exchange is a long-standing and ongoing process that can have a variety of outcomes including the creation of hybrid identities: "Such populations and voices have been there for some time, thanks to the globalized process set in motion by modern imperialism; to ignore or otherwise discount the overlapping experience of Westerners and Orientals, the interdependence of cultural terrains in which colonizer and colonized co-existed and battled each other through projections as well as rival geographies, narratives, and histories, is to miss what is essential about the world in the past century."[64]

The recognition of the possibility for an alternative history, one that significantly differs from the simplified and misrepresentative history presented by Orientalism, may be a significant step toward developing social relations less marked by exploitation and conflict. In an increasingly globalized and culturally diverse world, plural societies may offer the promise of new understandings of human difference, less coloured by misrepresentation of the other. Such a re-imagination of social relations should not involve forgetting a history marked by exploitation and conflict but rather unpacking that history and re-articulating it in what is undoubtedly a richer picture of social relations, one marked by both war and co-operation and by exploitation and exchange.

Today, Canada is presented as one of the world's more successful culturally plural states – a state that has successfully developed multiculturalism, unlike many others. According to the Aga Khan, the religious leader of more than 14 million Ismaili Muslims, Canada is the state that got pluralism right. He has stated, "What the Canadian experience suggests to me is that honouring one's own identity need not mean rejecting others."[65] The question for the next chapter is whether such praise is deserved.

4

Canadian Muslims and Xenoracism

Thus far the book has reviewed some of the existing research on race and racism and focused on how scholars have explained the dynamic nature of racism in the late twentieth and early twenty-first centuries. It has expounded on xenoracism and how it can be applied to racism that affects Western Muslims. The book will now move from the conceptual and theoretical to the specific, as it directly engages with the experiences of Canadian Muslims in the multicultural framework and critically examines the presupposition that multiculturalism in Canada has avoided the "crisis" experienced in much of the Western world. The question for this chapter is this: What do the life experiences of Canadian Muslims tell us about manifestations of xenoracism in Canada?

As an ideology that operates on multiple levels, both the societal and institutional, xenoracism is produced through policy and bureaucratic function and in everyday social relations. In chapter 2 it was pointed out that ideas of difference, patterns of racialization, and ideologies of racism are shaped by local conditions and geopolitical trends. Thus, Canada, marked by differing local, political, social, economic, and historical conditions, displays a unique set of social relations, although it remains subject to the same larger global political trends. Analyzing these relations and the presence or absence of xenoracism in a particular case study poses several challenges.

For instance, when examining individual-level experiences with racism it may be difficult for individuals to discern the reasons why they have been targeted. As with other social experiences, racism has a subjective element: individuals filter experiences through their own unique perspective moderated by their attitudes, outlooks, and life history. Moreover, as shown through sociological and anthropological study, individuals are situated within multiple communities and social identities. For example, a second-generation Canadian Muslim may be planted within the cultural mores and norms of the first generation, the cultural expectations and standards of the larger Canadian host culture, and a variety of overlapping identities related to gender, class, profession, and their immediate peer network.

With these complexities in mind, this chapter will examine experiences with xenoracism, first through an examination of survey data, primarily from Statistics Canada's Ethnic Diversity Survey (EDS) from 2003 and Environics' Survey of Muslims in Canada (SMC), which compares data collected from 2006 and 2016. What these sources lack is contextualization of individualized perspective on experiences with racism. With this limitation in mind, findings from the semi-structured interviews will be used to elucidate subjective experiences with xenoracism. Here individual stories are presented in greater detail, offering glimpses of how ideologies of racism operate in a particular time and place and affect individuals through the ambiguities, perplexities, and personal costs many experience through racism. However, before entering into the research itself, the book will first examine the diversity and complexity of the Canadian Muslim community.

THE CANADIAN MUSLIM COMMUNITY

Muslims in the West have been the subject of countless works, with a new wave of writing appearing after the events of 9/11. Orientalism continues to hold considerable sway in these analyses, often portraying the community as homogenous, marked by a uniform set of values and cultural practices. At one end of the spectrum, works such as Bruce Bawer's *While Europe Slept: How Radical Islam Is Destroying the West from Within* portray Muslims as a "peril" that could potentially destroy everything that the Europe and the West stands for.[1] At the other end of the spectrum, scholars like Jocelyne Cesari have attempted to highlight the heterogeneity found in Muslim communities in the West, the varying cultural identities, practices, and religious interpretations that exist in a diverse religious community, "to relocate the debate on the individualization of religious practice within the larger context of shifting boundaries of Islamic tradition that are being challenged in various ways throughout the Muslim world."[2]

As indicated by the evidence presented below, Cesari's understanding is far more reflective of the cultural identities and experiences of communities whose complexity disallows facile generalizations.

Globally, Muslim communities represent a remarkable diversity of cultural, national, tribal, and religious groups, whether it be sects such as Shi'a, Sunni, or Ismaili or ethnicities and nationalities such as Indonesian, Arab, or Persian. Islam is represented by individuals, families, and communities who display very different cultural traditions. Furthermore, as Paul Bramadat notes, these multiple identities are "'inextricably linked where various practices and traditions are intertwined making it difficult to discern where they originated."[3] Within the Muslim faith itself, during some periods there have been as many as thirty religious interpretations of Islam (religious traditions and schools of jurisprudence).[4] One interviewee, Usama al-Atar, a Shi'a Imam, drew a picture of the heterogeneity found in the Muslim community:

Islam is a way of life, there is the misconception that when people hear *Islam* they think of Arabic countries or Middle Eastern countries, but in fact Arabs consist of twenty percent of the Muslim population worldwide. Indonesia is a non-Arabic country that has the biggest Muslim population, China has a huge Muslim population, Malaysia, Turkey, Iran, and ... so there is a misconception that Islam is associated with the Arab world. If you go to the Indonesian culture, or the Indian culture, or the Malaysian culture, or the Chinese culture, or the Iranian culture, for a matter of fact, you will find they are celebrating their [own] cultural traditions.

Indeed, individuals may identify with Islam culturally without prescribing to the religion itself.[5] As Said observes, "Islam defines a relatively small proportion of what actually takes place in the Islamic world, which numbers a billion people and includes dozens of countries, societies, traditions, languages, and of course, an infinite number of experiences."[6] On the basis of the recognition of the complexities that exist in such identities, Werbner, a long-time observer of the Muslim diaspora, specifically South Asian communities in Britain, has called for "a revised conceptualisation of community, one which allows for internal diversity and conflict, for cross-cutting ties, for multiple identities citizens bear within a critical community."[7]

As in other religious traditions there are individuals who practise religion from a variety of perspectives and display varying degrees of religiosity. Tariq Ramadan, who has written extensively on the experience of Muslims in the West, identifies three primary categories that represent the majority of Muslims:

1   Those who refer to themselves as believers, practice Muslim traditions and observances but do not necessarily regularly attend religious services in places such a mosque.
2   Those who may refer to themselves as believers but do not respect or adhere to obligations and prohibitions of the faith such as the ban on the consumption of alcohol.
3   Those who define themselves as atheistic or agnostic but adhere culturally to Muslim traditions and practices despite having no formal religious affiliation.[8]

He claims that these categories represent, depending on locality, roughly 75–80 per cent of Muslims living in the west; the remainder, 20–25 per cent of Muslims, adhere strictly to religious precepts and attend religious services regularly.[9]

In general, Canadian Muslims, like their counterparts in other Muslim communities, display diversity in culture, ethnicity, race, sect, and degree of religiosity. However, in the context of Canada, this heterogeneity is especially pronounced, as noted by Saeed Rahnema:

> Muslims in Canada are highly diversified in terms of ethnic and national background. Over 212,000 or 36 per cent are from South Asia. Arabs constitute over 122,130, or 21 per cent of the Muslim population, followed by other west Asians, including Iranians, with over 81,000, and over 51,000 Muslims, identified as 'Black' in the Census. Canadian Muslims also come from other parts of the world, including South East Asia, China, Korea and the Philippines, with a small number from the United States. Canadian Muslims are further differentiated on the basis of sectarian affiliations (Sunni, Shi'i, Ismaili, Ahmadi, etc.) and degrees of religious convictions.[10]

EDS data roughly corroborate these numbers, with 85 per cent of Canadian Muslims counted as visible minorities, close to 38 per cent as being of South Asian descent, 35.6 per cent Arab or "West Asian," and 7.6 per cent Black.[11]

The first Canadian Muslims arrived in the late nineteenth century from states such as Syria and Lebanon, and some worked as goods traders in the "frontier."[12] Immigrants in the first waves of migration were primarily Sunni; however, waves of Shi'a came in the 1970s, especially from Iran.[13] One interviewee, Imam Sadique Pathan, who is the head of outreach and public relations in Western Canada at Islamic Relief Canada and the outreach Imam at the al-Rashid Mosque in Alberta (which is the oldest standing mosque in Canada), noted that "Muslims have been here since 1871. So, we have to ask the question what does it mean to be Canadian? Muslims were here, they were here with their families, many of them were assimilated – and some of them even anglicized their names. They have contributed meaningfully politically, [and] economically." McDonough and Hoodfar claim that during the initial influx of immigration there was little knowledge among members of the host culture about Islam: "Before the 1980s, Muslims in Canada lived in a society that was largely ignorant of Islam, but generally hospitable." However, starting with the 1979 Iranian revolution, the media began disseminating stories that linked the religion to conflict and political violence.[14]

Today, Canadians Muslims are marked not only by their heterogeneity but also by their youth, relative to the rest of the Canadian population. According to federal census data the Muslim population is the fastest growing religious group in the country, nearly doubling in size between 1991 and 2001, and today the population is more than 1 million or roughly 3.2 per cent of the Canadian population.[15] The median age for Canadian Muslims is roughly 28 years, whereas that of the Canadian population is closer to 37 years. Canadian Muslims are also well educated, with 56 per cent of them possessing some post-secondary schooling in comparison with 44 per cent of the general population.[16]

However, Canadian Muslims' higher level of education has not resulted in higher employment rates. In 2007 unemployment among Canadian Muslims was 14 per cent, compared with a national average of 7.4 per cent.[17] Moreover, many of the jobs that Canadian Muslims occupy tend toward the traditionally non-skilled area of the sales and service industry, where 27 per cent find employment.[18] Despite these challenges, Canadian Muslims represent a growing segment of the population that is young and well educated – a valuable human resource for any state marked by aging populations and a shrinking labour force.

The "Muslim Diaspora"

To reiterate, Canadian Muslims represent a diverse mosaic of communities. But according to some scholars, since 9/11 there has been a unifying trend within the larger community, which, on some levels, has brought communities closer together under a shared religious identity. For instance, Moghissi, Rahnema, and Goodman, in their 2009 work *Diaspora by Design: Muslim Immigrants in Canada and Beyond,* have used the term diaspora to describe a larger and unifying conception of identity centred around Islam,[19] but some scholars have asked whether this description is appropriate, especially when we speak of highly diverse religious communities.

Etymologically, the term diaspora is traced to the Greek word for dispersion and is most commonly associated with the Jewish community. It carries with it an idea of displacement and return to a preferred homeland.[20] According to Knight, the term diaspora is typically used to "describe any population that is considered transnational or 'deterritorialized' (i.e., which has originated in a country other than the one in which it currently resides and whose socioeconomic and political networks transcend state borders)."[21] Therefore, the term has been applied to peoples who have been forced from a "homeland" as a result of war or some form of persecution leading to their displacement.[22] However, as currently employed in much of the migration literature, the term seems somewhat open to interpretation – applying to virtually any and all minority groups that can be described as a diaspora without much consideration to the meaning of the term, something that Knight believes has led to the overuse of the term.[23]

Similarly Bramadat views the concept as problematic when it is applied to some religious communities and believes that for a group to be part of a diaspora there must be a communal preference to call another place home – a view of one's current place of residence as temporary.[24] Thus, when projected on multi-generational communities, this principle becomes increasingly problematic. Bramadat's concern is that the heuristic use of the term diaspora becomes "unintentionally exclusionary," a way "to distinguish between people who really belong here ... and people who are just visiting."[25]

In this sense the more problematic usage of the term diaspora can be placed within the larger context of what has been called the crisis of representation related to the (mis)representation of communities in many academic studies. As an alternative, scholars have suggested the term transnationalism, which, rather than denoting a desire for return or a sense of impermanence, refers to a more modern global reality, in which many of us have, as Bramadat writes, a "sense of living between two or more kinds of national or ethnic identities."[26] Indeed, in an increasingly globalized world, migrants and even families whose Canadian citizenship extends back several generations may carry multiple loyalties and cultural, national, ethnic, or racial identities (not to mention class, gender, or other forms of identity).[27]

Given the academic debate over the applicability of the term diaspora to religious communities (outside of the Jewish community), interviewees were asked about their views on the appropriateness of the usage of the term in the Canadian Muslim context. As pointed out by Baha Abu-Laban, professor of sociology at the University of Alberta and a long-time observer of the Muslim community in Canada and the United States, the use of the term diaspora is problematic in that "it is not clear if Muslims have intentions of returning to their home countries, even if their home countries stabilize politically." In his own prior research on Arabs and Muslims he found that "after a length of stay in Canada or in the United States the urge to go back and settle in the home country dissipates." For Abu-Laban a primary reason for migrants to lay down more permanent roots can be related to the birth of the second generation: "The point of focus becomes the children and their future and they say, 'Well I can't go back to Lebanon or Egypt or Syria' [because] my children are here, they were born here, they know the language here, they don't speak the native language, so this is where I am, and this is where my future is going to be."

Echoing Bramadat's and Abu-Laban's objection to the wider usage of the term on the basis that it infers a sense of impermanence, one interviewee, Dalal Daoud of the Canadian Islamic Congress, stated, "I don't like what it means, I don't like the term itself, it inhibits Muslims from seeing this as home." Repeating this sentiment was Usama al-Atar, a Shi'a Imam: "The Muslim community in general would not fit under [the] definition of diaspora ... they have a very strong sense of belonging to Canada." Usama al-Atar drew on the example of the Lebanese community in northern Alberta, in the town of Lac La Biche, who recently celebrated their 100th year of residency in the community and then posed the question, "So, do we consider that as a community living away from home? I mean it has been here for a century." Supporting this idea, scholars Sheila McDonough and Homa Hoodfar view the Muslim identity in Canada as shifting less toward diasporic tendencies but instead toward a national sense of belonging: "Through the transformation of their religious identity, roles, and institutions, as well as groups or voluntary associations, Muslims of diverse ethnic groups redefine themselves as primarily Canadian Muslims."[28]

Another interviewee, Shaykh Zak, who works as a Muslim "chaplain," objected to what he saw as a double standard in the usage of the term: "This diaspora thing was first coined for the Jewish community. Over time, I have found out that Judaism turned into ethnicity so the religion has really conformed to an ethnic concept in which you find it is not like a gene thing but it is the heritage – an ethnic concept ... now Christianity on the other hand ... you cannot talk about diaspora in this sense, you have to break it down into ethnicity to discuss it."

The conflation of religious with ethnic identity within a diasporic identity may be highly problematic when considering the heterogeneity found in the Muslim world in general and the Canadian Muslim community in particular. As interviewee Baha Abu-Laban pointed out, "When you think of a diverse community such as the Muslim Canadian one homeland means almost every country in the world." In turn the conflation of ethnic with religious identity may lead to a common misconception when we refer to the "Islamic world" or Muslims in general: the common association of Muslims with Arabs. Interviewee Yasmeen Nisam, a lawyer, noted that since Muslim communities are so heterogeneous, "I don't think there's a real, single Muslim identity because all these groups are so diverse in their traditions – in their practices – in the way they see the world. There are some very mainstream Muslims, there are some who don't even practice ... but they identify themselves as Muslims. Then there's practicing Muslims ... people that are more religious and their views differ quite dramatically ... so there's no one voice."

Interviewee Shayda Nanji, an Ismaili Muslim and member of the Edmonton Council of Muslim Communities, similarly objected to what she saw as a misrepresentation: "When Muslims are described in a very monolithic way, Muslims are put in one box, or whatever ... we have to de-mystify all of that because Muslims are diverse in their languages, and their cultures, in the interpretations of their faith, in the practice of their faith, in the food they eat – there is no such thing as a monolithic group of 1.4 billion people."

Interviewee Zavhar Tejpar, an accountant, brought up another critical point in relation to discussing group identity: "Muslims are largely spread out and yet the public perception is one of the Arab world, so we have an issue. I have trouble when Muslims are earmarked because they are Muslim … you are Irish, yet nobody looks at you and says, 'You are a Christian' – they say … Caucasian and that's where it stops … We get into defensive mode … I wish that Muslims would not push their cause by using religion … they should portray themselves as individuals, rather than saying they are Muslims."

With these opinions and findings in mind, returning to the idea of Moghissi, Rahnema, and Goodman that there is a "diasporic impulse" among Canadian Muslims, despite the noted heterogeneity in the community there is said to be an increasing desire to identify with fellow Muslims on the basis of faith. The reason for this impulse, according to academics is, at least partially, experiences with racism and marginalization and negative public attitudes toward Muslims: "Indeed, we are increasingly witnessing in the West the formation of a diasporic impulse among the earlier and new migrants of Muslim cultures who collectively carry the insinuatingly negative identity marker of 'Muslim.'"[29] Here a diasporic identity offers a potential source of empowerment in the face of experiences with discrimination and prejudice: "The formation of a collective identity and solidarity in the Diaspora more often manifests a response to political frustration and the blossoming of deep-seated resentment to the continuing colonial and neocolonial aggression against Muslim societies, accentuated by an inhospitable climate in the new country."[30] Knight similarly believes that these impulses can be driven by marginalization (in relation to the host culture where they reside) and that "feelings of alienation and exclusion in the host country can therefore feed the desire to go back to the country of origin."[31]

The possibility that racism and alienation may lead to the development of solidarity should also not be viewed as unique to Muslims. Historically, we can pull out a number of examples where racism has led to the development of solidarity movements, such as the civil rights movement or Black Power movement in the United States, or the Catholic Irish civil rights and militant Republican movements in Northern Ireland, as a response to racism and segregation. When subject to discrimination and general social insecurity, individuals may seek solidarity in an empowering broader identity, and certainly religion provides an avenue for the development of a unifying and universalistic identity, for example as found in the Islamic principle of the "umma." Ramadan draws on some of these notions when he writes, "The fear of losing one's religion and culture at the core of Western societies has led to natural attitudes of withdrawal and self-isolation. All immigrants have gone through similar experiences in terms of culture, but for Muslims religious questionings are also often mixed with such cultural considerations."[32] Ramadan links a series of events, many of them shaped by the phenomenon of xenoracism, that have stimulated this reaction: the Rushdie affair, the head-scarf issue, the Danish cartoons, and terrorist attacks: "They experience this daily: being a visible Muslim in the West today is no easy matter. In such an atmosphere, a crisis of confidence is inevitable: some have decided to isolate themselves, believing that there is nothing to hope for in society that rejects them; others have decided to become invisible by disappearing into the crowd; last, others have committed themselves to facing the problem and opening spaces for encounter and dialogue.[33]

From this perspective, Muslims, like individuals in all other immigrant communities, seek the support networks that cultural and religious communities offer, but this "impulse" is further re-enforced by a sometimes unwelcoming environment, one that fails to offer avenues to belonging in the wider community. Drawing out some of these ideas, one interviewee, Ahmed Abdulkadir, a community organizer and the executive director of the Ogaden Somali Community of Alberta Residents, identified some of the advantages of belonging to the broader Canadian Muslim community: "The advantage of being a Muslim is that you have a close community who likes to help each other – who bonds together during a crisis. There is a sense of community."

Thus, as revealed by the opinions of the interviewees, there are a number of different interpretations of what it means to be Muslim in Canada. Like the members of any other cultural or religious group with limited resources and numbers, Canadian Muslims have formed communal spaces to maintain their traditions, their sense of community, and their religious practices in a multicultural state, and these observations lead to the conclusion that scholars must use caution when speaking of identity. The Canadian Muslim community should be recognized as having a heterogeneous identity containing a multitude of individual experiences. This leads us back to Werbner's observation that religious identity groups like Muslims must be considered in a way that allows for internal diversity "for cross-cutting ties" and the multiple identities that people engender in a community.[34]

Part of breaking with the Orientalist traditions of the past will be to eschew attempts to discover an essential nature of Islam, a monolithic image from which generalizations are formed. Instead, religious identities should be viewed in the context of diverse traditions, practices, and cultures. As Cesari notes, "One must examine the social and historical contexts within which Muslims create their discourse on what is important or unimportant in Islam, in their Islam."[35]

Moreover, through exploring the idea of a Muslim diaspora the research has revealed how suggestions of impermanence draw defensive reactions, as interviewees consistently mobilized ideas of diversity, national belonging, and transnationality. A common, knee-jerk reaction to the idea was to highlight a sense of permanence, multigenerational family roots in Canada, and national affinity. With this complex portrait of the communities in mind, the book now moves on to look at experiences with xenoracism.

EXPLORING XENORACISM IN CANADA

As already noted, specific ideologies of racism can only be understood within economic and political conditions that shape social relations.[36] Furthermore, as shown in previous chapters, contemporary forms of racism can be traced back to historical trends – for example, the formation of modern political communities. Foster has recognized how the historical development of the nation-state, within the context of modernity, was essential to the establishment of hierarchical, racist ideologies.[37] Race and racism scholars in Canada have identified similar trends in the historical development of racism in the Canadian state, while acknowledging the unique political, economic, and social features of Canada. Moreover, pertinent to this analysis, a number of scholars in Canada have explored how racism has been historically embedded in the Canadian government's approach to immigration, integration, and, more generally, nation building.

For example, Angus McLaren, in his study of racism in Canadian immigration policy, noted how pre-war immigration policy prioritized white, Anglo-Saxon immigrants when admitting newcomers. However, as immigration has long been interlinked with economic priority in Canada, at times this preference was relaxed to meet labour needs. Describing the clear racial hierarchy that was exhibited within Canada's policy in this area, McLaren states, "British and Americans were viewed as the most desirable, next northern and western Europeans, after them the central and eastern Europeans (including the Jews), and last of all the Asians and blacks."[38] The state's approach to the integration of newcomers also reflected this cultural and racial hierarchy because during this period the priority was "Anglo-conformity," in other words, the assimilation into what was perceived by some as the superior English-Canadian ideal.[39]

Racially discriminatory and assimilationist practices were most blatantly obvious in Canadian immigration and integration policy up until the adoption of the points system in 1967 and official multiculturalism in 1971. However, before this, Satzewich notes that after the Second World War there was a slow shift away from racialized policy, at least in terms of immigration. For instance, the post-war repeal of the Chinese Immigration Act in 1947 began to, albeit painfully slowly, open the door to immigrants from East Asia.[40]

Walker notes that the shift in Canadian policy during this period can be linked not only to economic necessity (i.e., the need for labour during the post-war economic boom) but also to changing norms at the international level where the shock of the Holocaust, which had been in part driven by the negative influence of the pseudo-science of eugenics and "scientific racism," led to the adoption of the 1948 Universal Declaration of Human Rights by the United Nations.[41] Later these norms and ideas were adopted into domestic document legislation such as Ontario's 1944 Racial Discrimination Act and Saskatchewan's 1947 Bill of Rights.[42]

While 1967 and 1971 are the dates when the Canadian federal government adopted the "race-neutral" points system and multiculturalism, curbing overtly racist practices in immigration and integration, race and racism scholars continue to point to manifestations of racism in the Canadian state, its economy and society. For example, according to Backhouse, racism is ubiquitous in Canadian society, permeating its culture and institutions.[43] Other scholars such as Satzewich have pointed to more targeted and specific manifestations of racism in Canada, such as the "moral panic" over immigrants from certain racial backgrounds, specifically in the 1980s and 1990s when black communities suffered demonization over media portrayals of criminalization of the community.[44]

There are numerous studies focusing on manifestations of racism in Canadian society that target specific communities. For example, Wortley and Julian focused on racial profiling in Toronto, where almost half of black male respondents have reported involuntary police contact, in comparison with 12 per cent of white males.[45] Creese and Ngene Kambere, in their study of the experience of African immigrant women in Canada, found that racialized accents constitute borders of belonging and regulate access to power and resources in the Canadian state and economy.[46]

It should be noted that a sizeable portion of the Canadian race and racism literature, specifically related to the experience of the black community, has focused on what was previously described in this book as colour-coded racism. Increasingly, race and racism scholars in Canada are turning their attention to the experience of Canadian Muslims. As Satzewich claims, much of this change in focus is related to the perceived threat or risk posed by certain communities. He states, "Muslims more recently have nudged black people aside and have moved up the list of 'risk' groups."[47] Previous studies have taken note of discrimination and racism that targets Canadian Muslims. For instance, Seljak et al., in their study of religious discrimination in Canada, conclude that "sizeable minorities express negative attitudes towards certain religious groups, especially Muslims."[48] Bahdi found in a study on racial profiling after 9/11 that workplace discrimination against workers who appear Arab was taking place in Ontario.[49]

A number of these studies were conducted around a particularly acute period of negative public attention for Canadian Muslims during the province of Ontario's debate over Shari'a law, which began in 2003. At that time the Islamic Institute of Civil Justice had stated that it would offer arbitration of family and business disputes in accordance with Shari'a law and Ontario's Arbitration Act, 1991.[50] The idea of introducing Shari'a law in Ontario was examined as early as 1994; however, as it came closer to being a reality, as Khan puts it, the "the politics of fear" were employed to stir up concerns of Muslim groups setting up a state within a state.[51]

In response to the public controversy, the Ontario provincial government commissioned former attorney general Marion Boyd to review the Arbitration Act. Surprising many observers, Boyd recommended allowing the practice of Shari'a law within the Act. However, despite this recommendation the Ontario provincial government, under the leadership of Dalton McGuinty, rejected Boyd's arguments and subsequently took the extreme measure of banning all religious arbitration under the Act.[52]

At the heart of the Shari'a debate was a dispute between civil society groups within and outside the Muslim community that primarily focused on gender rights and concerns that Muslim religious arbitration would countermand the Charter of Rights and Freedom's gender protection. For example, the National Association of Women and the Law, the Canadian Council of Muslim Women, and the National Organization of Immigrant and Visible Minority Women of Canada all raised concerns that gender equality would not be ensured under Shari'a law.[53] There were also concerns that Shari'a law would countermand section 15 of the Charter (which applies to equality of rights) and section 28, which is intended to guarantee equality of rights for both sexes, stating, "Notwithstanding anything in this Charter, the rights and freedoms referred to in it are guaranteed equally to male and female persons."[54] Some Muslim community groups, including a number of Ismaili organizations, also objected to the Islamic Institute of Civil Justice's particular religious leanings.[55]

Noting the diverse array of interest groups engaged in the controversy, it can be observed that on one hand, the Shari'a debate served to illustrate the diversity of views and factions that exist within the Canadian Muslim community and Canadian Muslim civil society. On the other hand, the debate demonstrated the contentiousness, fear, and arbitrariness that surround ideas of religious accommodation for Muslims in Canada. In the end, McGuinty's dramatic and reactionary outright ban of all religious arbitration, despite Boyd's recommendation, was described by Siddiqui as an example of "a creeping irrationality in our own public discourse, public opinion and public policy when dealing with Muslims."[56]

The Shari'a law debate has been subject to extensive journalistic and scholarly analysis, but what is most important for this chapter is how the episode revealed deep discomfort with Islam among some segments of the Canadian population. In a sense, the Shari'a law debate in Canada drew a similar, if appropriately muted, reaction to what was seen in the Rushdie affair in Britain. For some Canadians, the fact that Ontario even considered the implementation of Muslim religious arbitration was evidence that accommodation and multiculturalism had simply gone too far. And for some Canadian Muslims, the debate clearly demonstrated the extent to which xenoracism had permeated Canadian society. Yet, it represents only one example of the kind of controversy and contentiousness that has appeared over the accommodation of Muslims in Canadian society. As mentioned in previous chapters, these kinds of episodes were often generated not by local but rather by global events: the Israeli-Palestinian conflict, the Iranian revolution, the Gulf Wars, and so on.

Controversies like the Shari'a law debate have received considerable attention from journalists and academics, yet there are overlooked trends that speak to the kind of xenoracism that Canadian Muslims increasingly face in Canada. Many of these events, incidences, and political trends are discussed within the context of the specific subject matters in the book, for example, in relation to security and integration policy. However, one trend that is often overlooked in the literature on "Islamophobia" and xenoracism, which is worth reviewing here, is the growing impact of the anti-Islamic social movement. In many ways that movement has been stimulated by the evolution of online technologies and the spread of ideas and ideologies across borders within the broader context of globalization.

As discussed in the introduction, a growing and amorphous anti-Islamic social movement is fomenting xenoracism in Europe and North America. As so painfully and terribly evident in the example of the Quebec mosque shooting of 2017, Canada is not immune from the militant outbursts of this movement, with its many organized groups and individual adherents. Triggered and encouraged by a series of local and international events, Canadians are increasingly involved in a plethora of social media, vigilante, and civil society based groups focused on anti-Muslim hatred.

A series of white nationalist and supremacist groups, and more explicitly anti-Muslim groups, are responsible for distributing anti-immigrant and anti-Muslim writings through numerous mediums and venues, including well-publicized posters in Canadian universities, social media platforms, and Internet forums like Stormfront and Blood and Honour.[57] More established groups such as the Ku Klux Klan and Aryan Guard have been joined by European imports more firmly grounded in the hatred of Muslims such as the Patriotic Europeans against the Islamization of the West and Soldiers of Odin who have carried out anti-Muslim protests and vigilante-style patrols in Canada.[58] A growing "alt-right" movement has sanitized the hateful language and appearance of their neo-Nazi predecessors – cleverly using the language of cultural pride rather than hate – but even the shallowest scratch on their veneer reveals a violent opposition to immigration of non-Europeans, Muslims in particular. The message that is shared and propagated by these groups is clear: Muslims are undesirable, dangerous, and unwelcome in Canadian society, which should be defined by it European and Anglo-Saxon heritage.

The impact of right wing extremism, and a growing anti-Islamic social movement in Canada, is largely unknown as only a handful of journalistic and academic articles have examined the groups and individuals who define the movements. Furthermore, what exists in terms of study is really no more than an environmental scan of groups and movements rather than an analysis of their impacts on Canadian society, its newcomers, and its minority communities. There is also no pre-existing analysis of how the movement is stimulating hate crimes and incidents. However, what has been measured in recent years has been a startling spike in hate crimes and incidents that target Muslims in Canada. For instance, in 2015 Statistics Canada reported a 60 per cent year-over-year increase in police-reported hate crimes and a staggering 253 per cent increase from 2012 to 2015. A number of Canadian Muslim civil society groups attributed the rise in reported hate crimes to the divisive rhetoric around the 2015 federal election, while others believed the trend, similar to what was seen around 9/11, is a response to an increase in mass-casualty terrorist attacks in Europe.[59]

It is difficult for academics to identify correlations between the rise of right-wing extremism, the anti-Islamic social movement, and the substantive spike in reported hate crimes targeting Muslims, but it would be naïve to believe that the fear-mongering, vitriolic, and hateful sentiments being propagated through YouTube videos, Facebook posts, pamphlets, posters, and graffiti were not having an impact on these trends. When looking at institutional and political manifestations of xenoracism, like what was seen in the Shari'a law debate or the controversy over the niqab leading up to the 2015 federal election, and what is being seen at a more grassroots level, it is clear that there is a confluence of institutional, political, and societal elements that promote and stimulate xenoracism that targets Muslims.

Thus, one may ask, how have these episodic examples and trends related to xenoracism directly impacted the lived experiences of Muslims and how can we directly measure experiences with racism in the Canadian Muslim population? To begin to answer these questions the book now turns to its various sources of research, starting with statistical data.

MEASURING EXPERIENCES WITH DISCRIMINATION AMONG CANADIAN MUSLIM COMMUNITIES

Significant data sources that reveal historical experiences with racism among Canada Muslims are the dated but rich Ethnic Diversity Study (EDS) and the more recent Survey of Muslims in Canada (SMC). The following section provides descriptive statistics related to experiences with discrimination among Canadian Muslims from 2002 to 2016.

In particular, the 2003 EDS provides a rich body of data related to Canadian Muslims and their opinions, attitudes, and experiences. In terms of demographics, the EDS data for Muslims were made up primarily of data from immigrants (the sample was 90.1 per cent immigrants). A majority of respondents were also visible minorities, with 85 per cent indicating visible-minority status. Moreover, revealing the relative youth of Muslims in comparison with the general Canadian population, 64 per cent of immigrant respondents and 71.4 per cent of non-immigrant respondents were between the ages of 18 and 44 years. Finally, the sample reveals that Muslims are most likely to live in larger urban centres rather than in rural areas.[60]

Turning to important measurements of discrimination, according to the EDS, 32 percent of Canadian Muslims reported experiencing discrimination in the last 5 years in comparison with 37 per cent of Canadian Hindus, 31 per cent of Canadian Buddhists and 23 per cent of Jehovah's Witnesses. Significantly, of the 32 per cent of Muslim respondents, only 34 per cent reported religion as the reason for discrimination, in comparison with 70 per cent of Canadian Jews and 75 percent of Jehovah's Witnesses (Table 4.1).[61] These findings suggest that religion is a somewhat muted source of discrimination in the Canadian context. The obvious question arising from the EDS data is what is the primary reason Muslims experienced discrimination? The answer to this question is speculative, although one may posit that discrimination was linked to visible-minority status, considering the makeup of the sample group, rather than religious identity.

When respondents were asked whether they felt out of place because of their religion, 43 per cent of Muslims who were not members of a visible minority and 32 per cent of visible-minority Muslims reported

Table 4.1 Experiences with discrimination among religious communities in the Ethnic Diversity Survey

Religious affiliation	Percentage of respondents who reported discrimination in the last 5 years*	Percentage of respondents who reported discrimination who indicated religion was the reason*	Unweighted count
No religious affiliation	16	8	7,821
Roman Catholic	12	8	13,157
Other Catholic	9	5	1,508
Anglican	12	7	2,456
Baptist	14	24	883
Jehovah's Witnesses	23	75	224
Lutheran	8	17	1,047
Mennonite	9	40	303
Pentecostal	21	17	503
Presbyterian	11	9	774
United Church	8	8	2,880
Other Protestant	15	22	2,442
Greek Orthodox	21	15	417
Other Orthodox	21	13	415
Other Christian	18	23	2,527
Muslim	32	34	806
Jewish	25	70	657
Buddhist	31	10	542
Hindu	37	9	506
Sikh	29	30	612
Other religion	31	49	123

*Percentage based on weighted values from Statistics Canada's Ethnic Diversity Survey.
Source: Ethnic Diversity Survey Public Use Metafile 2002.

that they did feel out of place because of their religion (Table 4.2). When asked whether they worried about hate crimes, 58 per cent of Muslims who were not members of a visible minority said they were not worried at all and 2 per cent were very worried. In comparison, 55 per cent of visible-minority Muslims responded that they were not worried at all and 5 per cent were very worried. Respondents from non-Muslim visible minorities had comparable numbers, with 55 per cent not worried at all and 7 per cent very worried (Table 4.3).[62]

The more recent Environics surveys from 2006 and 2016 examined inter-community perceptions and attitudes among the host society

Table 4.2 Experiences with feeling uncomfortable or out of place because of religion in the Ethnic Diversity Survey

Classification	Percentage of respondents who felt uncomfortable	Percentage of respondents who felt uncomfortable who indicated religion was the reason for their discomfort
NON-VISIBLE MINORITIES		
No religion	19	11
Christian	18	13
Muslim	*31*	*43*
Hindu	–	–
Sikh	–	–
Other faith	35	71
VISIBLE MINORITIES		
No religion	50	3
Christian	44	7
Muslim	*41*	*32*
Hindu	43	12
Sikh	35	26
Other faith	37	8

Source: Ethnic Diversity Survey Public Use Metafile 2002.

Table 4.3 Worries about hate crimes in the Ethnic Diversity Survey

Classification	Percentage of respondents who expressed this degree of worry				
	1 – Not worried at all	2	3	4	5 – Very worried
NON-VISIBLE MINORITY					
Muslim	58	23	11	6	2
Non-Muslim	76	14	7	2	2
VISIBLE MINORITY					
Muslim	55	19	15	5	5
Non-Muslim	55	21	13	5	7

Source: Ethnic Diversity Survey Public Use Metafile 2002.

and among the Muslim community, together with the experiences of Canadian Muslims with discrimination. The 2006 survey involved 500 self-identified Canadian Muslims, and the 2016 follow-up involved 600 self-identified Canadian Muslims. In the 2006 survey, when asked what aspect of Canada they "like the least," 12 per cent of Canadian Muslim respondents cited discrimination, while 24 per cent indicated "cold weather/climate." When asked what they were "most worried" about, the top two worries among Canadian Muslims were discrimination (66 per cent) and unemployment (65 per cent).[63]

Comparing the 2006 data with the 2016 SMC survey, when asked "What do you like least about Canada?" 9 per cent named experiences with discrimination and 31 per cent named climate/cold weather.[64] However, when asked directly (unprompted) "What do you believe are the most important issues facing Muslims in your local community today?" 35 per cent named discrimination. The second most cited issue, identified by 8 per cent of the sample, was "interaction between cultures."[65] In addition, when asked, "In the past five years, have you experienced discrimination or been treated unfairly by others in Canada because of any of the following: Your religion … Your ethnicity or culture … Your sex … Your language?" 35 per cent indicated in the 2016 survey that they had experienced discrimination (for any reason), 22 percent attributed the experience to their religious identity, and 22 per cent attributed it to ethnicity or culture.[66]

Both the EDS and Environics data indicate that a sizeable minority of Canadian Muslims have experienced discrimination, although only some of these individuals indicate that those experiences are related to religious identity. The surveys show that experiences with discrimination have remained relatively constant from 2002 to 2016. For example, 32 per cent of Canadian Muslims indicated that they had experienced discrimination in the past 5 years in the 2003 EDS (conducted in 2002), in comparison with 35 per cent in the 2016 SMC (conducted between 2015 and 2016).

Other polls have focused on negative societal attitudes toward Muslims. For example, in terms of feelings of trust among the general Canadian population toward Canadian Muslims, a March 2012 joint poll (conducted by the Association for Canadian Studies and the Canadian Race Relations Foundation) of over 1,500 Canadians found that 52 per cent of Canadians trusted Muslims "not at all" or only "a little." In comparison, 71 per cent trusted Protestants, 69 per cent trusted Catholics, and 64 per cent trusted Jews "a lot" or "somewhat." Asked whether these groups were to blame for their lack of trust,

42 per cent agreed that Muslims were to blame, again representing the highest level of any group.[67]

Another survey conducted around the time of 9/11 by the Canadian chapter of the Council on American-Islamic Relations in 2002 detected higher levels of experience with discrimination (when compared with the EDS and SMC); that survey found that 60 per cent of Canadian Muslim respondents reported having experienced "bias or discrimination since the 9/11 terrorist attacks." Another poll conducted in 2002 found that 41 per cent of 253 Arab-origin respondents thought that Canadians "do not like Muslims" while 84.6 per cent believed that Canadians regard Muslims as violent.[68] At least in the immediate aftermath of 9/11, these trends may have been associated with hate crimes; Muslim Canadians living in the Greater Toronto Area experienced a 66 per cent increase in hate crimes, with Muslims experiencing close to half of all reported hate crimes in 2001, according to the Toronto Police Service.[69]

It is difficult to find directly comparable data from other states in terms of sample composition and the structure of the survey questions. As a rough comparison, one European Union study that focused on experiences of discrimination among youth in three European Union states found that, when comparing non-Muslim and Muslim youth, "religion rarely featured as a reason for discrimination against non-Muslims, but was one of the most commonly cited reasons for discrimination among Muslims."[70] In that same study, in terms of national findings, 31 per cent of Muslim youth in France reported discrimination on the basis of religion in comparison with 44 per cent in the United Kingdom and 64 per cent in Spain.[71] Another study, the Pew Global Attitudes Project of 2006, asked Muslims whether they believed the general population (in their country of residence) was generally hostile toward Muslims. That study found that 42 per cent of British Muslims, 39 per cent of French Muslims, and 51 per cent of German Muslims viewed the host society as hostile.[72]

The statistical data ultimately reveal a mixed picture of discrimination and negative perceptions toward the Canadian Muslim community. The best-quality data sources, for instance the more rigorous EDS, reveal that Canadian Muslims report somewhat lower rates of discrimination than other religious groups and do not relate existing discrimination to their religious belief, perhaps indicating that xenoracism remains a more muted source of discrimination in Canada. The results of the more recent SMC are generally supportive of these findings. The fact that a third of Canadian Muslims were indicating experiences with discrimination, and that much of that discrimination was not based on religion, can be seen as a somewhat positive indication, even if those levels are still uncomfortably high. Also, a small number of respondents stated that they were "very worried" about hate crimes (although as shown in Table 4.3 a significant number expressed at least some concern over hate crimes).

On the other hand, a fairly significant number of Canadian Muslims expressed some unease with public perception of their religion or a sense of feeling out of place, numbers that are comparable to levels of perceived host society hostility in some European states. The more recent survey of inter-community trust by Environics also demonstrates relatively low levels of host-society trust for Canadian Muslims, whom non-Muslims blame for this lack of trust.

Ultimately one can only glean so much from statistical data, and the book now turns to the interview data to gain a more in-depth understanding of the Canadian Muslim experience vis-à-vis racism. This data source offers particular advantages over survey data, as Essed recognizes: "Experiences are a suitable source of information for the study of everyday racism because they include personal experiences as well as vicarious experiences of racism. In addition, the notion of experience includes general knowledge of racism, which is an important source of information to qualify whether specific events can be generalized.[73]

Interviewees and Their Perceptions of Racism in Canada

All interviewees were informed that they could speak to "experiences with racism in Canada from either a community or individual perspective." Of the respondents in the Canadian Muslim community sample, 78 per cent expressed at least some concern over discrimination and prejudice at either the individual or community level and 47 per cent reported direct personal experience with some form of racism in Canada. Outside of these numbers, interviewees expressed varied and sometimes divergent opinions the extent to which they viewed racism as a significant problem in Canada and whether they believed it was based on religion, visible-minority status, or other factors.

Following on a point raised in the chapter on xenoracism, a common theme for interviewees was that racism directed toward Muslims was linked to global political events. From this perspective, racism peaks after particular events. For example, according to Ahmed Shoker, a director at the Canadian Islamic Congress, since 9/11 there has been what Canadian Muslims perceive as "a subtle sense of discomfort ... and this will require some years to really, sort of, remove this stain altogether – where we feel as we did before September 11th." Yasmeen Nisam believes that "discrimination based on religion [is] definitely more pronounced since 9/11." Ali Maher Shawwa, a retired Muslim chaplain, remembers how on 9/11 he overheard two older women discussing Islam: "One says to the other, 'What is this Islam?' The other lady says, 'This is a religion that kills Jews and Christians.'" Azim Jeraj, a business owner, believes that after 9/11 there were "a lot of changes, where a lot of negative things have been said about Islam. I have heard of people walking in, going for a job interview with a beard, the chances of getting a job are fewer." For Azim Jeraj there was a distinct change in the general Canadian population's perception of Muslims after that event, something that was driven by misinformation: "I think a lot of that has happened because of the media, you know, how does your attitude change overnight, so all these influences certainly have worked into the population."

However, Azim Jeraj believes that some of the negative sentiment that was generated after 9/11 is now beginning to dissipate: "I think it is beginning to get better now, but for the first 5 years after 9/11 things were tough ... you could notice that you could see graffiti on the walls of mosques and things like that, a lot of that happened. It's not happening anymore, so I think people are again going back to our Canadian nature." Baha Abu-Laban shares Azim Jeraj's view, stating that in relation to the prejudice that existed directly after 9/11, "In part the relevance of discrimination lessened, the challenges to the larger community did not seem to exist in the same way they had before, the fears did not exist in the same way, so in that sense it began to dissipate." However, he also notes that "the discrimination existed long before 9/11, long before the First Gulf War and the '67 war."

Soraya Hafez, a president of the Canadian Council of Muslim Women, also believes that racism in Canada has been driven by international political events: "During the first Gulf War the Muslim communities across Canada suffered from racism, and the Second Gulf War and September 11th again." Working as an elementary school teacher, she recalled how these events would be transferred to the playground. Referring to the American bombing of Libya in 1986, she stated: "During the attack on Libya, on the playground at the school some students would approach students of Arabic or Muslim background and say, 'We will beat the heck out of you guys' ... okay those little kids were born here and raised here – why would they be guilty, they are feeling and asking what did we do? ... The other students were supporting the Americans: that was one incident way before 9/11 or the Gulf War."

A few interviewees thought that racism was not a significant issue in Canada. Bashir Ahmed, executive director of the Somali Canadian Education and Rural Development Organization, believes that "there is not that much direct racism" and notes that his organization has "found one incident 20 years ago." He notes that he has found little in terms of "outward racism." "If I cannot see you hate me because of how I look or my religion I cannot tell." Similarly, Sohail Quadri, a former Progressive Conservative member of the Legislative Assembly of Alberta for Edmonton-Mill Woods, stated, "For the last two decades I did not encounter that at all. I'm not saying it's not there – but I did not encounter that."

For others, there was the perception that xenoracism was present but remained a more muted issue in Canada. For example, according to one anonymous interviewee, a leader in the Ontario Somali community who is as an academic and engaged in international governmental work, this kind of racism is present, "but, it's a question of degree – it's hard to quantify and qualify ... I have not experienced discrimination directly." The interviewee followed up on his answer by acknowledging that some of his family members, specifically a woman wearing the hijab, had experienced some minor discourtesies.

Others had no direct experience with racism in Canada but viewed it as a reality for the larger community. For example, Dalal Daoud stated, "It hasn't really affected me negatively." However, "as for Muslim men I think the whole thing with the War on Terror was an obstacle ... I have heard of numerous cases of Muslim men being treated differently with a beard ... but again, I think it is based on misunderstanding." A common theme in the interviews was expressed by one anonymous interviewee, a prominent member of a Muslim cultural association: "A lot depends on individual experience. I am not sure whether you can generalize that – some of us have been fortunate who hardly notice any of that and others who notice those kinds of things ... and you say is it really truly discrimination or is it something else?" In this statement, the interviewee draws out what was an overriding theme in the interview data: experiences are highly individual and there are inherent difficulties in trying to distinguish between discrimination on the basis of religion, colour-coded racism, prejudice, stereotyping, ignorance, or even curiosity.

Another theme explored in the interviews with Canadian Muslims was whether experiences with racism were generated by visible-minority status or by religion. For some, colour-coded racism was still the predominant form of racism in Canada. As Ali Maher Shawwa bluntly observed, "Yes – there is discrimination ... Canada, in reality, is a white country." Shaykh Zak recounted one experience he had shortly after he immigrated to Canada when he tried to purchase a vehicle in a private sale: "A woman answered the call and we agreed on a time to meet. When I arrived there and knocked on the door a man opened the door and looked at me, and I still remember his face ... and he looked at me and said 'What?' and I replied that I was there to see the car. And he looked back inside and said, "Look at what your ad has brought us" and I stood there watching him intensely and he left the door ajar and just walked away and I waited there for the woman to come, but she never did."

For Shaykh Zak, the reason behind this experience was clear: "And this was definitely a case of discrimination based on nothing but a concept in this man's mind. Basically just a non-white, non-Caucasian person ... it had nothing to do with anything but how I looked. But this I carried with me for a long time because I always tried to see that face in the crowd and there are a lot of them. But the thing is, over the last 30 years or so ... this attitude has changed, I mean, dramatically improved – but it didn't completely go, right?"

Yasmeen Nisam recounts her experiences growing up; echoing the sentiments expressed by Shaykh Zak, she believes that colour-coded racism exists but has become less pronounced in recent years, something she relates directly to greater diversity and multiculturalism:

I saw a lot of racism growing up. I was the only non-white student at school and I felt it a lot. My kids, they don't say anything to me about it, and I think it's because there are so many different peoples, cultures, colours ... I remember going to school and thinking I can't take my food for lunch because it's so different and has a different smell ... my kids they want to take their food – and there's so many different foods being brought, they're happy at school. I had a lot of girlfriends but boys didn't accept me and I was too ashamed to tell my parents, and then one day

I just couldn't take it anymore and I just burst out crying and my parents couldn't believe this. They went to my teachers and told them and the teachers talked to the boys and it got a little better, quite a lot better, but it was so traumatic. I still remember this to this day, and my kids – they love school, their friends – they love going to school. I think it's the multicultural society – they're accepted more than I ever was.

However, according to Yasmeen Nisam, while colour-coded racism may be dissipating, it is being replaced by another form of racism: "I can tell you what I have observed and I think discrimination is alive and well – it always has been, but now more so towards the religion – because Muslims come from many different ethnic backgrounds. I can speak for the East Indian community because I am an East Indian Muslim woman and I did feel racism growing up. I don't feel colour racism very much anymore, but I see my community being affected by discrimination based on religion more now."

She goes on to describe how this form of racism is manifested through the targeting of cultural and religious symbols: "Women who wear the hijab have felt a lot of discrimination and in fact, articling, I had a conversation with my principal and I asked him, 'What would you do if I wore the hijab?' And he was not happy with that. He said, 'Well, you'd look like a nun' ... they make judgments based on physical appearance ... it's definitely more pronounced since 9/11 ... discrimination based on religion." Ahmed Shoker supports this idea: "Muslims do have negative experience, they are there, yes, unfortunately ... however, I should say that there are many who report exactly the reverse ... but because of their religion, or the wearing of the hijab, or anything connected to faith does this sometimes cause discomfort? Unfortunately, yes." Recounting a story of a woman who had a negative experience at a local supermarket, he stated, "It's usually a look or a comment that offends or hurts – that's what we usually get from Muslim women, particularly those who wear the hijab."

Further drawing out the gendered element of contemporary xenoracism and the targeting of visual symbols of religious faith, Ahmed Abdulkadir believes that while he has not personally been targeted with discrimination on the basis of religion, community members are experiencing it: "From the community perspective – I hear they feel racism, especially the women who wear the hijab – there are incidents – like people having their hijab pulled off, or not being allowed to pray during work hours." Citing specific incidents of hate crimes, he described how one community member "was wearing a hijab in front of 7/11 [and] someone came and verbally abused her and later physically assaulted her – specifically because she was wearing a hijab," and in another case, "a woman had a coke from McDonald's thrown at her and they yelled 'go back to your country, you terrorist.'"

Imam Sadique Pathan's answer to the question of whether discrimination on the basis of religion is a reality for Canadian Muslims was emphatic: "Absolutely, we have a number of examples ... we have the NCCM [National Council of Canadians Muslims] saying that hate crimes surpassed the [previous] highest rate this year." Imam Sadique then went on to describe what he specifically saw as manifestations of xenoracism in Canada: "We are seeing terrorism being described as Islamic. We are seeing it in the [2017 leadership] race with the Conservatives – the way that Muslims are being described – they are being painted as uncivilized."

Unfortunately, the Imam has also been a victim of this kind of racism in Canada: "I have experienced it, definitely, myself. Someone yells at you when you are walking by. Or sometimes it's just the way you are treated, the derogatory statements." He then went on to recount a specific experience he had while employed as a social worker: "Post 9/11 I experienced [racism] personally with workplace discrimination, when one client refused to work with me after she knew I was Muslim. The biases were there."

Soraya Hafez described a number of personal experiences with racism in Canada, including an episode where she was asked by a local newspaper to give an interview after 9/11. She received a threatening phone call the morning after her interview was published and was told, "Why don't you go back to where you come from." Another anonymous interviewee, a board member at a settlement agency and professional engineer, recounted how the first generation, specifically her parents, had experienced racism: "My parents don't look back on it in a negative way, but they do have some recollections of racist experiences. My mom being in the hospital and them serving her ham and bacon and saying to her, 'It's just meat, what's the problem?' And right now, of course, in our day and age that would be, 'Oh, I'm so sorry!' You might not even have to say anything – they might know just from you being Muslim that there are dietary concerns."

The same interviewee recounted how when she began attending university her parents, on the basis of prior experiences with racism, were concerned that she might be targeted because of her choice to wear the hijab:

> [They] were very concerned about racism, what I might experience, I was, you know, in my last year of engineering; the next year I would be looking for work. I wasn't married yet and they thought this was going to really set me back. They started saying, 'Well you know there is racism you don't know about, we experienced it, we know.' So that's when I heard them being really anxious, worried about racism impacting my life. Before they would kind of just blow it off and say, 'Oh you people are just, whatever … carry on, you know?'… But I decided to wear it and I didn't experience any racism that I can recall. The only thing that I experienced … I don't know if it's racism … but people have stereotypes.

Usama al-Atar, a Shi'a Imam who holds a doctorate in chemistry, links discrimination directed toward Muslims to larger secular trends in society. He states, "Is there discrimination against Muslims? I think there is discrimination against religion; although they say we live in a free society people who practise religion are considered to be backwards, in this society. At the same time, because Islam is strict in its social stand, then there is a greater discrimination against Islamic values." The essence of his argument is that in an increasingly secular society – secular in the decline-of-religion usage of the term – religion, especially religion that requires strict lifestyle choices, can be viewed as regressive in comparison with what many people consider to be progressive secular standards.

He elaborates on this point by highlighting how, because Islam has adhered to a more strict moral code of conduct than some other branches of Abrahamic religions, it has been viewed as intolerant, and this is the source of much of the discrimination Muslims experience today:

> Islam in general rejects abortion, it rejects same-gender marriages and so on and so forth … and I think that has made people take a stronger stand against Muslims. Because some people say, for instance, that I can still be a Christian and have an abortion … I can still be a Jew and I can do that, I can be a liberal Jew and do that, you can't be an Orthodox Jew and do that. But in Islam

you can't, there is no option, so you either remain as a Muslim, or convert and join another religion. And that is what makes people say, 'Okay so Islam does not tolerate all of this.'

Usama al-Atar went on to point out how some issues, for example, same-sex marriage and abortion, are issues that are taboo in other religions as well.

Another point raised by a few interviewees was that experiences with racism in the Muslim community were moderated by class. A speculative point raised by Azim Jeraj was that "direct racism is affected in labour jobs, you find, once you get into the civil service, or, you know, management jobs in the private sector, if there is racism it is not out in the open, so you don't see it. Some people may feel it at work – as long as you keep producing and keep doing what you are supposed to do, you are fine." As a successful individual who had few issues integrating into the labour market after emigrating, he believes that it is individuals in working-class positions who likely to suffer the majority of racism. Shawkat Hassan, a member of the British Columbia Muslim Association, an organization with a 40-year presence in the province, and a chaplain at a penitentiary in the Greater Vancouver Area, recalled a discussion he had with a construction worker he met in prison: "One of the guys, who happened to be from Bosnia and came to this Masjid, he was working in construction and doing a good job – he had a boss who was teasing him about being a Muslim terrorist. And this guy also wanted to tease him [back] and he said 'If you don't shut up I'll shoot you.' So he went right away to the police and said he said so on and so on and right away he ended up in the prison for uttering threats."

Demonstrating the complex nature of racism in a multicultural society, a few interviewees brought up issues with discrimination within the Muslim community itself. This was a common sentiment expressed by members of cultural associations or other umbrella groups that were trying to build intra-community consensus. Shaykh Zak, who considers himself a non-sectarian Muslim chaplain, recounted how, despite his "good contacts with all kinds of Muslims," because of divisions, often of cultural rather than core religious beliefs, "based on that I have been discriminated against ... the issue we were discussing about Muslims discriminating against other Muslims this is very rampant, very clear – that if you are not with us you are against us." One anonymous interviewee sought to challenge what he saw as the common-sense understanding of racism: "I think that one thinks discrimination is from the whites to the non-whites – [but] that's not the case ... there is discrimination from the brown to the black ... even today when I see a black guy ... I'm on the defensive and there's no reason ... they are good human beings ... but there is this stigma attached to people."

Other interviewees brought up concerns that religious-based discrimination had worsened in recent years, something that was linked specifically to the political climate under the former Conservative government. For example, according to Shawkat Hassan, "I didn't feel that way, but I feel it now. I have been here for 15 years and I have never felt that way, except now with this government ... In fact I am also working as a chaplain and sometimes I feel such kind of, not prejudice, but ignorance I would say – from CIC [Citizen and Immigration Canada] staff members – which is because I am a Muslim, because some inmates are Muslims. Sometimes I feel like I have to work harder than others to prove the needs for those inmates and for my services, because I am a Muslim."

Shawkat Hassan expressed great concern, indeed emotional angst, that not only he and his community would continue to experience this but also his children: "This kind of policy is not healthy, because we came here to become citizens, I don't want to feel, or my kids to feel excluded ... my kids were born and grew up here, went to school here, and so on. I want them to feel as though this is their country, that their future is here, for them and for their kids and generations to come. And I don't feel, I don't feel, at all, that somebody that came here 200 years ahead of me should have more rights than I do."

A common concern, expressed by roughly half of the interviewees, and noteworthy in that the theme was not directly related to the interview questions and was brought up independently, was that, under the Conservative government of Stephen Harper, the country was diverging from key cultural values and the government was openly hostile toward Muslims. In particular, negative perceptions of foreign policy priorities were a common theme raised by interviewees. On this theme Dalal Daoud noted, "For example, if we talk about the Israeli Palestinian issue and how the Harper government is taking a very strong position with Israel, [for] the Muslim or Palestinian population, it just pushes them away, it isolates them. As a Canadian I have always been proud [of our record] like supporting human rights, peacekeeping, diplomacy and all of that – the moderation – and that's what really attracts me." An anonymous interviewee expressed similar concerns related to the Conservative government: "Quite frankly that's a major concern for us. A lot of people in the Muslim community felt very comfortable with the Canadian model in the past, but they are getting quite uncomfortable with this situation." Soraya Hafez singled out the former prime minister for contributing to what she saw as a divisive narrative, "There are people that still say 'you people,' even the prime minister when he was in Brandon or something said 'you people' what do you mean 'you people,' *we people* we are all here, we are all Canadians."

Shayda Nanji, an Ismaili Muslim and member of the Edmonton Council of Muslim Communities, stated that in terms of discrimination, "I don't feel it on a personal level." However, she prefaced this statement as follows:

> What I find worrisome is our current government, and their shift in policy, particularly related to foreign policy in the Middle East and the peace process and all of that. When you see the way the media portrays things [for instance] Sun TV and Ezra Levant's television show. That tells me that there are some elements there, some undercurrents … they have the money, they have the power, they have the opportunity … so what they are doing is constantly stirring up negativity … but there was just as much good on the other side, so it is like taking a backwards step. The minority view, the quick sound bites, they have a much broader impact.

Shayda Nanji's comments were generally indicative of many of the opinions expressed in the interviews that at the societal level Canadians are generally quite welcoming of diversity, but at the political level, and through the media, there are concerns over what is seen as negative stereotyping.

With the election of the Trudeau Liberals in 2015 there is an open question of how much the negative perception of the federal government among Canadian Muslims has been altered. Interviewed after the events of 2015, Ahmed Abdulkadir identified what he sees as a considerable change in the rhetoric and style of the government: "It's all about the government, and the government has changed – its attitude is different." Positively citing a specific cabinet appointment, he stated that "Trudeau is viewed positively in the Somali community

– especially since the first Somali minister of immigration [was appointed] – this has major implications for how the community sees the government."

While the change in the federal government seems to have been warmly welcomed by many segments of the broader Canadian Muslim community, there are concerns that some more recent trends and events are fomenting ill will toward Muslims globally. For example, Ahmed Abudlkadir, while noting some positive trends locally, indicated how the "hysteria, the fear of refuges and the impact of Donald Trump's election have [all] amplified Islamophobia." He singled out the role of social media in driving some negative perceptions: "People hear news faster than before – people are just saying 'you hear what happened – this is what happened.'"

CONCLUDING REMARKS

The Canadian Muslim community is not a homogenous entity; it is representative of a multiplicity of experiences that are drawn together by a world religion. In a globalized and transnational world, many Canadian Muslims, like members of other minority migrant communities, exist between two or more worlds. When individuals are told (to paraphrase the experience of some of the interviewees), "you don't belong here, why don't you go back to where you belong," when they are referred to as "you people," and when they experience discrimination, racism, and xenoracism, belonging is called into question. For a multicultural society and for a multicultural state this observation has particular ramifications: it challenges the premise of equity.

The opinions of the Canadian Muslim interviewees were in some ways as diverse as their community; however, they also drew on common experiences. Not surprisingly, considering how much attention has been brought to the community in the post-9/11 world, a shared view was that xenoracism was connected to global political events, in particular, conflict, war, and terrorism. Most interviewees believed that since 9/11 xenoracism had been gaining traction (although several interviewees believed that it had dissipated somewhat since 2001).

The survey and interview data indicate that a sizable minority of Canadian Muslims have directly experienced some form of racism in Canada: 32 per cent according to EDS data, 35 per cent according to the 2016 SMC, and 47 per cent of the interviewees. It is noteworthy, considering the composition of the elite-level Muslim community sample in the study conducted for this book, which included religious leaders, professionals, successful entrepreneurs, and so on, that such a high number of individuals experienced racism directly. If, as suggested by some interviewees, manifestations of racism were more acute among the working class and more marginalized segments of the communities, there might be much higher levels among the population as a whole. Of course, without further research this is a purely speculative statement. Other noteworthy findings from the EDS and SMC data are that 37.5 per cent of Muslims (cumulatively for immigrant and non-immigrant samples) felt out of place in Canada, 29 per cent of the Canadian population held negative views of Muslims, and a small majority of Canadians lacked a sense of trust in the community. But how much of these attitudes and experiences can be linked to xenoracism?

At the societal or everyday level the fact that, as indicated by the EDS, only 34 per cent of Muslims who reported discrimination believed it was based on religion and that only 29 per cent felt out of place (i.e., not foreign) may indicate that xenoracism remains a more muted source of discrimination at the societal level. These findings are opposed to the results of studies in the European Union, which found that a significant source of discrimination for Muslim youth was religious identity. After reviewing all of these findings we can conclude that at the societal level, xenoracism that targets Muslim communities exists alongside other forms of racism, such as colour-coded racism.

When interviewees did speak of societal-level experiences with xenoracism they attributed those experiences to outward symbols of faith – the hijab or other types of head covering for Muslim women and beards for men. There is a gendered element to these experiences, a finding that speaks to the need for further study of specific experiences with xenoracism among men and women.

Some interviewees directly referenced multiculturalism as providing a defence or a barrier against racism. They believed that multiculturalism, and a Canadian tradition for respect for cultural diversity, had made Canadians less ignorant of each other's traditions and more open to difference. Yet, at the same time, there were also significant concerns that some politicians and the media were challenging many of the values that Canadian Muslims associated with this positive image of Canada. There were concerns that politicians and the media were encouraging divisiveness in a society that is generally marked by receptivity and respect of cultural difference. This perceived hostility challenged their sense of belonging and worryingly generated fears for future generations. In the next three chapters the political-institutional level will become the focus of the book as it examines areas of policy including multiculturalism, integration, and security.

5

The Crisis of Multiculturalism:
The Canadian Exception?

The years that followed 9/11 were marked not only by the War on Terror and the so-called Great Recession but also a "crisis of multiculturalism" and the re-emergence of mainstream far-right anti-immigrant politics in Europe and elsewhere. In some states, for instance the Netherlands, the response to the crisis of multiculturalism and growing anti-immigrant sentiment has been migration controls, re-imagined citizenship, and required viewing of films intended to expose newcomers to Dutch values. Through pieces of legislation like the 2006 Civic Integration Act the burden of integration in the Netherlands was shifted squarely to newcomers *and* more long-time residents, requiring them to pass rigorous civic integration and language proficiency tests. By the late spring of 2011, reflecting an increasingly commonly held position among Western European politicians, the Dutch disavowed multiculturalism.

As Kenan Malik pointed out in an article on these trends in the *New York Times*, "The real target of much of this criticism, however, is not multiculturalism but immigration and immigrants – especially Muslims. Mr Wilders, leader of the Freedom Party, the third largest in the Dutch Parliament, has campaigned for an end to all non-Western immigration, a ban on mosque building and the outlawing of the Koran."[1] By 2016, in the context of an unfolding "migrant crisis" in Europe and a series of terrorist attacks on European soil, the Freedom Party had rocketed to the lead in national polling, joining far-right political parties from Austria to Sweden that threaten to ascend to power.[2] Despite disappointing election results in 2016 and 2017 these parties retain elevated levels of public support and are having an increasing influence on public policy.

The question is how did we get here? As Lentin and Titley contend in *The Crises of Multiculturalism: Racism in a Neoliberal Age*, "Multiculturalism has inspired a long history of backlash; however, since 11 September 2001 commentators, politicians and media coverage in a range of European and Western contexts have increasingly drawn on narratives of the 'crisis of multiculturalism' to make sense of a broad range of events and political developments, and to justify political initiatives, rhetoric and aspirations in any given context."[3]

According to Lentin and Titley, the repudiation of multiculturalism in Europe has been part of an initiative to "define cultural boundaries – and hierarchies – between 'nationals and immigrants,' drawing on established tropes of national cultures endangered by the demographic challenge and confidence of immigrant cultures in general, and Islam in particular."[4] In this narrative Muslims can become the undesirable and disintegrated foreign other – proof of the "failed" multicultural project and the need for a re-imagined and more homogenous state. As Lepinard observes, "Islam, rather than race or ethnicity, is at the centre of the new politics of inclusion and has become the main focal point of policy making and constitutional politics ... In this context religious identities may be used to replace the national-foreigner divide and the markers of ethnic difference that previously structured integration politics and policy."[5]

The primary question for this section of the book is this: Has Canada "bucked" the trend? Has Canada avoided the crisis of multiculturalism? Parallel to this question, has the state's unique approach to diversity helped to mitigate xenoracism toward Canadian Muslims? The optimistic assertion, albeit a qualified one, is that state multiculturalism in Canada has been resilient in the face of the wider crisis of multiculturalism and xenoracism witnessed elsewhere, most especially in Western Europe. However, such resilience must be tested in relation to the experience of Canadian Muslims within that framework.

To begin to assess these assertions the chapter will explore the meanings and historical development of multiculturalism in Canada and review of some of the arguments made in favour of and in opposition to official multiculturalism in Canada.

DEFINING MULTICULTURALISM

For many, multiculturalism is simply a social reality – something we experience on a daily basis in an increasingly globalized and cosmopolitan world. Pitcher writes that this lived multiculturalism "does not describe an abstract ideal of social organization, but rather an already-existing sociopolitical reality of which cultural difference has become a defining feature."[6] But "lived multiculturalism" is not the focus of the book; rather, the focus is state, or, as it has been referred to in Canada, "official" multiculturalism, a set of public policies that aim to manage cultural diversity. This is, in fact, the original meaning of the term: as Abu-Laban and Gabriel reflect on the etymology, "It is notable that the actual term 'multiculturalism' was first coined in Canada as a result of the federal policy."[7]

According to Fleras and Kunz, state multiculturalism "consists of specific government initiatives to transform multicultural ideals into official programs and practices that acknowledge diversity as different yet equal. A new symbolic order, along with a corresponding mythology, is constructed under multicultural policies that help to paper over any inconsistencies at odds with present realties."[8] In other words, state multiculturalism is a normative set of policies that seeks to match public policy with an ideology and the realities of an increasingly multicultural society. By comparison, Castle and Miller distill state multiculturalism down to its practical applications and believe it is "based on the idea that immigrants need services that address their special needs with regard to education, language and housing. The absence of such measures can put immigrants and their children at a disadvantage, and deny them opportunities for upward mobility. The key assumption of multiculturalism is that specific policies do not lead to separatism but, on the contrary, are the precondition for successful integration."[9]

In the above descriptions we find two important points. First, state multiculturalism is a normative policy that is closely associated with nation building. It is an attempt to imagine a new political community that replaces a pre-existing identity that no longer corresponds to the social reality on the ground. In other words, it seeks to address a contradiction between the idea of the nation and the social relations it contains; it is an attempt to define new parameters for belonging at the national level. In this sense it is an ideology that is intrinsically tied to ideas of Canadian nationalism, forming an ideal of what national culture *ought* to look like.

Second, in the quote from Castles and Miller we find the practical side of this normative vision: the interconnection between multiculturalism and integration. In constructing a new symbolic order the

inequities of past social and economic relations marked by discrimination, prejudice, and the uneven distribution of public resources
must be addressed to meet the normative vision. For Baldwin Wong,
an interviewee from the policy sample group and social planner at
the City of Vancouver, the ability of multicultural policy to address
these inequities is critical in judging the policy's success: "If multiculturalism does not contribute to equity then it's meaningless, because
for me it's really about access."

Will Kymlicka, arguably the most influential multicultural theorist
in Canada, identifies what he sees as the essence of a multicultural
state: "A state is multicultural if its members either belong to different nations (a multinational state), or have emigrated from different
nations (a polyethnic state), and if this fact is an important aspect
of *personal identity* and *political life*."[10] With this straightforward
definition in mind there are a number of forms that state multiculturalism can take. It may vary in terms of the normative aspirations
it engenders and the policies it contains. To highlight this diversity,
Abu-Laban and Gabriel use the example of a very narrow conception
of multiculturalism in the United States where multicultural policies
tend to refer "to educational practices and to efforts by ethnic minorities ... and other groups to foster a more inclusive curriculum in
universities and public schools."[11] Here, in effect, are policies that
are far more focused than those witnessed in Canada. By comparison,
Castles and Miller believe that there are two "key variants" of multiculturalism: (1) the United States style variant accepts diversity but
does not give the state the role of enforcing social justice and main-
tainer of cultures, and (2) multiculturalism is seen as a public policy
variant where multiculturalism implies the willingness of the majority
group to both accept cultural difference and state action to secure
equal rights for minorities.[12]

Under Kymlicka's definition, the first model, the US approach to
multiculturalism, would not meet the standards of a multicultural
state because multiculturalism is not an important aspect of American
identity, and multicultural policy is limited to narrow segments of
public policy. By comparison, in Canada multiculturalism is said to
be a defining feature of identity and public policy. Of course, this was
not always the case; as a relatively new state Canada has contained
a number of competing visions of national identity.

It was in the early 1970s, in an atmosphere of global social and
political upheaval, marked by generational change and shifts in

societal values in the Western world, that the Canadian state first developed state multiculturalism, establishing the prototypal version of the policy. For Dallmayr, "Several aspects render the Canadian case noteworthy. One is the high political saliency of cultural pluralism and diversity. More than elsewhere (in the West), multiculturalism has been the topic of intense public constitutional debates, which may have to do with the fact that Canada has never fully subscribed to the assimilationist or "melting-pot" ideal of its neighbour."[13]

THE HISTORICAL DEVELOPMENT OF OFFICIAL MULTICULTURALISM IN CANADA

As US political scientist Francis Fukuyama has observed, multiculturalism "was born in Canada" and its principles of tolerance and diversity spread, at least for a time, to much of the world's liberal democracies.[14] To trace the historical development of state multiculturalism in Canada one needs to return to the post-war years when, according to Biles and Ibrahim, the Canadian government had been "overtly tackling issues arising from their diversity since at least the end of World War II."[15] As noted in the preceding chapter, during the post-war years, despite growing diversity, immigration policies in Canada, as in the rest of the Western world, were overtly racist and assimilationist in orientation. Before the institution of the points system in 1967, immigration standards distinctly favoured British and Western European migrants and secondarily white migrants from areas such as Central and Eastern Europe, while limiting non-white migrants; therefore, it contained a clear racist/hierarchical ideology within its immigration system. Discriminatory and assimilationist policies during this period sought to establish cultural conformity, and the government was largely dismissive of societal inequities based on race.[16]

Moreover, before 1967, immigration policy was discriminatory on religious grounds, exemplified by Canada's refusal to accept Jewish refugees fleeing the Nazi persecution and the Holocaust during the Second World War.[17] However, by the 1960s, declining numbers of immigrants from dominant cultural groups, such as the British, growing diversity among newcomers, and an increasingly assertive Québécois minority led to a renewed effort of nation building.[18] Subsequently, by 1963, then prime minister Lester Pearson established the Royal Commission on Bilingualism and Biculturalism to re-examine confederation and the idea of national identity and belonging in Canada.

In 1969 the B & B commission, as it became known, released a report entitled *The Cultural Contribution of other Ethnic Groups,* which recommended the recognition of the increasingly multicultural nature of Canada. As McRoberts recognizes, in the report of the B and B commission "there was the general recognition of the need to recognize the rights and contributions of cultural and ethnic groups that fell outside of the bi-cultural framework."[19] Consequently, in 1971 Trudeau used some of these recommendations as justification for the establishment of a new vision of Canadian identity – one that maintained the bilingual character of the state yet adopted multiculturalism, rather than biculturalism, as a normative vision of national identity. As Abu-Laban and Gabriel note, "The couching of multiculturalism within a bilingual framework may be seen as an indication of the continued dominance of British – and to a lesser extent French-origin groups in Canada."[20]

There was of course a utilitarian motive for the adoption of state multiculturalism, and this was especially true for Trudeau. As Winter notes, it has been an overlooked "coincidence" that Canadian multiculturalism was implemented during a period of "profound conflict" between the two dominant linguistic-cultural political forces: English Canada and an increasingly assertive, nationalistic, and, in the case of the Front de Libération du Québec, sometimes militant Quebec.[21] Undoubtedly, Trudeau's strategic adoption of multiculturalism was related in large part to what has been commonly referred to as the Quebec question in Canada.

Not surprisingly, Trudeau's multicultural vision of Canada was not well received by Quebec provincial governments that have, regardless of their position on confederation, consistently rejected state multiculturalism in favour of a loose commitment to what has been referred to as interculturalism. In short, that alternative policy maintains a more distinct cultural core into which newcomers are expected to integrate. Dupré contends that interculturalism was intended to promote "common public language and … the recognition of ethnocultural pluralism … while encouraging convergence with the French Canadian majority."[22] Thus, state multiculturalism in the rest of Canada exists alongside the intercultural approach adopted in Quebec where interculturalism offers a different vision of integration and belonging.[23]

The Quebec government's rejection of the multicultural model and adoption of interculturalism can be seen as a decision that was grounded in Québécois nationalism and fears of the diminution of language and identity in the face of the economic, political, and cultural power of English Canada. Chiefly, there was concern among nationalists that immigrants were increasingly being integrated into the Anglo minority in Quebec, a trend that was viewed as potentially detrimental to Québécois culture. State multiculturalism was seen as a threat, not only because it could empower communities that may have little interest in said culture but also because it contained an idea of cultural relativism that could challenge the idea of Quebec as a distinct or separate society.

Of relevance to this study, in the context of the overall crisis of multiculturalism, some Canadian scholars, members of the media, and international governments and organizations have recently made a case for interculturalism as a potential replacement for multiculturalism as a model for managing ethnocultural diversity. For example, within the European Union, the Committee of Ministers of the Council of Europe in an influential white paper on "intercultural dialogue" have argued that interculturalism is now the preferred model for Europe because multiculturalism is largely seen as having "failed."[24]

Prominent scholars such as Alain Gangnon and Raffaele Iacovino have offered a spirited defence of Quebec's bicultural approach to Canadian pluralism, stating, "Contrary to those who view minority nationalism in its nineteenth-century manifestation this is indeed the recipe for a genuine political relationship between political communities that share a long history, demonstrate similar values, and have expressed the will to live together."[25] Similar sentiments can be found in the opinion of the prominent sociologist Gerard Bouchard, who co-chaired the province's commission on reasonable accommodation, as he sees interculturalism as a viable alternative to multiculturalism.[26]

However, events such as the vitriolic debates over Quebec's charter of values in 2013 demonstrate the potential limits of interculturalism when it is exposed to assertive Québécois nationalism. Since 1995, when former Quebec premier Jacques Parizeau blamed the defeat of the sovereignty movement on "ethnic votes," xenoracism has appeared relatively frequently in the political discourse of Quebec. Some examples of this include the 2007 provincial elections where the Action démocratique du Québec employed an anti-immigration election

platform to gain a margin of support in rural ridings, and the introduction of Bill 195 (the Quebec Identity Act) by the Parti Québécois
(under the leadership of Pauline Marois).[27]

To an extent, Quebec's struggle in balancing cultural diversity with
Québécois nationalism mirrors some of the experiences of European
states during the "crisis of multiculturalism." Arguably, these issues
can be traced back to the historical development of Quebec nationalism and the province's struggles to define its place in the Canadian
state. That nationalism, before the 1960s, was tied to ideas of a French
Canadian "race" that was defined through a common language, religion and rural culture.[28] When Quebec went through its Quiet
Revolution, a period of rapid secularization where the provincial
government replaced the Roman Catholic Church as the most important institution in Quebec society, that society shifted its national
allegiance to the province and its political identity. Thus, according
to Dupré, at this point "a form of modern, territorially-based nationalism emerged and got diffused."[29] In this sense, Quebec nationalism,
at least to an extent, mirrors the ethnic nationalism and patterns of
secularism found in Europe.

Additionally, as Quebec exists as a "nation in a nation" and has
constantly struggled to gain recognition as a distinct society within
the Canadian state, the Quebec brand of nationalism is, by its very
nature, defensive. This is evidenced by a series of language laws (such
as Bill 22 and Bill 101) making French the official language, the denial
of public funds to non-French schools, the promotion by the Parti
Québécois of so-called identity acts such as Bill 195, simmering hostility from politicians toward ethnic minorities since the 1995 refer-
endum defeat, and a drive to establish a more formal and coercive
idea of belonging.[30]

Put simply, Quebec now stands as a curious extension of Western
European trends in Canada, as more assertive ethnic nationalism,
public angst over secularism and increased religious diversity, and the
mobilization of xenoracism in political platforms have become common features of public discourse in the province. These features can
be readily identified in the speeches and rhetoric of figures like Pauline
Marois, who in an interview published in Montreal's *Le Devoir* stated
that multiculturalism is undesirable and dangerous. According to
Marois, using language that is not dissimilar to that used by anti-
immigrant far-right parties in Europe, multiculturalism in Britain has
led to people "smashing each other in the face and throwing bombs."[31]

Of course, Quebec's experience with xenoracism, while perhaps more acute than what has been witnessed in the rest of Canada, is not unique to the province. For example, fears over religious symbolism (e.g., the niqab) and the exploitation of those fears by federal politicians were on full display in the 2015 election campaign. Undoubtedly these trends demonstrate that xenoracism is not isolated to Quebec and that state multiculturalism alone is not a sufficient bulwark against that particular ideology and a growing anti-Islamic social movement. Where we do find a significant difference between Quebec and the rest of Canada is in the former's adherence to a more ethnically rooted vision of national identity.

Paradigms of State Multiculturalism

According to Sugunasiri, in 1971 Canadian immigration and integration policies went from a paradigm of "classical racism" to one of "classical multiculturalism."[32] This dramatic paradigm shift in policy heralded an era of constitutional and legislative change that helped to ingrain multiculturalism in the fabric of the Canadian state. For instance, the 1980s saw the codification of multiculturalism in the 1988 Canadian Multiculturalism Act and in the 1982 Canadian Charter of Rights and Freedoms. During this period, a greater emphasis was put on "race relations" within the overall policy of the federal government. There was recognition among policy-makers, partly brought on by critics of the policy, that multiculturalism needed to do more to reduce the significant institutional barriers faced by minorities.[33] During this period of race-based politics, Biles and Ibrahim note that "the political strength of the anti-racism movement forced other dimensions of diversity to the margins. The Multiculturalism Program reflected this agenda by emphasizing its anti-racism policy."[34]

By the mid-1990s, in the context of the downsizing of the public service in the program review of 1994, state multiculturalism, like other government programs/ministries, was being re-examined and reduced in size. Policies like multiculturalism became measured in terms of outcome, impact, and return on investment, and since programs like anti-racism were difficult to measure, especially in terms of outcomes, it became more difficult for bureaucrats and ministers to justify funding. Colin Boyd, a director of multiculturalism programming with the federal government, outlines how these ideas were adopted into bureaucratic deliberations: "How do you know that an interfaith initiative or a program to address racism and discrimination actually increases understanding and reduces racism? It is very difficult to correlate the two, and so we are frankly struggling with that, in the federal government especially, in an environment where fiscal restraint means spending is scrutinized increasingly."

By 1997 the federal Liberal government began to restructure the multiculturalism program, shifting the emphasis away from antiracism to a "civic" form of multiculturalism with a focus on promoting political integration and a sense of belonging to Canada. This shift continued the trend away from a focus on direct funding for cultural organizations, under what some have termed the "song and dance" model of multiculturalism, toward programs that promoted the new priorities of integration. Fleras and Kunz characterize this new approach as follows: "It is based on fostering a sense of belonging and a shared sense of Canadian identity as one way of enhancing national unity without forsaking those differences that enrich or empower. Emphasis is on what we have in common as rights-bearing and equality-seeking individuals rather than on what separates and divides us. Policy objectives under civic multiculturalism include a commitment to the society-building goals of social justice, an emergent Canadian identity, citizenship and national unity, and increased civic participation."[35]

Whatever its goals, the multiculturalism program since the 1990s has been subject to downsizing within a political climate that promotes results-based public spending. Fleras and Kunz, writing in 2001 when the trend toward program downsizing was firmly in place, observed, "The government may remain officially committed to official multiculturalism; nevertheless, its support is increasingly muted, it reflects a disturbing trend towards complacency or expediency, and is not beyond the pale of axing costly multicultural programs."[36] Successive governments, including the Liberal governments of Jean Chrétien and Paul Martin and the Conservative government of Stephen Harper, armed with ideals of limited government and a reduced role for the public service, hollowed out the program. State multiculturalism has been downgraded from ministry to program and was transferred from the Department of Heritage to Citizenship and Immigration Canada in 2008, under Stephen Harper's Conservative government. In July of 2009 the Conservatives laid out several new objectives for the program as part of an ongoing program review that commenced in 2007. One of these objectives was "to build an integrated, socially cohesive society."[37] The Conservative government nearly halved the program's funding when it came into power, from $34 million in 2005–06 to $17 million the following fiscal year, and its funding had dwindled down to the $12 million range around the time of the Conservative defeat in 2015.[38]

However, despite the cuts of the recent decades, state multiculturalism has been a dynamic policy in the Canadian context that has endured through several paradigms, changing government priorities, and views on the appropriate role of the state in the arena of socioeconomic policy. Thus, the historical development of official multiculturalism has led to a series of compromises between somewhat conflicting goals. On the one hand, policy-makers sought to establish greater equity among cultural groups and reduce barriers to full participation in Canadian society. On the other hand, especially after the civic multicultural turn of the mid-1990s, policy-makers sought to develop a consensus around a core set of Canadian values and encourage active civic participation among minority groups who were viewed as being at least somewhat disengaged from this space.

THE POLITICAL ECONOMY
OF STATE MULTICULTURALISM

A sometimes-overlooked driving factor in the historical development of state multiculturalism in Canada has been economic and labour considerations. Yet, a review of the history of Canadian immigration, integration, and diversity policy reveals that economic priorities have never been far from considerations of who should be allowed into Canada and how those newcomers should be incorporated into the state and its labour market. From the turn of the twentieth century to the adoption of the points system in 1967, and with today's distinctly economically driven approach to immigration and integration, we find that Canada's approach to newcomers has always been shaped first and foremost by economic considerations.

This was certainly the chief consideration of Wilfrid Laurier's interior minister, Sir Clifford Sifton, who introduced an open-door immigration policy for Europeans at the turn of the twentieth century, bringing in millions of Europeans from across the continent and in the process significantly altering the cultural composition of the country. Sifton's concern was not *how* newcomers from Central and Eastern Europe would impact "Anglo-conformity"; rather, it was the need for settlement and economic growth in Western Canada.[39] Angus McLaren also points to the recruiting of Sikh and Chinese labour by railway companies in Western Canada as evidence that economic considerations have trumped issues of race in Canadian immigration policy. According to McLaren, in this particular example, "The practical political and economic concern of the federal government and the railways in settling the West necessarily ran counter to the ideological preoccupations of many Anglo-Canadian intellectuals."[40] Of course one must consider the dangerous labour conditions and acute racism these economic migrants faced in the labour market, and more generally in Canadian society of that time.

The post-war period in Canada, as in much of the world, was a period of economic boom that generated growing labour needs. To meet those needs the Canadian government opened its doors to successive waves of asylum seekers after the Second World War and later groups of Eastern European refugees fleeing mid-century unrest in the communist bloc.[41] By 1962, under the stewardship of John Diefenbaker, racial preferences were removed from immigration policy, paving the way for the adoption of the "colour-blind" points system in 1967.[42]

After 1967 Canadian immigration policy favoured skilled and wealthy migrants. By comparison, in many European states post-war immigrants and migrants have tended to be less skilled or "guest" workers.[43] Subsequently, these less skilled immigrants have tended to suffer from significant disparities in terms of employment and wages in comparison with the host culture and occupy economically depressed regions, cities, and neighborhoods, creating a distinct spatial concentration of poverty or "ghettoization" in states like the United Kingdom and France. According to Joppke this historical pattern of immigration in Europe cannot be separated from "the generally more coercive and control-minded integration and citizenship policies in Europe."[44] In comparison, immigration and integration policy in Canada after 1967 has been shaped by the points system that has privileged skilled, educated, and wealthier applicants. As Joppke notes, in Canada, it would be "incoherent to harass chosen, high-skilled new world immigrants with coercive and restrictive citizenship rules at the tail-end of the immigration process."[45]

This is not to say that Canada's approach to immigration, integration, and diversity has been problem free – in 1896, 1967, or 2017. Since the adoption of state multiculturalism in Canada, the state has committed itself to pursuing equity for cultural minorities. Yet, according to a range of studies, despite Canada's points system, adoption of official multiculturalism, and the more skilled, educated, and wealthy nature of Canadian newcomers, such equity remains elusive. For example, visible minorities or "racialized" groups display a significant income gap with the Canadian mainstream, with incomes roughly 15 per cent lower than the national average in 1995, even if that gap has seemingly narrowed over recent decades.[46] According to Samuel and Basavarajappa, foreign-born members of visible minorities continue to face challenges in terms of workplace integration, such as a lack of fluency in an official language and issues with credential and work-experience recognition. As a reflection of these challenges, foreign-born Canadians have experienced a significant gap in unemployment in comparison with Canadian-born workers, even though this gap began to narrow in the early 2000s.[47]

In their study, Samuel and Basavarajappa, employing EDS data, also suggest that a distinct gap in labour market outcomes for foreign-born visible-minority groups may be related to "incidents of discrimination or unfair treatment" related to ethnicity, culture, skin colour, language, accent, or religion.[48] Pendakur and Pendakur also note the role of discrimination in creating a structural disadvantage for visible-minority groups in Canada, specifically related to income.[49] These inequities are certainly a challenge to the underlying priorities of state multiculturalism.

Another potential challenge to the goals of official multiculturalism in Canada can be found in more recent attempts by the previous, Harper-led Conservative government of Canada to meet labour needs through the admission of foreign temporary workers with little access to permanent residency status or citizenship, and thus little access to the rights-based framework of state multiculturalism. By the mid-1990s larger groups of temporary foreign workers entered the Canadian labour market and lower paid areas of work in the domestic- and service-based sectors of the economy. By the mid to late 2000s these temporary workers were making up a significant percentage of workers in the domestic labour sector.[50]

Numerous studies and media pieces have highlighted the negligible rights and subsequently poor working conditions to which these workers have been subject. However, of potentially equal concern is the restricted immigration status of these workers, which according to Stasiulis and Bakan, has a "profound impact on their working and living conditions in Canada. More specifically, the greater the restriction faced at the border, the greater the risk of intense exploitation and discrimination."[51] A larger discussion of the potential effects of Canada's increasing reliance on foreign temporary workers on state multiculturalism is beyond the scope of this book. However, it should be noted that as this segment of the Canadian population grows, an increasing percentage of Canadian residents exist in a grey area where citizenship, belonging, and individual rights are elusive.

There are other trends among visible minority or "racialized" groups that demonstrate more positive experiences in Canada's labour market and society. As already noted, gaps in unemployment and income that became more pronounced in the 1980s and 1990s for visible minorities began to moderate by the early 2000s. But there are other reasons for optimism. By the early 2000s scholars like Monica Boyd were noting higher levels of educational success among second-generation Canadians,[52] and subsequent studies, including numerous studies by Statistics Canada, have confirmed this trend. For example, according to Picot and Hou, the percentage of individuals who possess a university degree is higher among visible-minority second-generation Canadians than among second-generation Canadians who are not members of a visible minority.[53] Following a review of existing data they conclude that "the children of immigrants in Canada (second-generation Canadians) have a significantly higher level of educational attainment than the children of Canadian-born parents (third-and-higher generations)."[54] One can speculate that this success in the Canadian education system may serve to reduce discrepancies in income and unemployment among multi-generational Canadian minority communities in the future.

Finally, another positive observation on the economic experience of newcomers and minority groups is the fact that Canada does not display the sort of spatial segregation or "ghettoization" found in some European states and the United States. Since Abdolmohammad Kazemipur and Shiva Halli released their provocatively entitled work *The New Poverty in Canada: Ethnic Groups and Ghetto Neighbourhoods* in 2000 there has been a significant debate over whether Canada suffers from the sort of ghettoization found elsewhere. Yet a close review of Kazemipur and Halli's study reveals that they detect high levels of "spatial concentration of poverty" in only two cities (Montreal and Winnipeg) and furthermore that they acknowledge that Canada "has not followed patterns detected in the research on American cities."[55] Follow-up studies, for instance by Balakrishnan and Gyimah, found little evidence of spatial concentration of poverty.[56] Similarly, Walks and Bourne found that "the majority of Canadian urban areas reveal degrees of segregation lower than many cities in the United States and Britain."[57] As these researchers point out, there tends to be some conflation in the literature, where there is little distinguishing between ghettos and what have been referred to as ethnic enclaves, with the latter representing a typical, established pattern of spatial settlement for minorities that does not necessarily result in a spatial concentration of poverty.[58]

Overall, this brief review of the economic facets of multiculturalism and immigration policy reveals that economic considerations have long been at the heart of Canadian immigration, integration, and nation-building policy, and that since the late nineteenth century such considerations have often trumped racist ideologies in terms of policy design. However, despite this, visible-minority communities continue to suffer distinct structural disadvantages in the labour market – disadvantages that any state committed to multiculturalism should be mindful of. As noted previously, Canadian Muslims, despite their higher levels of education (i.e., when compared with non-Muslim Canadians) experience higher levels of unemployment and of employment in lower paid service-sector jobs.

A key question moving forward in these areas of policy is how Canada can balance economic considerations with more normative and ethical considerations. Peter Li, in his work *Destination Canada: Immigration Debates and Issues* has suggested that the Canadian government shift its fixation on the economic benefits of immigration to a more holistic understanding of the benefits of immigration and multiculturalism, where the social and cultural capital that immigrants bring to Canada is valued as well as economic benefit.[59] With these observations in mind, the next section will delve deeper into debates over the efficacy and desirability of state multiculturalism.

STATE MULTICULTURALISM IN CANADA: THE PROPONENT'S CASE

Canada has 45 years of experience with multicultural policy. No other state has gone as far in institutionalizing state multiculturalism and making it part of national life. Respected religious studies scholar Paul Bramadat believes that multiculturalism, what he calls "the

Canadian diversity model" represents an international example "which promotes a relatively new and broadly inclusive approach to cultural differences ... It is no accident that many international scholars, policy analysts, and politicians consider that Canada's current policies on multiculturalism represent some of the most practical, dignified, and progressive approaches to modern citizenship in the world."[60] The following section will focus on five key points that indicate the relative strength and success of the made-in-Canada approach to diversity and national identity.

There Is Public Support for Multiculturalism

A compelling indication of the success of Canadian multiculturalism can be found in the support it enjoys among the general public. According to data compiled by the polling firm Environics, in 1997 74 per cent of Canadians agreed that multiculturalism was important to Canadian identity, but in 2003 this number jumped to 85 per cent; multiculturalism ranked above Canada's popular pastime, ice hockey.[61] Multiculturalism has also become something in which Canadians express great pride. Since 1985 Environics has asked Canadians to describe in their own words what makes them "proud to be Canadian." In 1985 they cited things such as "the beauty of the land" and multiculturalism ranked in tenth place; by 2006 multiculturalism had climbed to second place.[62]

Findings from a 2012 joint study by the Mosaic Institute and the Association of Canadian Studies on Multiculturalism identified a difference in generational support for the policy. The survey of 1,522 respondents found that, overall, 58 per cent of Canadians hold a positive view of Canada's multiculturalism policy. However, among respondents between the ages of 18 and 24 years, that number was 74 per cent, while among the 65 years and older group it was 47 per cent. When asked whether it was easy for Canadians from different racial, religious, and cultural communities to form close relationships, 80 per cent of 18- to 24-year-olds agreed, versus only 46 per cent of respondents aged 65 years and older.[63] These figures speak of both positive perceptions of multicultural policy and of the experience of "lived multiculturalism" among young adults in Canada. Reflecting on these findings, the report concludes, "The results suggest that multiculturalism enjoys its strongest support amongst those who have grown up knowing nothing else. Emerging out of the most diverse classrooms in Canadian history, young people feel comfortable transcending ethnic and religious boundaries."[64]

Multiculturalism Has Become Part of Canadian National Identity and This Creates a More Welcoming Environment for Newcomers

It has been argued that multiculturalism's popular support and its relationship with Canadian national identity help to create a welcoming environment for newcomers who seek to find a place in the country. Commenting on the pride that Canadians and immigrants to Canada find in multiculturalism, Kymlicka states, "The fact that Canada has officially defined itself as a multicultural nation means that immigrants are a constituent part of the nation that citizens feel pride in, so multiculturalism helps native-born citizens to link national identity to solidarity with immigrants and minorities. And, conversely, multiculturalism provides a link by which immigrants and minorities come to identify with, and feel pride in, Canada."[65]

For Fleras and Kunz, pluralism is part of what it means to be a Canadian, unlike the situation in other Western states: "Cultural differences are not disparaged as being incompatible with national goals, but are endorsed as integral components of a national mosaic, a reflection of the Canadian ideal, and a source of enrichment and strength."[66]

According to these scholars the net result of state multiculturalism in Canada is the creation of a more welcoming environment – an environment in which newcomers can experience a sense of inclusion that may not exist in other states, at least to the same extent. To illustrate this point Esses et al., in their comparative study of national identity and attitudes toward immigrants in Canada and Germany, found that: "In terms of attitudes toward immigrants and immigration, this research supports the view that national identity can have a significant impact on these attitudes. It is indeed promising that focusing on inclusive perceptions of national identity can have positive effects, at least among citizens of nations that acknowledge the importance of immigrants in their development."[67]

Another aspect of Canadian national identity that may be attractive for newcomers is the relatively open-ended nature of Canadian nationalism. A question that many Canadians still struggle with is what it means to be Canadian. As seen in the work of Michael Adams and Environics, multiculturalism, our natural heritage, our landscapes, and our national pastimes such as ice hockey tend to rank high on the list for much of the public. As a relatively young state, Canada possesses a still somewhat undefined and malleable identity – one that is more amenable to growing ethnocultural diversity and migration. Soroka, Helliwell, and Johnston believe that this "thinner" sense of Canadian national identity may allow newcomers to more easily find identification and belonging.[68]

Multiculturalism Attracts More Newcomers to Citizenship and Civic Life

There are also a number of empirical studies that have heralded the potential efficacy and desirability of multiculturalism in terms of attracting newcomers to citizenship, arguably the most important measurement of political integration. For instance, Bloemraad, in her comparative study of citizenship in the United States and Canada, found that immigrants in Canada are more likely to become citizens than immigrants to the United States.[69] Bloemraad, who combined a series of interviews with immigrants from the Portuguese and Vietnamese communities in Boston and Toronto with statistical research, found that official multiculturalism, settlement support services, and civic participation in the Canadian context led to an easier path to citizenship than in the United States.[70] Citing a 2005 study, Banting, Courchene, and Seidle note that 84 per cent of eligible immigrants in Canada pursued citizenship in comparison to 56 per cent in the United Kingdom and 40 per cent in the United States.[71]

In addition, examining participation in civic life, Paul Howe found that new citizens in Canada were more likely to be engaged in formal politics.[72] This engagement has resulted in greater representation of newcomers among elected officials according to Adams: "Canada's lower house is ... closest to being representative of the overall population." In the House of Commons roughly 13 per cent of members were born outside of Canada (in comparison with 19 per cent of the population as a whole) whereas in the United States, close to 15 per cent of the population was born outside of the country but only 2 per cent of members of the House of Representatives were born elsewhere. In France roughly 11 per cent of the population was born elsewhere, yet roughly 6 per cent of deputies in the National Assembly were foreign born.[73] While the Canadian Parliament still has a long way to go to meet the realities of Canadian society in terms of diversity, it still outperforms other national political systems.[74] Further, it is worth noting that since the defeat of the Conservatives and election of the Liberals in 2015 there have been some high-profile appointments of ministers from minority communities, including the young Canadian-Somali lawyer Ahmed Hussen as minister of Immigration, Refugees and Citizenship.

Putting these studies within the context of the civic multicultural paradigm, there seems to have been a great deal of success, especially in terms of promoting access and desirability of citizenship and political participation. For Colin Boyd, "The acquisition of citizenship in Canada for newcomers is one of the highest in the world. Newcomers become voters ... [This] has created in Canada the conditions for a more inclusive sense of citizenship. In Europe, where there is a much more rigid [system], in some countries, France/Germany, where you have, for instance, Turkish people living for over 30 years that are not citizens – that encourages [a climate] where people may co-exist but they're not integrated as we are in Canada ... the acquisition of citizenship is a powerful tool for integration."

Multiculturalism Is Codified into the Constitution

Another factor that differentiates Canadian state multiculturalism from the policies of other states is the fact that it is part of the country's constitutional and legislative framework, specifically in the Canadian Charter of Rights and Freedoms and the Canadian Multiculturalism Act. Even if hostile political forces possessing a pronounced distaste for multiculturalism on ideological grounds come into power, there is little prospect for altering the policy at the constitutional level. The Act and the Charter ensure that important aspects of multiculturalism remain intact, and this is especially true in terms of the role the courts play in supporting these rights. Of particular importance in this regard is Section 27 of the Charter, which reads simply, "This Charter shall be interpreted in a manner consistent with the preservation and enhancement of the multicultural heritage of Canadians."[75] Together with the Charter, the Act further codifies and institutionalizes multiculturalism. The Act recognizes the protection of not only "cultural" rights but also religious and racial rights: "AND WHEREAS the Government of Canada recognizes the diversity of Canadians as regards race, national or ethnic origin, colour and religion as a fundamental characteristic of Canadian society and is

committed to a policy of multiculturalism designed to preserve and
enhance the multicultural heritage of Canadians while working to
achieve the equality of all Canadians in the economic, social, cultural
and political life of Canada."[76]

According to Anna Chiappa, an interviewee from the policy sample
and executive director of the Canadian Ethnocultural Council (a
group that advocates for multiculturalism in Canada), "The act provides that vision of the level playing field and says to institutions that
you have an obligation to ensure that the service you provide, the
employment that you offer, the information you provide ... reflects
that vision. Multiculturalism is under the Charter and the Charter
says we are all equal ... no one culture can trump the other." Chiappa
points to other pieces of legislation such as the Broadcasting Act of
1991 that requires broadcasters to offer "ethnic" programming as
being important, together with the Charter, in implementing multicultural policy at the societal level. These constitutional and legislative
protections make the Canadian approach to multiculturalism more
robust than that of its peers in the Western world.

Canadian Muslims Have a Favourable View of the Program

As the minority group that has been singled out in the failure of
multiculturalism narrative, Muslims have been highlighted by xenoracists as exemplifying the incompatibility of some religious minority
groups and liberal-secular values. But as indicated by the interview
sample group from the Muslim community, Canadian Muslims have
an overwhelmingly favourable view of state multiculturalism in
Canada. For Baha Abu-Laban, who was an active participant in the
founding stages of state multiculturalism, the policy offered a route
to political power for minorities who had been left out of the old
bicultural model. On what the policy means to him, he remarked,
"For me multiculturalism is to level the playing field and allows us
to be involved in a way that we were deprived of in the past."

Ahmed Shoker, director at the Canadian Islamic Congress, com-
mented, "In my judgment Canada is in the top of the world when it
comes to multiculturalism, there is no question about it." Bashir
Ahmed, executive director of the Somali Canadian Education and
Rural Development Organization shared similar sentiments: "It is the
best policy that I have seen in the Western world." One anonymous

interviewee, a prominent member of a Muslim cultural association, echoed these statements: "We think that is one of the strongest values in Canada, as much as it gets a bad name, we think it has helped us to bring a number of communities together." Dalal Daoud, of the Canadian Islamic Congress, views multiculturalism as part of Canadian identity, an aspect of national identity that differentiates Canada from other states: "It has been a Canadian value. I think that is what makes us different than European nations."

For first-generation Canadians like Shawkat Hassan of the British Columbia Muslim Association, state multiculturalism was an attractive national attribute that helped him to decide to immigrate to Canada: "Let me be frank with you, I have worked with the UN and travelled to many places ... but I like Canada for its policy on multiculturalism. The United States I felt as though I am in a melting pot, here in Canada I feel as though you have your own identity, we respect your identity, but it has to fit with the rest of the people, with the rest of others ... so you fit with the system here and that is because of the multicultural policy that exists in this country."

Community organizer Ahmed Abdulkadir also believes that official multiculturalism is attractive for newcomers: "Because of multiculturalism, that is why we are here. From the community perspective, *Canada is multiculturalism* – it is intertwined."

Azar Syed, also of the British Columbia Muslim Association, believes that state multiculturalism was essential in improving the situation for migrants in the late twentieth century: "I moved here in '73 and that time, if I compare it to the later years, the 70s were very hard for the immigrants, maybe because the multicultural philosophy had not taken hold ... But later on in the 1980s everything was very smooth, there was hardly any discrimination." He then went on to qualify this statement by saying that discrimination returned as an issue for the community after 9/11.

It should be noted that a few interviewees in the Muslim community did believe that the policy had issues, or required some changes. For example, Azim Jeraj, a business owner who emigrated in the 1970s, believes that "multiculturalism was great when we first came to Canada, it was wonderful to get some money to preserve my singing and dancing and all that." However, today he believes that with the second generation growing up in Canada, learning official languages and participating in its traditions, multiculturalism needs to change: "I think a lot of ideas with multiculturalism were trying to freeze that [culture], saying here keep your song and dance, instead of having it evolve naturally ... Let culture grow from within rather than having exported, having it brought here, because that is what multiculturalism did." Some interviewees viewed multiculturalism as an ongoing project, a work in progress, but the vast majority expressed support for the policy.

STATE MULTICULTURALISM IN CANADA: THE OPPONENT'S CASE

The book will now turn to the perspective of those who are opposed to state multiculturalism in Canada: those who view multiculturalism as a highly flawed approach to diversity or simply as a failed policy. Multiculturalism in Canada has been critiqued from an array of perspectives originating from a number of often divergent scholarly and ideological positions. Phil Ryan, in his aptly titled work *Multicultiphobia*, reviews some of these arguments: "It stifles individualism, imposing conformity by endorsing the illiberal practices of minority groups. Yet it is also the handmaiden of excessive individualism. It promotes moral relativism, and it fosters a rigid moral absolutism that denounces racists in every corner of Canadian society and makes no allowance for the mores of earlier times."[77] Ryan's brief summation draws out the varied and sometimes contradictory grounds on which state multiculturalism has been attacked. In the early twenty-first century the narrative of the crisis or "failure" of multiculturalism has been used to single out a host of socio-economic issues in Western states; however, in this section the analysis will focus on four key points.

Multiculturalism Creates Separateness

Perhaps the most prominent and long-standing critique of multiculturalism is that it promotes separateness and divisiveness among Canadians who belong to various cultural, ethnic, and religious communities. The Canadian Charter of Rights and Freedoms and the Canadian Multiculturalism Act have been singled out as promoting communalism and factionalism to the determinant of shared values and identity.[78] For critics of state multiculturalism, the policy emphasizes difference leading to separateness represented physically by, for example, ethnic enclaves. For Drury, today's multiculturalism has departed from the original vision of Trudeau, what she describes as a skin-deep "aesthetic plurality," where newcomers were free to maintain cultural traditions.[79] More recently she believes "pluralist enthusiasts" have built a form of multiculturalism that can be "an obstacle not only to integration but also to social mobility." Furthermore, she holds that conflicts are being generated among cultural groups over sometimes conflicting values, and certain values "might even pose a threat to peace, order and good government."[80]

Another theory holds that the policy creates separateness by projecting an artificial image of a culturally divided society that is out of step with how individuals live their day-to-day lives. Neil Bissoondath's work *Selling Illusions: The Cult of Multiculturalism in Canada* is one of the oldest and most cited works to levy this charge. Bissoondath claims that multiculturalism was a politically expedient tool for politicians looking to manage a diverse society that has ultimately led to the stereotyping of cultural groups and the highlighting of difference that creates societal divisions.[81]

Himani Bannerji's work *The Dark Side of the Nation: Essays on Multiculturalism, Nationalism and Gender* also contends that state multiculturalism projects stereotypical identities that are subsumed under the label of culture (and in doing so neglects other forms of identity such as class and gender). She rejects this form of social engineering and calls for the model to be abandoned: "We could leave behind the Weberian paradigm of tradition-modernity and a facile post-colonialism which threatens to become a form of culturalism."[82] For Marxist-feminists like Bannerji, state multiculturalism serves to deflect "critical attention from a constantly racializing Canadian political economy," thereby maintaining hegemony.[83]

Multiculturalism Opens a Space for Radicalism and Extremism to Flourish

Contained within the narrative of the "failure" of multiculturalism is the charge that multiculturalism has allowed religious minority communities, such as Muslims, to pursue illiberal policies, and in the most damning charges, the policy is said to have allowed a space for extremism and terrorism to flourish. State multiculturalism is said to promote cultural and/or moral relativism where all cultures and their beliefs, values, and practices are viewed as equally valid and valued. This is said, in turn, to encourage cultural practices that are opposed to liberal democracy and the norms, values, and laws of the host society. Reitz et al. claim that while diversity can bring new ideas, so too "immigrant newcomers who bring values that depart or appear to depart very substantially from those of the host society may lead to the creation of social boundaries that are difficult to transcend."[84]

The more serious charge, that state multiculturalism opens a space for extremism, has frequently been cited in Europe, for example after violent demonstrations among minority communities, or after incidences of violent extremism and terrorism. The violent reactions to Salman Rushdie's *The Satanic Verses*, terrorist acts like the London transit bombings of 2005, and the murder of Theo van Gogh in the Netherlands are all seen as examples of the kind of violent extremism that will occur when there is too much accommodation of difference and too little assimilation of newcomers and their values. Reflecting these ideas, Malik wrote in the *New York Times* that "in neither Britain nor Germany did multiculturalism create militant Islam, but in both it helped clear a space for it among Muslims."[85]

In Canada these concerns have been more muted; however, recent violence such as the attacks in Quebec and Ontario in October 2014 has drawn attention to individuals committing political acts of violence in the name of Islam. Also of concern have been the arrests and prosecutions of members of the Toronto 18 terrorism plot and the more recent Via Rail plot that resulted in prosecutions, both of which were linked to Canadian Muslims. These events have led to worries over security and the accommodation of religious and cultural traditions. These concerns, and the subsequent securitization of immigration and integration policy, will be explored at greater length in chapter 7.

The Policy Is Inadequate in Addressing Inequality and Racism, and "Reforms" to State Multiculturalism May Provide an Avenue for Institutionalized Racism

Another criticism of multiculturalism is that it is really only a surface-level policy that has done little to address the underlying inequities and racisms that limit the policy's goals. Here critics have derisively referred to a "song and dance" form of multiculturalism that promotes the celebration of difference, for example at festivals and cultural events, and basic tolerance of difference, but that fails to substantively address inequity or generate meaningful intercultural exchange and understanding. On this Lentin and Titley believe that state multiculturalism may provide "license to ignore and negate continuing and shifting racism in multicultural societies."[86] Reflecting Foucault's views of the modern state, they view multiculturalism as "a mode of management and control securing the legitimacy of the status quo through a deflection of questions of power and inequality into the relatively more malleable economy of cultural recognition."[87]

Moreover, a concern cited by Lentin and Titley is that the failure-of-multiculturalism narrative may be used by politicians to institutionalize racist practices that are presented as remedies needed to address the socio-economic damage wrought by state multiculturalism. In their 2011 book *The Crises of Multiculturalism: Racism in a Neoliberal Age* they state: "Lamenting it [multiculturalism] as a benevolent if somewhat naïve attempt to manage the problem of difference allows for securitized migration regimes, assimilative integrationism and neo-nationalist politics to be presented as nothing more than rehabilitative action."[88] Pertinent to this analysis, their primary critique of multiculturalism focuses "on the ways in which renditions of multiculturalism provide a space for the redrawing and laundering of contemporary racisms."[89] Thus, state multiculturalism is viewed as inadequate (in terms of pursuing goals related to anti-racism), and the shallowness of the policy is said to provide fertile ground for politicians to pursue problematic reform initiatives.

The Former Conservative Government Undermined the Policy

As outlined in the previous chapter, there is concern among some minority communities that the Conservative government under Stephen Harper significantly altered and undermined state multiculturalism while in power. In point of fact, there was evidence of a shift in federal policy vis-à-vis state multiculturalism during the Harper years. As recognized in prior analyses (such as Phil Ryan's *Multicultiphobia*) the Conservatives granted multiculturalism tacit support insofar as it helped to generate support among minority voting blocs whose votes were needed to garner electoral success in large urban centres like Vancouver and Toronto.[90] But alongside this strategic calculation the Harper government instituted a series of measures that altered multiculturalism policy and related policies associated with immigration and citizenship, all of which aimed to reshape ideas of Canadian identity and national belonging.

According to one anonymous interviewee, a former employee at Citizenship and Immigration Canada with over a decade of experience in the multiculturalism program, the program was neglected in favour of other priorities in the department, such as settlement: "They started cutting down the budget of the program – in 1993 it was about $27 million, which is still not much, but a decent amount ... It kept going down and down and down until it became $10 million ... which is nothing because the settlement budget is about $1 billion ... we have stopped funding." Speaking on the cutbacks and the abandonment of the anti-racism element, the same interviewee remarked on the multiculturalism program, "As I left, it only exists on paper, the program doesn't fund any more, there is nothing. They cancelled the racism policy: the action plan against racism was cancelled, just shut down. The program is just lasting on a few threads, even this year they cut back on the events budget: so what's left?"

Kamal Seghal, executive director at the Alberta Network of Immigrant Women, also believes that the Harper government purposely undermined the multiculturalism program, reducing its importance in relation to other priorities: "The respect for multiculturalism policy is now fading away ... multiculturalism is not being upheld. The government of Canada had a department that was totally geared towards multiculturalism and heritage – over a period of years the funding for that area kept on getting depleted, the budget cuts kept happening and right now multiculturalism is part of 'settlement.'"

Under the stewardship of former minister Jason Kenney there were significant changes to immigration and citizenship policies at Citizenship and Immigration Canada. According to the anonymous interviewee from Citizenship and Immigration Canada, many of those changes could be related to the role of the minister. On this point the interviewee stated, "The minister wants more hands on ... he wants tangible outcomes ... The way he was dealing with the program was he had to approve every single file – very micro managed." Part of the changes at Citizenship and Immigration Canada focused on areas related to immigration, such as the reduction of the number of family-class immigrants admitted to the country. For example, between 2011 and 2012 the federal government reduced family reunification visas by roughly a third, from 16,000 to 11,000 visas. According to some immigration lawyers, applicants for reunification at this time were facing wait times of up to 13 years.[91] Admittedly, the reduction in the number of family-class immigrants began long before the Conservatives came into power. In 1990 family-class immigrants made up roughly 60 per cent of arrivals, but since that time the balance between family- and economic-class immigrants has essentially been flipped. By the early 2010s, with Conservative policies accelerating the trend toward economic immigration, family-class immigrants made up less than 30 per cent of all arrivals and economic immigrants more than 60 per cent.[92]

Yasmeen Nisam, a lawyer and interviewee from the Canadian Muslim community, remarked on the curtailments at Citizenship and Immigration Canada, "I do immigration work and lately I have seen people refused for ridiculous reasons ... the officers are so powerful – once their decision is made that's it, the appeal process takes years. I feel they are trying to cut back on immigration." Following on cutbacks to family reunifications, refugees were also singled out under the former government as they had their health funding cut by $100 million (over 5 years), much to the dismay of the refugees themselves, physicians, and immigration and refugee lawyers.[93]

More directly related to the multiculturalism program, as indicated by interviewees, funding to ethnic, cultural, and religious groups was also tightly controlled and reduced under the Conservatives. Relating this trend back to the Canadian Muslim community, funding controls and reductions can in part be tied to the events of 2008–09 and a controversy over the Canadian Islamic Congress and Canadian Arab Federation, which publicly criticized Israel's offensive in Gaza, which in turn led to Kenney's statement on the groups that they "do not deserve and have no right to taxpayers' dollars to promote their kind of extremism."[94] Ryan notes that the Conservative government employed strategic funding to promote groups that more closely reflected their dominant views and as a means of isolating groups they wished to silence. As an example, he highlights the shift in money from the Canadian Islamic Congress to the Canadian Muslim Congress and the Canadian Council of Muslim Women.[95]

Therefore, the relationship between the Canadian Muslim community and the Conservatives was a driving force behind some of the changes in the multiculturalism program, specifically the closer scrutiny and curtailed distribution of funding to cultural associations and groups. According to the anonymous interviewee who is a former employee of Citizenship and Immigration Canada, "Religion plays a big role in multiculturalism now, for the federal government. And there was a scandal a few years back with the Arabic community and the minister, the CIC [Citizenship and Immigration Canada], and because of that the funding has stopped for the religious groups and the Arabic community in particular." The anonymous interviewee from a Muslim cultural association confirmed this trend and complained of a funding cut to the association from the multicultural program that resulted in the cancellation of a successful pilot program mentoring young people.

In addition to the changes to the multiculturalism program itself, the Conservative Party had initiatives that aimed to reframe national identity toward a more monoculturalist and assimilationist vision of Canada. This strategy can be found in several initiatives launched after 2011 that were specifically aimed at highlighting the history and prominence of English Canada. One example of this was the return of the word "Royal" to the titles of the branches of the Canadian Armed Forces. Another move to promote the same vision of national identity was the return of portraits of the Queen to prominent places in government buildings and Canadian embassies.

The Conservative government highlighted the country's colonial history through the funding of historical initiatives like the commemoration of the 200th anniversary of the War of 1812, granting $11.5 million to the initiative, which at the time represented roughly 70 per cent of the funding granted to the multiculturalism program.[96] As shown by McKay and Swift, the Harper government actively engaged in a re-branding of Canada to what they referred to as a "warrior nation" – one that was framed by British identity and symbolism.[97] According to McCoy and Knight, these policies were "part of a broader strategy by the Conservative government to place greater emphasis on our Commonwealth historical linkages," to the detriment of a multicultural vision of nationalism.[98] Of course, this re-branding neglected the seminal history of Indigenous peoples in Canada and the foundational role of the Québécois in Confederation and beyond. Additionally, Canada's growing immigrant and minority communities of non-British origin found themselves with little stake in the Conservative's re-imagined national vision.

This new image of Canada found its way into citizenship examinations and documents. For example, the former Conservative government introduced a 146-page citizenship guide for newcomers entitled *Welcome to Canada: What You Should Know* that put greater emphasis on the English monarchy and the history of the "royal" armed forces as key symbols of Canadian nationhood. In the 2013 version of the document, several "barbaric" practices were singled out as being unacceptable in Canada, including female genital mutilation and "honour-based crimes."[99] While these practices, under Canadian liberal mores, values, and laws, are illegal and morally reprehensible, the use of the term "barbaric" and the fact that many of the singled-out cultural practices have been associated with Islam in prior xenoracist narratives brought up the possibility of profiling certain groups.

Additionally, the changes to citizenship documents like the *Welcome Guide* mirrored earlier changes to citizenship examinations that reflected a new emphasis on military and English colonial history. When released in 2010 the new examinations produced a "massive" spike in failure rates, up to 30 per cent, among newcomers.[100] Confirming the rationale behind some of these trends, Tolley et al. identify how "questions about religious accommodation and about balancing of rights and responsibilities" were influencing Citizenship and Immigration Canada's approach to citizenship documents and examinations.[101]

Taken as a whole, the strategy of the former Conservative government under Prime Minister Stephen Harper was clear – it was a symbolic manipulation of Canadian national identity that promoted British colonial artifacts while simultaneously singling out what was seen as less desirable cultural traditions. In initiatives like the commemoration of the War of 1812 and the re-branding of the military, the Conservatives sought to celebrate an image of Canada that was largely regressive. Keeping with the party's ideological foundations, they sought to depart from the celebration of social and cultural history in favour of a far narrower interpretation of national history.

Certainly, much of this strategy consisted of rhetoric – statements and symbolic changes to Canadian institutions. However, substantive changes were also made to immigration and refugee programs and to citizenship tests and related documents. There is an argument to be made that the Conservatives, unable or unwilling to make direct legislative and constitutional challenges to the multicultural framework, attempted to undermine the policy on symbolic grounds and through alternative legislative channels. Thus, the question for many, one that will arguably remain unanswered for some time, is how effective these strategies were in altering Canadian identity and the way in which Canadians perceive immigrants, diversity, and multiculturalism.

It should be noted that the trends and policies outlined above have been examined in other works, such as by University of Alberta political scientist Yasmeen Abu-Laban, a long-term and astute observer of multicultural policy in Canada. In her article "Reform by Stealth: The Harper Conservatives and Canadian Multiculturalism" she identified what she described as "a systematic remaking of select symbols and discourses relating to 'Canadian Identity'" and acknowledged that this identity remaking sought to "resurrect elements of Canada's colonial links with Britain."[102] Similarly Abu-Laban identified policy changes to immigration and citizenship and micromanaged shifts in funding priorities as key components in the Harper government's reforms to multicultural policy. As Abu-Laban rightly observes, "Since its inception, multiculturalism has mainly been a symbolic policy."[103] This point is important as it speaks to the potentially highly detrimental manipulation of that symbolism and what it means to be Canadian.

CONCLUDING REMARKS

What is the take-away message from this chapter? Has Canada bucked the trend in the crisis of multiculturalism? State multiculturalism has now been stress-tested in Canada for 40 years. What the Canadian state and Canadians in general have accomplished seems impressive when considering the nature of intercultural relations in much of the world.[104] In a 2010 article entitled "Testing the Liberal Multiculturalist Hypothesis," Will Kymlicka, much like in the above discussion, weighed the arguments for and against state multiculturalism. He concluded, "I want to raise a bold and surprising possibility: namely, that the evidence to date, far from refuting the liberal multiculturalist hypothesis, actually supports it. Despite the widespread presumption that greater attention to empirical evidence would lead to greater skepticism about the merits of liberal multiculturalism, I want to suggest that the evidence bolsters the case."[105]

As shown by a number of prior studies (cited above), Canada offers a more expeditious path to citizenship than most other Western countries. As indicated by polling data, Canadians remain supportive of multiculturalism and value the contribution of immigrants. Moreover, among mainstream politicians there has been no explicit failure-of-multiculturalism narrative. Historically, state multiculturalism has been closely associated with nation building and an attempt to create a new symbolic order that can replace the assimilationist and racialized hierarchical model that preceded it. Importantly, state multiculturalism in Canada was generated by the agency of minority groups whose avenues to political resources had been constrained under prior arrangements. According to Elke, the historical development of multiculturalism has created a more open public space in terms of the acceptance of diversity and the recognition of minority rights – something that has curtailed "Islamophobia" in Canada.[106]

In addition, constitutional protection of the policy in the Charter and the Act both distinguish Canadian multiculturalism from other state approaches and afford some protections against refutation. The Act in particular has promoted diversity and equality in government institutions.[107]

Canadian Muslims, as indicated by the opinions of the interviewees, view the policy in a favourable light; they identify it as part of the national identity, an aspect of Canadian identity that drew them to the state as immigrants, even if there were worries about what was happening to the policy under the previous government and what the second and third generations of Canadian Muslims might experience.

The connection between multiculturalism and national identity is of particular note, especially in relation to the focus of this book. Identity is relational: how we define the "other" says a great deal about how we define ourselves. Canadian nationalism contains a positive association with difference and diversity, and in that sense it is the photographic negative of some European nationalisms that assign belonging on the basis of ethnocultural exclusivity. Critically, Canadian nationalism is less developed historically; it is more open to and welcoming of difference. With this particular vision of nationalism in mind, it is more problematic to paint peoples as foreign on the basis of cultural, racial, or religious difference, because difference is a defining feature of the state. It logically follows that an ideology like xenoracism that targets its victims on the basis of the quality of foreignness would find less fertile soil in a national space defined by a multicultural identity. Of course, what is presented here is the ideal vision, and like other ideals it never quite matches with reality.

Charges that state multiculturalism leads to separatism and is overly accommodative to illiberal practices emerged shortly after the policy was created, and by the mid-1990s concerns over a lack of civic integration among minority communities led to changes to the framework and the development of the "civic" paradigm. Allegations that Canada's approach to immigration, integration, and diversity generates issues such as ghettoization have also been levelled by some scholars.

However, none of these debates have generated the kind of hand wringing witnessed in Europe. And, despite some legitimate concerns over disparities in income and unemployment between the visible-minority communities and the general population, Canada does not display the kind of ghettoization found in the United States or some European states. There is also encouraging evidence that second-generation Canadians from visible-minority groups are excelling in comparison with their peers in terms of educational outcomes.

On the other hand, there is little doubt that the shift in state multiculturalism policy under the former Conservative government mirrored some of the trends seen in other states experiencing the "crisis of multiculturalism." A less accommodative approach to the usual victims of xenoracism (such as refugees and Muslims) can be found in those policy changes, as can the adoption of a more monocultural image of nationhood. Liz Fekete believes that it is "via the debate on national identity" that the state seeks to steer race policy away from multicultural vision to cultural homogenization and "one consistent element of all the debates is the implicit premise that Muslims are collectively responsible for the reactionary cultural practices and customs upheld by a few."[108]

The active promotion of the symbols of English Canada in public spaces, in the military, and in citizenship documents represents an active attempt to alter what it means to be a Canadian. This new image of identity did not reflect Canadian pluralistic traditions and biculturalism; it omitted the role of Indigenous communities and was out of touch with the contemporary lived reality of multiculturalism. Hypocrisy was evident in the former federal government, which employed multicultural rhetoric as a tool for electoral gain while simultaneously reducing the flow of resources and pathways to citizenship for minority groups. Canadian Muslims in particular were targeted as funding through the multiculturalism program was curtailed, at least partially over ideological disagreements related to foreign policy.

An important observation on these changes to citizenship, immigration, and multiculturalism policy is that they were *not* outwardly presented as rehabilitative actions that aimed to repair the damage done by failed multicultural policy. Rather, many of the changes took place at the bureaucratic level, instituted by a micromanaging former minister (Jason Kenney) and a government that carefully controlled the public message through the Privy Council Office and the Prime

Minister's Office.[109] Therefore, in Canada the rehabilitative actions were carried out without the employment of a crisis narrative, complete with the use of securitized speech. Rather, politicians pursued an agenda through bureaucratic back channels and symbolic shifts within state institutions.

This raises the question as to why the former federal government pursued these strategies through bureaucratic channels. Here it is argued that much of the answer to this question can be found in two points. First, in the context of electoral politics, directly attacking a policy that enjoys majority support does not represent an option for a political party seeking to retain power (something that the Conservative Party ironically achieved in 2011 in part through garnering the support of the "ethnic ridings").[110] Second, the constitutional entrenchment of multiculturalism blocks direct legislative avenues that would directly undermine or rescind the policy. Therefore, at least some of the legislative reforms that were, for example, instituted by the Dutch, are far less viable in the Canadian political context.

Thus, on balance, despite concerns generated by the actions of the former federal government there are more reasons to be optimistic than pessimistic on the future of Canadian multiculturalism. The Conservative-attempted implantation of a monocultural, nationalistic symbolism in Canadian identity will probably wither given the strong support for multiculturalism among young adults. As Phil Ryan concludes in *Multicultiphobia*, "we have repeatedly noted the surprising fact that multiculturalism continues to enjoy broad support from Canadians, to the point of being identified as a central element of the Canadian identity, despite the strength of multicultiphobia in the media and some political circles."[111]

Having said this, there is no doubt that multiculturalism will need to adapt to a changing Canadian cultural landscape as multiple generations of minority groups establish themselves as part of the fabric of the state and its society. State multiculturalism has never been static, rather it is marked by dynamism, and much of the future of the policy will depend on the direction in which federal governments and relevant ministers decide to steer it. And here lies the caveat – state multiculturalism has been shown to be vulnerable to manipulation by political elites; speculatively, if successive governments were to continue to undermine the policy from within, some of the positives discussed above may be threatened.

But what of Canadian Muslims? How have they fared in the model? This book has already identified institutionalized or in situ racism in the rehabilitative strategies imposed on state multiculturalism by the former federal Conservative government. However, there are other potential avenues through which xenoracism can operate, for example in integration and security policy. Today, in the post-9/11, post-Daesh world these are areas of policy that are inseparable from debates surrounding multiculturalism and the "limits of diversity."

6

Integration and Assimilation

In Samuel Huntington's controversial 1996 work *The Clash of Civilizations: Remaking of the World Order* we find one of the most influential and divisive perspectives on cultural incompatibility between the "West" and the "Islamic" world. In that work Huntington demonstrates pessimism about the ability of Muslims to integrate into Western societies: "Muslim communities whether Turkish in Germany or Algerian in France have not been integrated into their host cultures, and, to the concern of Europeans, show few signs of becoming so."[1] More recently, conservative politicians, a resurgent anti-immigrant right, and an anti-Islamic social movement express similar concerns over the threats posed by "parallel immigrant communities." These concerns are commonly expressed around debates over how much the host culture should accommodate the values and practices of religious communities and how far those communities are willing to go in adapting to the cultural norms and mores of secular-liberal Western societies.

Public anxieties over newcomer integration, and the nativism and xenoracism that accompany those sentiments, have helped to transform the meaning of integration in public policy circles in two important ways. First, today, in many states, at the centre of integration policy reform efforts are priorities of security, conceived of in both physical and national terms. Integration has become another strategy for protecting the state from what are seen as dangerous foreigners, rather than a strategy that aims to promote the inclusion of newcomers in the economic, social, and political fabric of the state. Second, the scope of integration policy has been expanded beyond newcomers and immigrants to include multiple-generation minority communities who are seen as essentially separate peoples. In this sense integration has become disciplinary public policy that aims to subsume those who are born and raised in a society yet are still perceived of as foreign.

While states today may take divergent approaches to newcomer integration, what is undeniable is the increasing importance of this area of policy for politicians. Recognizing this, Banting and Soroka write, "The integration of immigrant minorities has surged to the top of the political agenda throughout many contemporary democracies. The potent mix of changing immigration flows, new forms of racial and religious diversity and the heightened politics of security has triggered intense debates about social integration and social cohesion."[2] In many ways, integration today, most especially social or cultural integration, is seen as necessary rehabilitative action – a potential panacea for the problems wrought by multiculturalism. Such policies are presented as necessary to address the divided loyalties immigrant communities possess – loyalties that may act to undermine the unity of the liberal-democratic state and national community.[3]

The questions for this chapter are as follows: What does integration and belonging mean in the Canadian context? Has Canada adopted some of the more coercive and assimilationist forms of integration witnessed elsewhere? How have Canadian Muslims fared in terms of integration in Canada? To answer these questions, this chapter will examine the various meanings of integration, specifically in the context of Canada, and it will identify benchmarks for "successful" integration of newcomers in Canada. Through the data from Statistics Canada's Ethnic Diversity Survey (EDS), publicly released in 2003, and Environics' 2016 Survey of Muslims in Canada (SMC) and the findings from the interviews it will critically examine the attitudes, opinions, and experiences of Canadian Muslims in relation to integration in Canada. It aims to better understand the experience of Canadian Muslims in the framework of state multiculturalism, to judge the relative success of that framework, and to examine potential manifestations of xenoracism in Canadian public policy.

DEFINING INTEGRATION

There is no single universal definition of integration as it applies to the study of the incorporation of newcomers into host societies. Depending on local context, integration policies can differ significantly from state to state, for example in terms of the end goal of the policy (i.e., assimilation vs. cultural pluralism), and priorities of integration (linguistic, economic, political, social, cultural, etc.).[4] Integration of newcomers may mean their inclusion into varied aspects of a state: its labour market, political institutions, and social fabric. Ultimately, Castles and Miller believe that the starting point for understanding state approaches to immigrant integration is "historical experiences of nation-state formation: the ways in which emerging states handled difference when dealing with internal ethnic or religious minorities."[5]

To date, the academic usage of the term integration has been quite loose, with many studies offering a cursory definition of the term. Further, a review of the literature on integration reveals that the meanings of the term differ, depending on the area of study. For instance, in studies focused on "racial integration" the term might simply refer to a rough parity between racial identities within a particular region, city, or neighbourhood.[6]

Wong and Tézli trace the academic study of integration to the 1920s and scholars such as Robert Park, Everett Hughes, and Luis Wirth at the Chicago School of Sociology.[7] In the mid to late twentieth century, Gordon influenced understandings of integration through his idea of "structural assimilation" in which newcomers seek economic parity and social incorporation with native-born citizens.[8] In this classical, predictive, and linear model of integration the process is distinctly tied to generational experiences. First-generation immigrants suffer acute disadvantages because of their more pronounced differences and their perceived foreignness in the eyes of the dominant culture. However, successive generations are said to become more and more integrated into the mainstream through intermarriage, through participation in public life (e.g., through the education system), and through socialization with the native population. In this distinctly US-based view of integration the end result is essentially assimilation as the perceived difference of successive generations fades into the melting pot.[9]

Quite apart from the classical understandings of structural assimilation offered by Gordon, contemporary integration theorists now widely recognize that integration is *not* a predictable and linear process, since in many cases newcomers may advance in the integration process only to take steps backwards, for example in later generations. Additionally, integration may vary depending on context and category; for instance, an individual may be fully integrated into the economy and labour market of a state yet feel marginalized in a societal context.[10]

It also can be observed that much of what we think of as integration is really just newcomers meeting their basic life needs. When immigrants are transplanted from one setting to another they must satisfy basic and immediate requirements – housing, a job, the ability to communicate, and new circles in which to socialize.[11] An individual newcomer will naturally prioritize, among other things, an income, housing, and education for his or her children. By comparison, state governments may prioritize integration in the labour market (to reduce immigrants' dependence on the state), and depending on the national context they may promote the acquisition of citizenship among newcomers to encourage civic integration. Where these interests most obviously converge is in the economic category of integration. Unsurprisingly, much of the scholarly focus has been on economic aspects of integration. A 2003 review of Canadian literature on newcomer integration found that roughly 60 per cent of all such research was focused on various economic aspects of integration.[12]

In the context of the recent debates surrounding the integration of Muslim communities in the West, the scholarly focus has shifted somewhat onto areas related to social and civic integration. According to Banting and Soroka, "The emphasis on social integration also reflects concerns that newcomers have only a weak sense of attachment and commitment to their new home, that they do not feel they really belong, and that they do not engage in the civic and political life of the society around them."[13] The shift in integration policy toward the social and civic spheres can be detected in state-based, international, and regional-organization definitions of integration. For example, the European Parliament's Committee on Civil Liberties, Justice and Home Affairs has defined integration as "a society's ability to integrate all its members into new arrangements of active citizenship that ensure the long-term well-being of all in a diverse society."[14]

Out of all of the identified categories or dimensions of integration, the social facet can be particularly difficult to conceptualize. Social aspects of integration are more opaque, and defining successful integration, especially in the context of multicultural states where identity is not tied to one specific culture, is difficult.[15] Other areas of integration are more clearly measurable, such as when newcomers try to satisfy immediate needs and requirements by finding employment and housing and learning a new language.[16] Recognizing these difficulties, Reitz settled on the following definition: "Social integration refers to the extent to which individuals become vested in the core institutions of society, participate in those institutions, and experience a sense of satisfaction."[17] With the importance his definition assigns to participation in "core institutions," Reitz hints at the value of involvement in civil society and the political life of the state in terms of promoting belonging.

Therefore, insofar as it applies to the incorporation of newcomers into a state and a society, integration is a term that carries multiple meanings. Yet, in the context of the crisis of multiculturalism the term integration has been heavily politicized in ways that often obscure or manipulate its meaning.

INTEGRATION ANXIETIES

Media coverage and academic literature on the topic of Muslim integration are pervasive and polarizing, especially in the European context. Aside from the more alarmist and distinctly anti-Islamic writers, there are journalists and scholars who critique or oppose, to varying degrees, accommodation and the influence of Muslim communities in the West. Most of these individuals promote a more assimilative approach to incorporating newcomers and "unintegrated" minority communities through mobilizing ideas related to secularism and liberal values. On the opposite end of the spectrum are writers and scholars who seek to counter the critics' and alarmists' position, often while pointing out the diverse nature of Muslim communities in the West and the generally Orientalist and racist character of the writings of the assimilationists. There is little in the way of middle ground in this debate.

On the far end of the spectrum, Bruce Bawer and other writers within the anti-Islamic social movement warn against appeasing Muslims and their requests for accommodation. In his alarmist, almost apocalyptic ramblings, Bawer warns that Western "elites" have "sacrificed freedom" by giving into radical and culturally incompatible communities that seek to reshape the West, from Europe to the United States, into a single Islamic society governed by Shari'a law.[18] In this narrative multiculturalism has not only failed, it has also created a space for assertive and distinctly adversarial cultures to establish themselves to the point that they represent an existential threat to Western, "European," American (etc.) culture.

In countries like the Netherlands a broad base of journalists, academics, and provocateurs have constructed distinctly xenoracist discourses around Muslim integration. Figures like Pim Fortuyn, Ayaan Hirsi Ali, Herman Philipse, Theo van Gogh, and Geert Wilders have presented a clear argument: multiculturalism has failed, it has opened the door to Muslim extremism, and one answer to this threat is the complete assimilation of Muslims, their religion, and their culture.[19]

Upon reasoned reflection the alarmist position seems absurd: the idea that a minority culture, which in most countries represents less than 5 or 10 per cent of a state's population, can represent an existential threat, a societal security threat (to use the language of the Copenhagen security school), to a host culture, their core values, and identity. One may ask whether "European," French, Dutch, or American identities are so insecure and so fragile at their core that they cannot cope with the presence of a small religious community.

Outside of the alarmist camp, there is another set of more intellectual writers and scholars who critique multicultural approaches to integration using a range of academic theories and empirical data. Among these figures is the liberal German sociologist Christian Joppke. While largely dismissive of the alarmist position, Joppke contends that "the future of Europe's Muslim populations is irrevocably tied up with the future of Europe itself."[20] He bases this argument on selective empirical data and two points: first, the growth in Muslim populations in Western Europe relative to declining birth rates among non-Muslim communities, and second, the divergence between Muslim immigrant communities and host cultures over attitudes toward gender issues and sexuality. Using studies such as Pippa Norris and Ronald Inglehart's analysis of the World Values Survey, Joppke contends that Muslim communities demonstrate some divergence from European host cultures in terms of values and attitudes, such as in relation to support for gender equality and sexual liberalization. Joppke cites Norris and Inglehart's conclusion that the "most basic fault line between the West and Islam ... involves issues of gender and sexual liberalization."[21]

In much of Europe today the opinions expressed by figures like Joppke are taken largely for granted – there is an increasingly common understanding that Muslim integration is a significant challenge for European states and societies and that certain values of Muslims challenge European traditions related to liberalism, secularism, and gender equality. There is also a growing belief in the salience of the demographic "threat" posed by Muslims, for example in relation to birth rates and population growth. The latter issue is a shared concern among figures like Joppke, the more alarmist writers like Bawer, the far-right in Europe, and the anti-Islamic social movement. Subsequently, within a political climate that favours these views, many European states have steadily moved toward an assimilationist model of new-comer incorporation. For example, states like the United Kingdom have been moving in this direction since at least the time of the riots in Northern England in 2001, a trend that only accelerated after the 7 July 2005 transit bombings in London. British politicians now show a preference for the language of "shared British values" and describe multiculturalism as a failed policy.[22]

Tellingly, David Cameron made his reference to multiculturalism as a failed policy in a speech on radicalization and "Islamic extremism" where he suggested that "muscular liberalism" should replace "state multiculturalism."[23] The conflation of these two areas of policy, of security and integration, is based on the growing belief among European policy-makers that integration is an antidote to radicalization and violent extremism among Muslim communities.

As seen in the United Kingdom and much of Europe, reforms to integration policy have tended to be reactive – a response to violence and unrest in minority communities (e.g., urban riots) or homegrown terrorism that is linked to religious communities. The obvious problem with this reactive approach is that since Muslims are singled out and subjected to calls for improved integration, the logic of securitized integration is applied uniformly to Muslim communities regardless of their beliefs or pre-existing levels of integration.[24] Commenting on this particular trend, Joppke observes, "Cameron's implicit mixing of culture with security concerns makes for a potent brew that achieves the exact opposite of what is intended – to keep 'Islam' out of the equation ... the 'active, muscular liberalism' offered as an alternative to the 'state multiculturalism' of old is mostly rhetorical."[25]

While the language of "muscular liberalism" might be new, and some of it largely rhetorical, it should be noted that the British approach, which calls on newcomers to learn the host country's language, norms, and history, is not wholly unlike the civic model of multiculturalism to which Canada has subscribed since the 1990s. As Banting observes, European policy-makers and bureaucrats seem to believe that civic integration and multiculturalism are incompatible. This position seems to be at odds with the Canadian experience because "these practices have been elements of the Canadian approach to immigrant integration for a very long time."[26]

The distinct difference between the Canadian and European trajectory on integration is the development of a far more coercive approach to incorporation in certain European states; in the Netherlands, for example, integration has become a mandatory duty and when that duty is not fulfilled newcomers can be denied social rights or even renewals of their residency. Moreover, in the Netherlands it is not only newcomers who must meet these standards of incorporation – settled residents, some of whom are Dutch citizens, and applicants for family reunification are also under increased scrutiny.[27] On this trend Fekete comments, "Many northern and western European countries began the process of revisiting integration policy, introducing new measures often referred to in popular parlance in terms of an 'integration contract.'"[28] Language and civic tests in the Netherlands and oaths of allegiance to the Queen in the United Kingdom are examples of the different forms these "contracts" take, depending on national context and historical experience with incorporating newcomers.[29]

Therefore, the answer to the crisis of multiculturalism in some states is not really integration per se, at least as it was once understood (i.e., as the gradual process of incorporating newcomers into a state and a society), rather it is more coercive and assimilative. At least to an extent it is a return to monoculturalism, where newcomers are expected to adapt to a (re)imagined Dutch, British, German, or other national identity. Integration, as conceived in these contexts, is not a two-sided process, rather it is increasingly a one-way requirement where less attention is paid to barriers to integration such as racism and difficulties in finding employment.

Arguably, the opaqueness of the term integration is an advantage for policy-makers who wish to reframe what belonging means in particular national contexts.[30] It should also be recognized that more coercive approaches to integration are incompatible with multiculturalism: as Banting observes, "Combining this more illiberal version of civic integration with a strong multicultural strategy would seem very difficult."[31]

With Banting's observation in mind, one may assume that Canadian public policy is relatively immune to the shifts in approaches to integration seen elsewhere. But as shown in previous chapters, Canada is not wholly immune to some of the trends associated with the wider crisis of multiculturalism, for example as seen in the adoption of some rhetoric and symbolism during the Harper years that promoted Canada's British heritage. According to Kymlicka, while Canada's approach to integration has long been the most successful in the world it is not immune to debates over the accommodation of minorities witnessed elsewhere.[32]

Haque contends that Canadian anxieties toward newcomer integration are articulated in more subtle ways. She gives examples of worries over the growing presence of non-official languages in Canada and the spatial concentration of ethnic communities in major urban centres like Toronto and Vancouver. According to Haque, these areas of concern are used to highlight the discomfort of the host society because "articulating these exclusions overtly in terms of race and ethnicity is seen as unacceptable in the public sphere."[33] On this last point Reitz et al. acknowledge in their study of social integration in Canada that religious characteristics, rather than racial origins, have been recently identified as potential barriers to successful integration.[34]

The picture that emerges from the analysis of contemporary public discourses on integration is often-divergent understandings of what integration means. Integration is frequently employed by those who seek to use the area of policy as a tool to reshape multicultural policies. Here multicultural policy is set up as a sort of straw man for its opponents to justify the need for more assimilative policies that target newcomers. To further elucidate the meanings of integration the following sections will examine two distinctly different approaches to the incorporation of newcomers in a host society.

THE ASSIMILATIVE MODEL

While there is no black-and-white division between integration and assimilation, the primary difference between the two is related to expectations. In short, assimilation contains expectations that newcomers will be incorporated into society through a more one-sided process of adaptation to the host society. In the most rigid forms of assimilation this involves the letting go of cultural identities and practices that migrants brought from their place of origin, with the end result being that newcomers become indistinguishable from the majority in their new home.[35] Taken to its extreme, assimilation represents the erasure of cultural difference and no space is allowed for the continuation of practices and values that are out of step with the dominant culture. In a world marked by transnationalism and multicultural societies, this approach to assimilation is simply unrealistic. Instead, what most states practice is what is referred to here as "targeted assimilation" in which a state prioritizes certain categories of assimilation – for example, linguistic, economic, or political.

States like France have long held to a more assimilative approach to newcomer incorporation. France's approach can be traced to national norms and values, established in its post-revolutionary period, which established principles of equality and the "rights of man," of the individual as an equal political subject, while rejecting special rights for identity groups.[36] As a result the French state prioritized homogeneity in its approach to incorporation. Today that ideal is seemingly quite distant from the reality on the ground of French cities and its troubled "banlieues" (essentially segregated suburban ghettos). As Cesari notes, in the case of France, despite the predictions of assimilationists, "ethnic boundaries, though they may be recomposed and reconstituted, do not disappear, even among second- and third- generation immigrants."[37] In the 1970s and 1980s some states recognized the limitations of a more assimilative approach to newcomers, such as Canada, Australia, the Netherlands, and Britain, and sought to develop a more multicultural approach to newcomer incorporation.[38]

Not surprisingly, integration policies leaning to the assimilative end of the spectrum have failed to produce the desired outcomes. The approach has proven problematic on a number of levels. Newcomers may be willing to adapt and to give up much of their past cultural practices and identities; however, inclusion requires acceptance from the host society and its institutions. Therefore, so long as prejudice, discrimination, and racism are experienced by newcomers and minorities, assimilation is impossible. As Wilkinson observes, "Academics and governments tend to de-emphasize the role that racism and discrimination plays in the integration process. While individuals may be successfully integrated in their work, school and ethno-cultural communities, they may become extremely isolated if racism is not addressed. The message we can take away from this and other similar studies is that despite 'success' in labour market and economic spheres, without cultural and social integration, there is the potential for discord."[39]

The multicultural paradigm that appeared in the 1970s contained recognition of some of these issues. As a policy framework it held to the idea that any form of incorporation of newcomers required not only efforts to lower barriers such as racism but also accommodation in shared institutions such as public schools, the labour market, and the media and in the institutions of the government.[40]

Yet in the context of the crisis of multiculturalism, assimilation has returned as states, especially in Western Europe, have re-prioritized incorporation into what is presented as more homogenous national identities. For instance, in the Netherlands and the United Kingdom, governments have put increased emphasis on developing a normative consensus around "core national values."[41] Importantly, not all minority communities are targeted with this new policy priority. On this point Fekete is clear: "One consistent element of all the debates is the implicit premise that Muslims are collectively responsible for the reactionary cultural practices and customs upheld by a few."[42] First and foremost it is Muslims who bear the burden of coercive assimilation.

As Lentin and Titley observe on the assimilative shift being undertaken by policy-makers, "The death of multiculturalism requires the rehabilitative discipline of integration, and a return to versions of the pre-experimental certainties, confidence in our values, without apologies."[43] In this repackaged and reformative brand of assimilation it is not only the newcomer who is subject to coercive incorporation but also the long-term resident minority whose non-integrated status is identified a priori.[44] In this paradigm there is little consideration of the barriers that newcomers and minorities face; the primary obligation rests with the unintegrated who must renounce past loyalties.[45]

The oft-raised question of the status of second- and even third-generation "immigrants" among the critics of multiculturalism is a reflection of the fact that some migrants are always deemed foreign in some societies regardless of where they were born or their citizenship status – as Wallerstein points out, this is a systematic confusion of "the notion of integration, that is, of belonging to a *de facto* historical and social entity, with that of conformity to a mythical 'national type,' which is supposed to be a guarantee against all possibility of conflict."[46] Canadian scholars like Banting, Courchene, and Seidle have contended that some European countries have been adopting illiberal policies to promote a more assimilative approach to incorporation, a trend that they believe is less pronounced in Canada.[47]

THE MULTICULTURAL MODEL: THE CANADIAN APPROACH

Race and racism scholars Michael Omi and Howard Winant characterize the philosophical difference that exists between "assimilationists" and "cultural pluralists" as the difference between promoting a unitary majority culture versus the belief that difference can and will be maintained in state-societies over time.[48] While more assimilative approaches to incorporation strive for a point where the cultural identities of migrants fade, integration in the multicultural model allows for the maintenance of cultural difference over time.[49] The classical model of structural assimilation associated with the United States, or the false promise of fraternalism and egalitarianism in the French approach, is quite distant from the vision of the mosaic that has long been used to describe the Canadian diversity model.[50] For interviewee Baha Abu-Laban, a professor of sociology at the University of Alberta who has studied both American and Canadian approaches to integration, the Canadian approach is unique and it has allowed "nostalgia for our heritage."

Not surprisingly, considering the cultural and geographical proximity between Canada and the United States, the idea of integration in Canada has often been framed in opposition to the American melting-pot model. On this point Ley observes that such a model "has been distinguished from assimilation, the key difference being that, while assimilation requires all the adjustment to be undertaken by immigrants toward an unchanging national culture and institutions, integration requires the mutual adjustment of native-born and immigrant societies to establish an evolving national project."[51] Reflecting this understanding, Wilkinson observes that in the Canadian case, "integration is a reciprocal process where newcomers are incorporated into a new society. During the process, both the newcomer and host society change as a result of interaction with one another ... the immigrant makes alterations to their behavior to 'fit in,' while the host society changes as a result of the incorporation of newcomers."[52] Thus, on a fundamental level, integration in the Canadian model, as opposed to the American assimilationist model, allows for migrants to maintain some of their cultural identity, which melds into an ever-evolving Canadian milieu or mosaic.[53]

In Canada, integration policy traces its origins to the nation-building and economic development projects that have required large influxes of newcomers since the nineteenth century.[54] Canada has been described as a nation of immigrants and, today, more than ever, newcomers represent an essential part of Canadian society and the Canadian economy: according to the 2011 census, roughly 20 per cent of the total population or 6.8 million people are foreign born/first-generation immigrants.[55] Moreover, Canada is a state that displays remarkable heterogeneity among its first-generation residents. Banting notes that Canada is a "classic settler society" and that "in contrast to some host countries in which immigration comes predominantly from one part of the world, creating a relatively homogenous 'other,' immigration to Canada comes from many different parts of the world, creating a 'diverse diversity' of ethnicities, races, and religions."[56]

As discussed in the previous chapter, with the introduction of the race-neutral points system in 1967 and the official policy of multiculturalism in 1971, Canada shifted away from an explicitly racist and assimilationist system of immigration and integration to one that prioritized the education, skills, and wealth of newcomers.[57] The points system was designed to bring in less economically disadvantaged newcomers, and in that sense it moderated economic integrative barriers. Of note, this approach to immigration and integration represents a sharp contrast to what is found in many Western European states like France, Britain, and Germany where migrants, including Muslim migrants, typically display lower levels of wealth, education, skills, and work experience.[58]

By comparison, in Canada, as Reitz points out, the points system has led to a "more favourable employment experience [for newcomers] compared to their counterparts in the US or Europe."[59] The priority given to economic integration in Canada is also apparent in how immigration policy has been "housed" over its history, for example at the Department of Manpower and Immigration, the Department of Employment and Immigration, and more recently shared between the former Citizenship and Immigration Canada and Human Resources and Skills Development Canada.[60]

While the overarching framework of multiculturalism has been influential as a guiding philosophy in immigration and integration policy, public policy has been complicated by the multiple levels of government engaged in the policy area. Given that Canada is a federal state with constitutionally divided powers of immigration and integration, federal, provincial/territorial, and municipal governments have shared responsibilities in these policy areas. Provinces and territories often take differing approaches to immigration, settlement, and integration, as is most clearly seen in the example of Quebec. While the federal government may have authority over naturalization, provinces and territories are far more engaged with settlement and the longer term integration of newcomers, for instance in labour markets, education, and social services.[61] As a result, Canada displays a complex and sometimes confusing approach to settlement and integration. For instance, newcomers face not only unique policy programs in Quebec and the Territories, but also nine provincial nomination programs, a variety of selection criteria and immigration fees, and a wide variety of settlement services.[62] With this observation in mind, scholarly work on integration in Canada can be challenging, and academics have often dealt with this challenge by looking at integration through the lens of various categories (i.e., social, economic, political, and linguistic).

In relation to linguistic integration, the Canadian government prioritizes language proficiency in one of the two official languages among newcomers.[63] Importantly, according to Millar, there is a difference between the way in which linguistic integration is conceived in Canada and the way that it is conceived in other states. On this point he writes, "Whereas in other national contexts, the public discourses of language and immigrant integration are based on exclusionary national language ideologies, in Canada the policy discourse is based on standard language ideology related to the functional importance of language ability for the economic integration of immigrants in Canada."[64] Therefore, there has long been an expectation in Canada that newcomers will be subject to "targeted assimilation" into the bilingual framework, and this form of assimilation is viewed as a basic functional necessity for participation in the social and economic life of the state. Within the multicultural framework, linguistic integration exists alongside of a set of cultural allowances where newcomers are encouraged to create ethnocultural organizations, celebrate cultural traditions, and share their culture with others.[65]

By the mid-1990s greater emphasis was being put on another area of integration: integration into the political life of the state under the civic multicultural paradigm.[66] Here, the emphasis was put on newcomers acquiring citizenship and exercising their new-found citizenship rights through voting and other forms of formal political participation. Supporting this vision of integration in Canada, Banting, Courchene, and Seidle contend that much of Canada's approach to integration since the 1990s has been directed toward the political sphere: "Canadian discourse highlights the central role of civic engagement and political participation in the integration of minority communities. Contemporary Canada is defined by multiple communities and identities, and the critical question is how the conflicts inherent in such diversity are resolved or managed. From this perspective, a key to social cohesion is consensus on the fundamental processes of collective deliberation, especially the institutions of liberal democracy, and the active participation of minorities in the processes of governance."[67]

A key aspect of this form of integration is the acquisition of citizenship and, as noted in the previous chapter, newcomers in Canada have pursued citizenship at a higher rate than that seen in some other Western states. Colin Boyd, an interviewee and director in multiculturalism with the federal government, believes that Canada's successful track record in attracting immigrants to citizenship demonstrates the success the state has enjoyed in integrating newcomers. He noted, "In Canada the acquisition of citizenship is a powerful tool for integration."

With these observations in mind, integration in Canada, at least in its ideal form, is seen as a two-way street that entails the need both for newcomers to adapt to the host society, its official languages, its labour market, and its political life *and* for the host society to provide opportunities for newcomers to equitably participate in Canadian social, political, and economic institutions.[68] Anderson and Black describe how at the centre of the two-way street model is the priority of political participation and expectations that newcomers "should become full members of the national political community by first naturalizing and then exercising their democratic rights while fulfilling their obligations to be interested and engaged citizens politically."[69] On the other side of the two-way street model, the Canadian government encourages settlement and integration through various programs and initiatives, for example Language Instruction for Newcomers, the Immigrant Settlement and Adaptation Program, and the Host Program.[70]

Historically, legislation like the Employment Equity Act aimed to address integrative issues, for example by reducing discriminatory barriers in employment.[71] As noted by Anna Chiappa, executive director of the Canadian Ethnocultural Council, multiculturalism (specifically the Canadian Multiculturalism Act) distinctly shapes the Canadian government's approach to accommodation and integration: "The act provides that vision of the level playing field and says to institutions that you have an obligation to ensure that the service you provide, the employment that you offer, the information you provide out there reflects that vision."

Non-governmental agencies and organizations also play a central role in the settlement and integration process. For instance, Biles and Ibrahim note that religious civil society groups play an important role in both settlement and integration for newcomers.[72] Naizghi Eyob, an interviewee and executive director at Mosaic BC, a non-governmental organization with over 35 years of experience in integration and settlement services, shares this vision of integration: "We look at integration as a two-way process – it's not a one-way street. We differentiate with the American model of assimilation." Baldwin Wong, an interviewee from the policy sample group and social planner at the City of Vancouver, outlined how integration is really a relational process, and in that sense the two-way street analogy is appropriate: "It's really more about mutual understanding and acceptance ... integration is a two-way street – you can't integrate until the other side wants to integrate with you – that is fundamentally important."

Following on these observations, how has integration been measured or gauged in the Canadian context? Banting, Courchene, and Seidle view the Canadian concept of integration as "contested" yet agree that "integration in Canada cannot demand adherence to a common culture or a single identity. It does not try to turn Canadians into a single people. Indeed, even the language of 'social and political integration' can be problematic. Rather, the predominant definition of the integration agenda focuses on the need to build a sense of belonging and attachment to a country that incorporates distinct identities."[73]

Outside of a "sense of belonging," measuring social integration is not a clear-cut undertaking. As Li has noted, measuring integration is "often based on a narrow understanding and a rigid expectation that treats integration solely in terms of the degree to which immigrants converge to the average performance of native-born Canadians and their normative and behavioural standards."[74] Here Li's conception of integration invokes Gordon's understanding of structural assimilation. As previously highlighted, Reitz has focused on social cohesion as a barometer of success for multiculturalism but also highlights what he views as the hallmark of successful social integration: "the extent to which individuals become vested in the core institutions of society, participate in those institutions, and experience a sense of satisfaction."[75]

Several existing studies have come to generally positive conclusions on the efficacy of Canada's approach to integration. For example, Banting, Courchene, and Seidle believe that Canadian integration has generally been a success, with less contentious points of debate focusing on deciding the means of fostering respect for differences rather than the need to develop a more cohesive society.[76] Kazemipur found in his research that a mutual sense of belonging and identification has strengthened social capital in Canada, representing an exception to the situation in other states, where diversity may negatively correlate with social capital.[77]

However, a few studies challenge these rosy findings. For instance, one prominent study by Reitz and Banerjee found that second-generation Canadians belonging to racial minorities were in fact less integrated than the first generation in terms of political participation and the sense of belonging they felt to Canada.[78] These findings provide some qualification to the positive conclusions from previous studies that showed how second-generation Canadians were excelling in certain areas, for example in relation to education.[79] Moreover, studies on the experience of second-generation Canadians further underline the non-linear and multi-dimensional nature of integration.

Leaving these issues to one side for the time being, a common theme can be discerned in several of these studies in terms of how social integration can be measured in Canada. For example, Banting and Soroka, in measuring social integration in Canada, identified what they saw as an important barometer for success: "A sense of belonging seems to capture two related feelings. In part, it reflects the person's sense of attachment to the country; but it also reflects the extent to which that person feels accepted by other denizens of the place."[80] Reinforcing this understanding, race and racism theorist Robert Miles believes that, at the national level, integration is ultimately about belonging.[81] Indeed, the concept of belonging or "a sense of belonging" is a common standard used by immigration scholars in Canada when measuring social integration in Canada.

Sense of belonging has also been used as a barometer for integration in policy circles. Wong and Tézli have identified how "the term 'sense of belonging' in Canada was developed in the mid-1990s by policymakers in the Canadian government shortly after the Department of Canadian Heritage was created in 1993."[82] In addition, sense of belonging was used as a benchmark in social integration in the 2005 report of the Global Commission on International Migration, which found that "integration recognizes and accommodates differences, but requires a sense of belonging amongst nationals and migrants alike."[83]

The focus on belonging in the Canadian integration literature demonstrates how, at its heart, social integration is related to social identity. Social integration in Canada can be gauged in the extent to which newcomers buy into a shared vision of national identity and the extent to which that belonging is reciprocated by the host population through tolerance, respect, and inclusion. Yet, problematically, considering the importance assigned to belonging in the literature, in a majority of studies the nature of belonging in a national context is left open to interpretation.

Citizenship in Canada

Thus far, citizenship and its meanings have largely been discussed within the overall context of multiculturalism and integration policy. Debates over citizenship and its meaning in a liberal-multicultural state have been a preoccupation among some of Canada's most prestigious political philosophers, including the likes of Charles Taylor, Will Kymlicka, and Michael Ignatieff. Given their coverage elsewhere, the philosophical nuances of these debates will be left largely unexplored in this book. What is of most importance here is the question of how citizenship and citizenship rights have been mobilized by policy-makers within the overall framework of the crisis of multiculturalism and how citizenship has shaped experiences with integration, particularly for Canadian Muslims.

A basic definition of citizenship is that it is a political contract between the individual and the state, where national allegiance is exchanged for certain rights.[84] Ideally, becoming a citizen means reaching a formal level of incorporation in the state where the individual becomes an accepted part of the national fabric who can enjoy the same rights as natural-born citizens.[85] With this in mind, citizenship contains both symbolic and legal ideas of belonging.[86] But in the context of the crisis of multiculturalism debates over belonging, questions over who belongs to a nation, who is native, and who is foreign have frequently been raised by those espousing xenoracism. Today citizenship does not necessarily equate into belonging or a sense of permanence and security for minorities, and formal citizenship, at least for some minority communities, does not equate into symbolic belonging to the host society.

As outlined in the section on nationalism, ideas of who belongs and who doesn't belong to an "imagined community" can be traced to how the nation has been framed historically in a particular state. When nationalism is tied to a single ethnic, racial, or cultural community this may create a highly exclusivist form of identity that easily lends itself to the construction of exclusionary rhetoric. This is a form of nationalism that historically grew from the early development of the modern nation-state and was intimately tied to political practices and ideologies such as imperialism, colonialism, and fascism in the twentieth century. According to Ignatieff, this form of ethnic nationalism has historically generated conflict, especially in culturally plural states or "multinational" states.[87]

As outlined above, part of the counter-reaction against multiculturalism in states like the Netherlands, for instance, has been the adoption of more stringent, coercive, and restrictive approaches to citizenship. Here citizenship and the symbolic belonging it is said to contain are centred on a Dutch cultural core where belonging can only be achieved through cultural adaptation. Therefore, within the crisis of multiculturalism, citizenship has become yet another area of policy through which the rehabilitation of multiculturalism has been pursued through the reassertion of "national values," As acknowledged by Joppke, at the policy level a fusion has taken place between policies that "previously belonged to two separate, if not lexically ordered policies and legal domains."[88] Together, these areas of policy have been used to establish greater control over newcomers and more established minority communities alike. More specifically, in the area of citizenship this control has been pursued through the tightening of naturalization rules and the use of more stringent citizenship tests for newcomers.[89]

By comparison, a multicultural state is said to contain a much different idea of symbolic belonging. In its idealized form, a multicultural state recognizes and values diversity, and formal membership in the community involves a commitment to a shared set of rights and values. In the Canadian model, citizenship rights are said to be equally extended to all cultural communities.[90] Gangnon and Iacovino describe this liberal ideal as "citizenship ... based on a set of universally-applied procedural rules [where] identity is relegated to individuals, privately pursuing their own conception of the good life."[91] This conception of national identity and belonging returns us to an idea raised in chapter 5 – that Canada engenders a much "thinner" sense of nationalism and national belonging than found in other states.

However, as was also acknowledged in the previous chapter, we have witnessed attempts by the former Conservative government under Stephen Harper to manipulate ideas of citizenship and symbolic belonging to the Canadian state. For instance, we saw this manipulation in the promotion of symbols of British identity within key institutions and activities, for example in the military and in citizenship tests and documents. Furthermore, issues related to the accommodation of religious minorities, like Canadian Muslims, were mobilized by the Conservatives around the question of who should and who should not have access to the rights of citizenship.

For example, starting in 2011, the Harper government began pushing for a ban of the niqab in public spaces, specifically at citizenship ceremonies and in government buildings. During the 2015 election campaign this wedge issue was brought to the fore and was used to elicit support for the Conservatives, in particular in Quebec.[92] This issue played out publicly in the legal battle over the right of a Pakistani immigrant (Zunera Ishaq) who fought and won the right to wear her niqab during the oath of citizenship, despite the fervent opposition of the Harper government.

The shift in public discourses around citizenship in Canada has drawn the attention of scholars like Joppke who in a 2013 academic journal article posed the question of whether the Canadian approach to citizenship was becoming reflective of the more coercive approaches found in Europe. After Joppke carefully considered this question, his answer was somewhat mixed: "In political rhetoric 'yes,' at least on the conservative end of the political spectrum; but with respect to policy 'no.' The latest amendment to the citizenship law in 2010, which has the ambitious purpose of 'strengthening the value of Canadian citizenship,' among other small changes, merely clarifies that applicants for citizenship must be 'physically present' in Canada during the required three years of residence."[93] Joppke believes that the Canadian citizenship model has largely adhered to its liberal-rights ideal.[94]

However, what Joppke couldn't have reflected on, when he wrote his comparative piece in 2013, were the legislative reforms that the Conservative Party initiated in 2015 when there were efforts to create grounds under which citizenship could be revoked. Tellingly this legislation (Bill C-24) was mobilized around security, the threat of terrorism, and the need to punish some Canadians for their transgressions.[95] Specifically Bill C-24 targeted dual citizens convicted of terrorism-based offences. While still in power the Conservatives moved quickly to revoke the citizenship of high-profile terrorists in Canada, including members of the Toronto 18 plot, such as Zakaria Amara.

After coming into power the Liberal government under Prime Minister Justin Trudeau and former immigration minister John McCallum moved to scrap the legislation on the basis of the idea that the bill devalues Canadian citizenship and creates differential standards in citizenship.[96] Yet, despite these actions, the introduction of Bill C-24 and the support that it enjoyed in some segments of the public are again indicative of the fact that Canada is not immune to some of the symptoms of the crisis of multiculturalism.

Belonging in a Multicultural State

Although the acquisition of citizenship among newcomers denotes a level of formal belonging to the state, it does not necessarily equate into a sense of belonging to a state-society. Ideas and sentiments of belonging have become increasingly multi-layered in an era where many individuals, families, and communities exhibit transnational social identities. As recognized by an increasing number of scholars, in the context of globalization ideas of belonging have become more complex because individuals increasingly display multiple belongings.[97]

Similar to the term integration, the meaning of belonging in academic study is largely taken for granted or loosely defined. As Vasta notes, belonging is used in scholarly work in a way in which its meaning is supposed to be apparent to everyone, denoting among other things affinity, acceptance, and togetherness.[98] Perhaps most generally, in a social context, belonging can be defined as a reciprocal relationship where individuals identify with a larger social identity group and gain some acceptance from that group. On this point Vasta elaborates as follows: "Belonging is not just a subjective matter. Crucially, it is formed between the interplay of the subjective self, collective agency and structural positioning ... people can have a sense of belonging as individuals as well as collective belonging; they can belong to a community, a locality or a nation; and they can have a transnational sense of belonging. Belonging can refer to the material, symbolic and emotional dimensions of life."[99]

Elaborating on this idea, individuals may identify with or find belonging in a variety of groups both big and small; they might identify with a nation, city, religion, race, and/or gender. Since human identities are multi-layered and complex, exhibiting characteristics of hybridity, individuals can feel a sense of belonging to multiple communities simultaneously.

In an increasingly globalized world, where people possess multiple loyalties, including multiple national loyalties, ideas of belonging become even more complex. Despite this complexity, as found by Vasta in her study, transnational identities and multiple belongings do not necessarily equate into a sense of confusion or "divided loyalties."[100] Similarly Hussain and Bagguley found in their study of British Pakistanis that individuals were developing concepts of belonging that accommodated multiple identities such as British, Pakistani, and Muslim.[101] Indeed, existing empirical studies confirm that transnationally situated individuals may be simultaneously "integrated" into multiple societies at the same time.[102]

Given this complexity, how then can personal belonging to a nation be defined? Yuval-Davis, Kannabiran, and Vieten point out that in the "politics of belonging" national identity is important: in other words, how nationalism is framed is important in terms of establishing an emotional component to belonging.[103] If a nation is defined in monocultural terms it is unlikely that outsiders or "foreigners" (as defined in relation to the dominant culture) can find belonging to the nation. On the other hand, when defined through the symbolism of cultural pluralism and multiculturalism, a national identity is more accessible for newcomers and minority communities, especially those who hold to transnational ideas of identity.

Some experiences can certainly negatively impact belonging for individuals and communities in a society. On this point Vasta observes that racism, and what she refers to as "the coercion of cultural assimilationism," can negate feelings of belonging and "not only contribute to the negation of a shared sense of belonging for some ethnic minority groups, but it also acts as a major destabilising force for the majority ethnic population. In this sense, the argument of the liberal nationalists that a shared sense of belonging is necessary to ensure social justice remains meaningless in the face of racism and exclusion by the majority cultural group and by its institutions."[104]

Reinforcing these findings, Hussain and Bagguley, in their study of British Pakistanis, found that an individual's sense of Britishness was challenged by racism that targeted Pakistanis and Muslims after 9/11.[105] Similarly, Wilcox, in her study of national identity and citizenship, found that immigrants and minorities who experience social exclusion found it difficult to identify with the institutions of the state.[106] From these studies it can be extrapolated that an ideology like xenoracism negatively correlates with a sense of belonging to a nation. And if a sense of belonging is the benchmark for social integration in the Canadian state, racism should be viewed as a significant barrier to the successful incorporation of newcomers.

This last point is of particular importance for this chapter in that it helps to explain some of the different sentiments that interviewees expressed in relation to a sense of belonging to the Canadian state. Modood, whose research has long focused on multicultural societies, believes that an emotional sense of belonging to a nation is critical for the success of a multicultural state.[107] By comparison, according to the findings of a study conducted by Ghorashi and Vieten, the renewed assimilative approaches to newcomers and minority communities adopted in Western Europe may act as a severe challenge to newcomers and minorities who seek to identify with the host society, as assimilation is very much opposed to the more multi-layered identities that many newcomers possess.[108] In the end, a sense of belonging comes down to subjective feelings and emotions where positive and negative social experiences and exchanges shape an individual's perception of themselves within a social milieu.

With these observations in mind, the next section will turn to the findings from the statistical data and the interview sample group of Canadian Muslims and focus on how Canadian Muslims understand their sense of belonging (or lack thereof) in the Canadian context.

CANADIAN MUSLIMS:
INTEGRATION AND BELONGING

The data from Statistics Canada's Ethnic Diversity Survey: Portrait of a Multicultural Society (EDS) provide a portrait of social relations and attitudes during a particularly difficult time for Canadian Muslims (shortly after the 9/11 attacks), but of course they do not reflect all of the integrative challenges that have emerged since that period. Nonetheless the EDS provides a rich source of data, a snapshot of social relations in Canada during its post-9/11 moment. By comparison, data for the 2006 Environics Survey of Muslims in Canada (ESM) were collected around the time of the Shari'a law debate in Ontario and Canada's escalating combat mission in Afghanistan, and data for the 2016 SMC were collected after a particularly divisive period of Canadian politics for Muslim communities (the 2015 federal election and its accompanying polarizing debates on the niqab and the admission of Syrian refugees). Noting the two previously identified priorities in integration – civic participation and a sense of belonging – the analysis will draw out data from the EDS and SMC focusing on these two key areas.

Earlier studies of integration among Canadian Muslims, for example Reitz (2009), have found that levels of integration in the population are higher than in some mainstream groups such as Catholics, especially in terms of a strong affinity for Canadian national identity.[109] Following on Reitz's contention that general life satisfaction is a good barometer for integration, when asked if they were "satisfied with life," 49.3 percent of Canadian Muslims said they were "very satisfied" in comparison with 47.6 per cent of non-Muslim Canadians (Table 6.1).[110] The EDS also measured a sense of national belonging, ranking respondents' sense of belonging to Canada on a scale of 1 to 5, with 5 representing a "very strong" sense of belonging. Of Canadian Muslim respondents 71 per cent reported a very strong sense of attachment. These levels were matched by the same percentage of Protestants (71) and were higher than those of Hindus (65), Jews (59), and non-religious groups (55) (Table 6.2). Finally, touching on another previously identified standard of integration, in terms of political participation, 66.8 per cent of Canadian Muslims voted federally and 63.8 per cent voted provincially, in comparison with 79.4 and 78.1 per cent, respectively, for non-Muslims (Table 6.3).[111]

While not providing the same depth of data as the Statistics Canada survey, the Environics SMC surveys from 2006 and 2016 draw out important findings on social integration among Canadian Muslims. While there are differences in question composition in the EDS and SMC, both surveys sought to measure a sense of national belonging. In addition the SMC looked at sentiments of national pride in Canadian Muslim communities when it asked, "Would you say you are very, somewhat, not very, or not at all proud to be a Canadian?" Here 83 per cent of Canadian Muslims indicated they were "very proud" to be Canadian in 2016. Of note, that number is a full ten percentage points higher than what was seen in the 2006 results. By comparison, 73 per cent of the "non-Muslim" sample group in the SMC survey indicated that they were "very proud" to be Canadian.[112]

The SMC also directly examined a sense of national belonging in Canadian Muslim communities when it asked respondents to describe their sense of belonging to Canada as either "very strong, generally

Table 6.1 Life satisfaction among Muslims and non-Muslims
in the Ethnic Diversity Survey

Classification	Percentage of respondents who expressed this degree of satisfaction				
	1 – Not satisfied at all	2	3	4	5 – Very Satisfied
MUSLIM					
Born in Canada	3.6	6.1	7.0	35.9	47.4
Born outside Canada	1.4	3.2	15.6	28.6	51.2
NON-MUSLIM					
Born in Canada	1.2	2.4	13.0	36.1	47.2
Born outside Canada	1.6	2.1	14.4	33.9	48.0

Source: Ethnic Diversity Survey Public Use Metafile 2002.

Table 6.2 Sense of belonging among religious communities
in the Ethnic Diversity Survey

Religious affiliation	Percentage of respondents who expressed this degree of a sense of belonging			Unweighted count
	Weak (1–2)	Somewhat strong (3–4)	Very strong (5)	
No religious affiliation	9	36	55	7,696
Catholic	10	35	55	14,321
Protestant	4	25	71	11,378
Christian Orthodox	2	22	76	808
Christian n.i.e.*	8	36	56	2,487
Muslim	4	24	71	766
Jewish	4	36	59	638
Buddhist	13	35	52	520
Hindu	5	31	65	487
Sikh	2	29	69	561
Other Eastern religions	14	33	53	75
Other religions	5	23	72	48

Source: Ethnic Diversity Survey Public Use Metafile 2002.

*Christian not otherwise stated.

Table 6.3 Voting in elections, as reported in the Ethnic Diversity Survey

Classification	Response	Percentage of respondents*	Count	Unweighted count
NON-MUSLIM				
Voted in federal election	Yes	79.4	15,366,659	27,052
	No	20.6	3,991,211	7,216
Voted in provincial election	Yes	78.1	15,051,300	26,296
	No	21.9	4,232,352	7,824
Voted in municipal election	Yes	64.1	12,333,449	21,386
	No	35.9	6,916,820	12,628
MUSLIM				
Voted in federal election	Yes	66.8	142,354	326
	No	33.2	70,693	176
Voted in provincial election	Yes	63.8	135,456	317
	No	36.2	76,709	182
Voted in municipal election	Yes	49.5	105,204	252
	No	50.5	107,499	249

Source: Ethnic Diversity Survey Public Use Metafile 2002.

*Percentage of respondents within each classification (e.g., non-Muslims who voted in a municipal election).

strong, generally weak or very weak." In this survey, 55 per cent of Canadian Muslim respondents expressed a very strong sense of belonging and 39 per cent expressed a "generally strong" sense of belonging (only 3 per cent identified themselves as having a "very weak" sense of belonging to Canada).[113] The EDS survey included a direct question on whether respondents' sense of belonging to Canada had "become stronger, become weaker, or hasn't really changed" over the past 5 years. It is noteworthy that close to 60 per cent (58 per cent) indicated that their sense of belonging had become stronger over the past 5 years, and only 5 per cent indicated that it had grown weaker.[114]

Similar to the EDS, the SMC also examined voting patterns in Canadian Muslim communities. Specifically, it focused on voting in the 2015 federal election. The survey asked its participants if they had voted in the federal election and close to 80 per cent (79 per cent) indicated that they did vote (only 16 per cent did not). Showing a clear partisan bias, 65 per cent of respondents indicated that they voted for the Liberal party, and only 2 per cent voted Conservative.[115]

In effect, the EDS and SMC provide a positive picture of social integration among Canadian Muslims from 2002 to 2016. As indicated by the data, in terms of critical metrics like life satisfaction and sense of belonging to Canada, Canadian Muslims have a higher level of integration than most non-Muslim Canadians. The high levels of belonging and life satisfaction should be viewed as a significant positive, especially considering the timing of the surveys and the importance assigned to belonging by a number of scholars focused on immigration and integration. However, significantly lower levels of political participation among the Canadian Muslim group (as indicated by the E D S) are a negative indicator in terms of integration into the critical political arena. On the other hand, remarkably, the 2016 S M C data show markedly higher levels of political participation, roughly a 20 per cent increase in voting. The next section will contextualize and update some of these findings by exploring the experiences, attitudes, and opinions of interviewees in relation to integration.

Muslim Canadian Interviewees and Their Opinions on Integration

Some interviewees expressed sentiments that reflect findings discussed earlier in the chapter, namely that individuals can display multiple forms of belonging in a way that does not undermine "loyalties." Interviewee Yasmeen Nisam, a lawyer with Indian heritage, spoke to this idea: "I grew up here, I love Canada – this is my home – I've lived all my life with the benefits of this country ... I have a pride for my country – this is my country. I have roots in India, I was born there and I still have affection for my birthplace, but this is my home and I think that's how a lot of people feel."

However, she went on to outline what she saw as a challenge for Canadian Muslims in terms of integrating into the Canadian state and society: "If you decide to assimilate would that culture care, even if you did that? It's like, 'Who do you think you are?' ... you'll always be different. I've lived here all my life but I get asked all the time, 'Where do you come from?' ... 'Canada' ... 'Yes ... but where do you *really* come from?' So it's like you'll never be truly accepted as the same, because you're not."

Some interviewees, reinforcing the image of the two-way street model of integration, believed that the key to successful integration remains mutual efforts on both sides – from the Canadian Muslim community and the host population. Dalal Daoud of the Canadian Islamic Congress pointed out that her organization encouraged members of the communities to get out into the broader community: "If you don't take that step and try and reach out you leave it to the media to build that image. Obviously we know if we leave it to the media we know what everyone is going to think, you know, that we are extremists, radicals, terrorists … on and on and on." Ahmed Shoker, director at the Canadian Islamic Congress, reinforced the view that Muslim communities and the host community need to find more common grounds for social engagement, where communities can build bridges and come together after the traumas of the past years: "The majority will say, yes, unfortunately, there are some good bonds that have been severed after September 11th and that will take some rebuilding, for sure. Part of it is our problem; we have to show the best of us. I wouldn't blame the Canadian government alone, we have a responsibility, and sometimes we play the card of apathy, we don't care … for us it's a 50/50 fault. We haven't done enough … But, it's a two way street and both parties have to work hard."

A common theme raised by several interviewees was that Muslim newcomers faced some challenges when adjusting to the political life of Canada. On this point Ahmed Shoker observed that

> When you bring people from a different culture where there is no democracy, where human rights are daily violated, and then you expect people to view themselves as equal partners, I know Canadians want it this way, that they are very proud of this attitude, but it took me 10 years to understand that is what is needed from us. The immigrants don't see that, because it is a cultural thing, it's like a language. They have to understand that 'we want you to be part of us' – they don't understand it, because they have lived in fear for decades, so they have to integrate slowly and gradually.

Supporting this view, Usama al-Atar, a Shi'a Imam, stated, "Here we have to understand something – that many of the individuals come from a system where there is no political freedom. A lot of them come from a system where, if you are involved with politics, it means you are with the government and you have to be really careful … Participating in the voting system is bad, it is evil, so you have to explain to them that is different here, it takes time."

Recognizing the difficulties that Canadian Muslims, especially those who come from societies with little in the way of liberal-democratic traditions, may face in terms of integrating into the political life of

Canada, there are examples of success in the political arena – of Canadian Muslims who have entered political life at its highest levels. An example of one of these individuals is an interviewee, Sohail Quadri, a former Progressive Conservative member of the Legislative Assembly of Alberta for Edmonton–Mill Woods. As he sees it, Canadian Muslims were faced with a choice after 9/11. Speaking of how the community felt after that time, he stated,

> They felt so frustrated because they were embarrassed about what's going around and they can't control it … so some people are thinking, 'back to isolation' but some are thinking 'isolation is no answer' – it's about time for us to get more active and become part of the process where we can go out and condemn all the stupid things that are happening on both sides. So a few of us got together and said … 'Be part of the process, what you can control is *you* – the best way for us is to get involved.' I'm not just talking about building bridges – though building bridges is wonderful … the only way to do it is to go out and have the nicest story to tell, and now I believe I have a very good story to tell about the Muslim community at large. We cannot be silent anymore. We cannot be bystanders – we have to get involved in order for us to change. It's the only way to let my neighbour know I'm not an alien; I'm another guy like you. The only way to do it is just meet, just talk … really try to understand each other.

Sohail Quadri's statement brought out a shared belief among some of the interviewees that there are two dominant impulses within the Muslim community when it comes to reacting to periods of divisiveness between Muslim and non-Muslim Canadians (i.e., around the time of 9/11): engagement and isolationism. Despite experiencing xenoracism and hostility at the political and societal level, many Canadian Muslims continue to reach out to try and overcome issues related to discrimination and stereotyping, primarily through intercultural engagement. This observation speaks to a remarkable level of resilience among a highly securitized community.

Azim Jeraj, a business owner, pointed out that in Alberta a number of Canadian Muslims from the Ismaili community have come to prominence in the political life of the province: "It's great, look at the number of people who participate in public offices from the Ismaili community, not only the mayor of Calgary, but you have also in the civil service a lot of Ismailis and on volunteer boards across the country." Soraya Hafez, a president of the Canadian Council of Muslim Women, also pointed to the noteworthy success of Canadian Muslims in elected politics and in prestigious positions in public and private life in general: "We are trying to be politically involved at every level, we have MLAS [members of the Legislative Assembly] here, at the federal level we have people running all the time, from the community you have now the professors at the universities, the lawyers, the doctors, so people are quite involved." However, as Azar Syed of the British Columbia Muslim Association pointed out, Canadian Muslims have found less success in other localities and provinces. Speaking in the context of British Columbia, he stated, "They tried in Surrey, there is one school trustee ... no great success so far." A few interviewees related how the acquisition of citizenship in Canada was a meaningful aspect of their own integration process. For example, one anonymous interviewee, a prominent member of a Muslim cultural association, spoke about how the experience of gaining Canadian citizenship had a lasting effect on him. On this he states, "Some of this was for me reinforced 15 years ago when I was first applying for my citizenship. The lady who was the citizenship judge ... They would interview you – in my case my family, myself, and my wife – and one of the things she emphasized was that you have to get involved with the broader community, and that stuck with me." That experience had led this interviewee to get involved in civil society, specifically by developing intra- and inter-cultural initiatives.

On the other hand, several interviewees noted some problematic experiences in terms of integration in Canada. For example, Ahmed Shoker pointed to the struggles of the Somali community in Canada: "Look at what is happening to the Somali community in Toronto ... here you have a youth that comes from a wartorn culture ... everything is wide open to them and they degenerate the wrong way into gangs." By comparison, Bashir Ahmed, who works with Somali youth, spoke of the great success that Somalis have found in Canada as academics and business people but also admitted that there were some difficulties: "There are always some difficulties, faced by the youth: the weather, the language, housing – since many families are five or six persons, so housing is expensive and they suffer some financial difficulties ... they come to school – they see their classmates who wear some very expensive clothes ... they get a little disappointed and their self-esteem might go down."

As Bashir Ahmed rightly points out, many Somalis come to Canada as refugees and subsequently face a unique set of challenges: "We should be fair, because people who come as refugees, they come from wartorn zones and their expectations when they go to European countries, especially Canada, they think it will be paradise, and people back at home they ask for help ... and people struggle." This last observation further underlines the need for scholars to be aware of the diversities and sometimes divergent experiences between various ethnic and cultural communities contained within the greater Canadian Muslim community.

Generational Issues

Another common theme related to integration that was drawn out by interviewees was the different experiences of first- and second-generation individuals. Many of the interviewees expressed the view that the first and second generations faced unique challenges in terms of "integration" in Canada. For example, Bashir Ahmed, whose work involves helping fellow Muslims settle and integrate into Canada, noted the considerable support that first-generation immigrants require when they first arrive: "When you are new to the environment you are like a child, you need guidance, you need caring, you need every aspect ... you need help ... So when I meet with immigrants I say, 'You know what? You are entering a very new environment.'"

Interviewees also identified the challenges faced by second-generation Canadian Muslims. For example, one anonymous interviewee, a board member at a settlement agency and professional engineer, spoke of some of the issues faced by second-generation Canadian Muslims during secondary education: "I wasn't to go out with a boy alone ... Dating was just not allowed for us, but everyone else was dating and you feel kind of drawn into that – so that's hard, and you can't drink or participate in any of that activity, so there's another level of things we can't do. So as a teenager – Islam and being a Muslim student quickly becomes being associated with all these things I can't do ... Rather than being about culture and what your parents want."

For that interviewee, the second generation exists in an awkward transition stage where they find a unique set of challenges in terms of establishing ideas of belonging in Canadian society: "They are going to go through that ugly time in high school ... they feel weird at home, it's such an awful stage for a second-generation kid. I have heard it said so many times that you feel as though you have two lives – the life you have to live at home to show your parents that you are still part of the culture and that you are not wanting to abandon their ways, but at the same time, when you go to school, you don't want to feel left out."

Another difficulty interviewees identified for second-generation youth was the fact that, despite being born in Canada, the children of immigrants often have their belonging called into question. For Ahmed Shoker, there is a double standard applied to second-generation Muslims who are born and raised in Canada: "My kids are all born here, they are Canadian, they love this country – no one should question their loyalty to the system, these are the kind of people that should have the trust ... [of] the government."

Canadian Muslims and National Sense of Belonging

This question was posed to all interviewees: In your opinion, how strong is the sense of belonging among the Canadian Muslim community to Canada? Some chose to speak from a personal level while others gave their impression of belonging at the community level. Although some interviewees had complex perspectives on belonging, a significant majority, or 74 per cent of the sample, expressed positive perspectives on a sense of belonging to Canada, roughly reflecting the numbers seen in the EDS and SMC statistical data. According to Baha Abu-Laban, a professor of sociology, "there really is a strong identification ... Muslims and Arabs – they tend to want to identify with the adopted country." On the basis of his own research, he believes that "identification historically with Canada has been strong, despite loyalty to the cultural heritage, despite notions that they may want to go back and retire in their home country, because most do not go back ... and I think that even the first generation, the immigrant generation, after a period of time of enjoying the liberties and the comfort of Canada, they feel as though this is their home."

Community organizer Ahmed Abdulkadir also drew out generational aspects of belonging and a growing sense of permanence for his community in Canada: "They believe they belong to Canada – especially the second generation – they fight for their rights ... 15 years ago you heard 'let's go back to our country' [but] you don't hear that any more. People want to fight for their rights here – they believe they are Canadian first and Muslim second."

While Bashir Ahmed saw some divides between Canadian Muslims and the general population directly after the events of 9/11, he believes that the sense of belonging in his community "is very high." To illustrate this, he went on to describe his community's annual celebration of Canada Day: "July first, they wore the Canadian flags, the children had face painting, there was so much pride." Drawing on a similar sense of belonging and patriotism, Imam Sadique Pathan of Islamic Relief Canada and al-Rashid Mosque observed, "I know that Muslims have great pride for Canada and this was indicated in a poll – that we are more patriotic than other groups in Canada." Outlining some of the transnational aspects of belonging among Canadian Muslims, Imam Sadique believes that "the identity of Muslims is very at home [in Canada], we have an identity that is both with the parents' homeland and with the newly adopted homeland."

For Usama al-Atar, belonging can be demonstrated by the long-term roots that most Canadian Muslims seek to lay down in Canada: "When people come here they really like it and I have not seen many Muslims who say, 'I am going to go back to where I came from.'" He further elaborated, "If we define integration as a sense of belonging, people belong here. When I travel abroad and people ask me where I come from I tell them I'm from Canada ... And many people feel that way."

An anonymous interviewee who is a Somali community leader in Ontario spoke about how his community views Canada in favourable terms, especially when compared with other potential destinations for newcomers. On this point he stated, "I think overall it [the sense of belonging] is good. If you talk to community members they sometimes draw comparisons between the US and here – and say that it's a better place."

For others, there was a more mixed perception of belonging. Dalal Daoud believes that a sense of belonging differed among generations: "It depends on the generation ... the youngest generation feel a stronger sense of belonging and they do really perceive Canada as a home." One anonymous interviewee believed that a sense of belonging was mixed in the community; reflecting the reciprocal nature of belonging, this interviewee identified how it was mostly dependent on how community members were received by the host culture: "My sense is that it is really diverse [the sentiment], I feel as though some people do have a kinship to this country and do feel part of it [but] resent when they are made to feel as though they are not part of it, that they are not part of the Canadian fabric."

Others spoke of belonging in quite negative terms. For example, Shaykh Zak, who works as a Muslim "chaplain," stated that "I haven't seen much of a sense of belonging. I have seen people come and take what is there to be taken but I don't see a sense of belonging and I am really sad to say that." Further elaborating on this point, he bluntly stated, "It is not a sense of belonging ... what they develop is a sense that Canada belongs to them."

Soraya Hafez problematized what belonging really means in Canada when she sees so many societal barriers for Canadian Muslims: "For me I feel I am a Canadian and I am a good Canadian, I work, I pay taxes, I follow the rules, I follow the law like any other good Canadian. Yet, I don't feel that there is that acceptance ...the first question that you get ... 'Where are you from?' I don't like that, I am very proud about where I am from but I don't like that, it eliminates me right away, and I want to be from here." Echoing this sentiment, an anonymous interviewee noted the problematic nature of the "where are you from" question. On this point, she found (while speaking with regard to second-generation Canadians), "People like me might resent it, they would say, 'I was born here.' People of my generation prefer to be thought of as just Canadian."

Imam Sadique Pathan, who clearly stated his belief that Muslims were some of the most patriotic Canadians, followed up on his comments by expressing concerns related to the acceptance of Muslims among the general public. Speaking of the negative experiences that some community members, have encountered, he stated, "It has led to many Muslims asking, 'Are we accepted?' There are many people who ask, 'Where do we belong?' The politics around the hijab, [and] portraying Muslims as disproportionately responsible for crime." Speaking about his concerns over growing discrimination and prejudice, he stated simply, "Muslims in general are very patriotic – but they are easily identifiable."

Shawkat Hassan, a member of the British Columbia Muslim Association, speaking in the context of what he saw as a rise of xenoracism and a hostile Conservative government, stated that "we have a lot of immigrants who came here recently at the same time. I know people who are living here and went back home. So even one of our leaders here, who has been very active for many, many years, pulled himself out and went back home with his family and he said, 'I don't want to see my kids suffer, I don't see a positive future because of this sentiment against Muslims.'" Expressing a high level of anxiety for his and his family's future in Canada, he continued, "Look, I tell my children ... this is a fearful future, if this trend keeps going I don't know, sometime the Muslims in the West will be like the Japanese in the concentration camps. Because there is no logic behind such a movement but it is pushing slowly and encouraged by the government unfortunately."

Speaking in the context of growing xenoracism, hate crimes, and an increasingly toxic political climate for Muslims internationally, Sadique Pathan expressed similar concerns for Muslims and the next generation: "With Trump ... he rationalizes [hatred], they can now justify the vilification, and then you have that 1 per cent who commit the violence, the vandalism ... quite frankly I am quite concerned for Muslim children." Sadique Pathan then went on to cite a specific violent attack in the United States: "We had a beautiful young Muslim girl in Virginia who was killed by a guy who was alleged to have road rage, but of course it was driven by anti-Muslim sentiment. To think that those things won't come to Canada – it's naïve – we are seeing the behaviours in America come to Canada."

Identifying concerns over the impacts of American political leadership and the impacts of the former Conservative government in Canada, one anonymous interviewee, a Somali community leader from Ontario, identified how a change in the Canadian government had led to a renewed sense of pride in Canada. On this point he observed, "I think it fluctuates with the developments in politics and security. Very recently, with the election of Trudeau, it has improved the [sense of] belonging – especially with a Somali community member acting as a minister [Ahmed Hussen] – with such developments we have had improved belonging."

Building on the findings from chapter 4, many of the interviewees who expressed more serious reservations about belonging in Canada were also individuals who expressed serious concerns over xenoracism in the community or experienced discrimination first-hand. This observation reinforces findings from the studies mentioned above – that racism negatively correlates with belonging.

CONCLUDING REMARKS

Newcomer integration in Canada has historically been described as a two-way street where newcomers are expected to adopt an official language, become citizens, and participate in the political life of the state. In return, it is assumed that Canadian society and the institutions of the state will promote equity and provide a space where newcomers can retain and maintain their culture. Grounded in a preference for cultural pluralism, the multicultural model of integration, in its idealized form, respects difference and allows newcomers *and* long-term resident communities to maintain a nostalgic connection to their place and culture of origin. Integration in Canada certainly contains elements of targeted assimilation, at least in terms of the promotion of language proficiency and civic participation. However, these areas of policy are largely functional insofar as they aim to promote inclusion into the critical economic and political aspects of the state.[116]

More to the point, how can we judge the efficacy of the Canadian model of newcomer integration and the experience of Canadian Muslims therein? Has integration devolved in Canada as it has elsewhere, becoming repackaged assimilationism that is layered with fear and xenoracism? Reitz believes that any assessment of multiculturalism must gauge the ability of the policy framework to influence public attitudes and opinions related to immigration and integration and the impacts (both positive and negative) of the framework on minority communities.[117] In his 2014 study of the impact of multiculturalism on experiences with immigration and integration he concluded that "popular multiculturalism creates a positive political environment for the development of Canada's expansionist immigration policy and helps immigrants integrate into the economy and society. In short, *support for multiculturalism represents social capital playing an important role in the development of Canadian immigration* [author's italics]. It constitutes a resource that enables policymakers to develop programs to assist immigrant integration and to address emerging problems affecting immigrants."[118]

Reitz believes that the "rubric" of multiculturalism, which is rooted in a philosophical commitment to support and maintain diversity, together with broad public support for multiculturalism, has helped to generate strong support for immigration and a more "flexible standard" for assessing immigrant integration.[119]

Thus, newcomer integration in Canada may be measured through indicators and standards that may *seem* inadequate in other national contexts, and as shown above, most existing studies on integration in Canada draw generally positive conclusions in terms of outcomes. Specifically, a number of Canadian integration and immigration scholars have focused on a sense of belonging among newcomers as an important barometer of social integration – a category of integration that now receives an increasing amount of attention in the academic literature, especially in relation to Muslims.

As indicated by the EDS and SMC data, Canadian Muslims compare favourably with the general population in terms of sense of national belonging. Together, the EDS and SMC offer snapshots of social and political integration within Canadian Muslim communities in 2002, 2006, and 2016 and indicate a consistently positive portrait of belonging in those communities. In fact, according to the EDS, Muslim Canadians display levels of national belonging that exceed those of most religious groups, except for Orthodox Christians and Protestants, with the latter "mainstream" religious group demonstrating the same level of national belonging as Muslims. Another important observation is that 58 per cent of Canadian Muslims participating in the 2016 SMC reported having developed a stronger sense of national belonging over the past 5 years. A significant majority (74 per cent) of Canadian Muslims in the sample group also spoke of having a strong sense of belonging to Canada; however, importantly, those who had directly experienced discrimination expressed very different sentiments.

These sentiments reinforce earlier common-sense findings that experiences with racism negatively impact feelings of belonging. While these experiences were not the norm for the interviewees, a sizeable minority spoke about significant challenges to their sense of belonging to Canada. Given that feelings of belonging have a reciprocal quality, when Canadian Muslims do not find acceptance, or indeed find quite the opposite, it should be of no surprise that some will express a highly tentative sense of belonging, or feelings of insecurity, marginalization, and rejection.

As discussed in the introduction, there is some evidence of increasing levels of anti-immigrant sentiment in Canadian society. For example, EKOS polling showed that in 2005, the year before the Conservatives came to power, 25 per cent of Canadians believed "there were too many immigrants" in the country; however, by 2015 that number had nearly doubled to 46 per cent.[120] Previous study has shown that a majority of Canadians express their discomfort around immigration and diversity on issues like perceived "ethnic enclaves," the growth of the use of non-official languages in Canadian society, and the perception that some religious minority groups, for example, some Muslim communities, possess values and norms that are out of step with "Canadian values."[121] The latter concern was, for instance, clearly on display during the Shari'a law controversy in Ontario in 2005.

Furthermore, as noted in the previous chapter, under the Conservative Party of Prime Minister Stephen Harper, the Canadian government had attempted to reframe Canadian national symbols toward a more distinctly militaristic and British vision of identity. Since integration is a relational process where newcomers and the Canadian society collectively shape ideas of who can belong to the nation, it follows that this new image of Canadian national identity may be both less appealing and less accessible to newcomers. More assimilative approaches to integration problematize belonging to a national culture, rendering newcomers who do not fit with an imagined homogenous community as foreign. It creates an idea of "us and them," a framing that is an impediment to the development of a sense of belonging.[122]

It is notable that some members of the Canadian Muslim sample group specifically expressed concerns about how they were treated under the former Conservative government. Since the interviews with much of this group were conducted, the situation has not improved: in the 2015 federal election the Conservatives introduced a series of wedge issues related to Muslims and citizenship. The Conservative rhetoric around the wearing of the niqab in citizenship ceremonies and the introduction of Bill C-24, which aimed to strip convicted dual-citizen terrorists of their citizenship, proved particularly divisive issues. As with other wedge issues there was political expediency behind these initiatives that sought to tap into a segment of the Canadian public that remains uncomfortable about some forms of diversity and opposed to the integration of cultures and peoples they view as outside of the Canadian norm. Again, these trends speak to the fact that Canada is not immune to trends witnessed elsewhere despite the inoculations offered by Canada's multicultural heritage.

Additionally, at the societal level, the awkward question that many face in casual conversation, "Where are you from … *no*, I mean where are you *really* from?" calls into question the belonging of people who otherwise consider themselves Canadian. While this question may come from a position of ignorance or simple curiosity (rather than blatant racism or xenoracism), this fact is largely irrelevant to individuals who are targeted with the question, because the effects on them are the same – frustration and a challenged sense of belonging.

Understandably, this experience is especially resonant among second-generation Canadians.

It must also be noted that findings on Canadian Muslim integration are less positive in terms of political participation, specifically in relation to voting, indicating that the communities are not as invested as other Canadians in electoral politics. In part, these findings can be explained by an observation from the Canadian Muslim sample group that many first-generation Muslim immigrants come from societies and states where the traditions of liberal democracy are undeveloped or absent. As these interviewees speculated, adaptation to a different political culture takes time, even decades, and in this sense political acculturation could be a multi-generational process. The 2016 SMC results provide a caveat here, indicating that Canadian Muslim communities have become significantly more engaged politically since 2002 – at least at the federal level. Although this point remains speculative without further study, the increased levels of participation and highly partisan voting patterns (in favour of the Liberal Party) may indicate that Canadian Muslims were energized by negative perceptions of the Conservative Party (which received negligible support from Canadian Muslims in the 2015 federal election).

Interviewees also drew out important differences in the experiences of first- and second-generation Canadian Muslims. For some, the experience of the second generation can represent a difficult transition as the cultural and religious ideas and expectations of parents can clash with the realities found among peer groups. Second-generation Canadian Muslims can find themselves in an awkward intergenerational position where they struggle to reconcile two cultural realties: the traditions and values of their parents and grandparents and a host society that may differ in terms of cultural values, norms, and mores. The successes and difficulties experienced by second-generation Canadians have now been well documented in immigration and integration scholarship. While this topic is not the focus of this book, findings of research in this area generally support the premise that second-generation Canadians occupy a difficult transitional phase of integration and that integration (although the term can be problematic when applied to non-newcomers) continues far beyond the settlement experiences of the first generation.

Yet, having recognized these many qualifications, there exist a number of reasons to remain optimistic. As shown by the research in this book and previous studies, multiculturalism and the norms and values it engenders in Canadian society are net positives for newcomers and their experiences with integration. Canada sets the bar lower than other countries when it comes to integration, offers a more open conception of national identity in which immigrants can find symbolic belonging, and employs limited assimilationist rhetoric in its immigration, settlement, and integration policy. There are meaningful differences to what is seen in other "former" multicultural states. The main difference between Canada and these states seems to be that Canada has normalized the idea of diversity, especially for the younger generations who have grown up in the era of state multiculturalism and subsequently have a sense of identity that is broadly sympathetic toward newcomers.[123] Therefore, the Canadian experience with integration represents a significant challenge to the alarmist, divisive, and xenoracist position of the anti-Islamic social movement and far right, which claim that accommodation and integration of Muslims into Western society are a recipe for societal discord and conflict.

Taken as a whole, the research findings presented in this chapter reinforce the idea that Canada has bucked some of the trends in the crisis of multiculturalism, namely the adoption of more coercive assimilative approaches to integration and settlement. For now, the image of a more open national identity and a system of integration that respects diversity remains attractive to newcomers and minority communities, including Muslims, who demonstrate high levels of social integration and resilience despite the many challenges they face in Canadian society.

7

Security

Modern globalized terrorism came to the West in the form of simultaneous explosions and coordinated attacks. Attacks in Madrid, London, Boston, Paris, and Brussels perpetrated by "homegrown" terrorists have brought domestic security concerns to the fore in the West, and they have broken down the barrier between domestic and global security. Those who carried out the attacks called themselves Muslims, even if their actions were wholly un-Islamic. They represented an ideology, a reactionary, revisionist, and distorted vision of Islam born of years of corruption, despotism, invasion, and interventionism in the Muslim world. For the far right and the anti-Islamic social movement the violence was confirmation of the validity of their long-standing claims that immigration from Muslim-majority countries was a threat to the West. The specter of modern terrorism coalesced with concerns over deficient integration strategies, parallel communities, and incompatible cultural practices in communities so long identified as the other in European history and identity.

For the proponents of xenoracism, the language of security gave greater urgency to their claims, as they told frightened publics that the demographic bomb of growing Muslim populations and the militant jihadist suicide bomber could no longer be ignored. A chorus of security "experts" focused on Islam in the West emerged to warn of Janus-faced immigrant communities. Terrorism studies scholar Lorenzo Vidino warned that Islamist organizations like the Muslim Brotherhood have infiltrated segregated Muslim communities and that while they "speak about interfaith dialogue and integration on television, the group's mosques preach hate and warn worshippers about the evils of integration into Western society. While they publicly condemn the murder of commuters in Madrid and school children in Russia, they continue to raise money for Hamas and other terrorist organisations."[1]

Supporting these views are the more vocal populist politicians like Geert Wilders, leader of the Dutch Freedom Party, who admonishes Westerners to "wake up" to the dangers that Muslim communities pose to Western society while suggesting that deportation of Muslims is a potential solution to the dangers they pose.[2] Other members of Europe's far right, such as Marine Le Pen, leader of France's anti-immigrant National Front party, have directly linked "unintegrated" communities to the terrorist threat while invoking the language of war; for example, in the immediate aftermath of the 2012 Toulouse terrorist attacks in France Le Pen stated, "Now we need to go to war" and warned that "entire districts are in the hands of Islamic fundamentalists."[3] These kinds of fears have also shaped public policy in the most powerful country in the world as President Donald Trump has instituted his "travel ban" on individuals from several Muslim-majority countries.[4]

Taken to its extreme, xenoracism and the anti-Islamic social movement have helped to produce right-wing extremist movements and the likes of Anders Behring Breivik, who confessed to the bombing and shootings that killed seventy-six people in Norway in 2011, and Alexandre Bissonnette, who murdered six Muslim men during evening prayers in Quebec City in 2017. As McCoy and Knight point out in the former case, "Breivik might have been delusional, but he is the product of a xenoracist movement, not only in Norway, but throughout Europe."[5]

In 2014 Canada experienced its first homegrown attacks linked to "lone wolf" assailants, at least one of whom, Martin Couture-Rouleau, was a supporter of the so-called Islamic State.[6] The second attack was carried out by Michael Zehaf-Bibeau, a 32-year-old Canadian citizen with a criminal record who had existed largely on the margins of Canadian society for much of his life. Zehaf-Bibeau shot and killed a Canadian Armed Forces reservist, Corporal Nathan Cirillo, who was standing on ceremonial sentry duty at the Canadian National War Memorial, and then entered the Centre Block building of the Canadian Parliament before being killed, in an apparent suicide mission. Zehaf-Bibeau made a video before the attack in which he outlined the political and ideological motives for his actions, which were primarily related to his anger over Canadian foreign policy.[7] Canadians have also been targeted in several failed terrorist plots, including the Toronto 18 plot in 2006, the liquid explosives plot originating in Britain that same year, and the 2013 Via Rail plot that aimed to attack passenger trains in Southern Ontario.[8] Demonstrating that domestic terrorism in Canada can originate from a variety of different ideological perspectives and communities, the Quebec City Mosque attack in 2017 showed the increasing threat posed by groups and individuals loosely or formally connected to the anti-Islamic social movement. For many Canadians these incidents had a meaningful psychological impact, and there are heated debates among politicians and in the media over an appropriate response to the threat of homegrown terrorism.

Responding to the events of 9/11 and the wave of homegrown terrorism which followed, the Canadian government, like governments in other Western states, significantly expanded security powers through, among other measures, the Anti-terrorism Act/Bill C-36 and Bill C-51. These legislative actions have led to a significant expansion and diffusion of security-related policy within the state and its bureaucracy. To highlight this trend, Murphy outlined the sheer scope of the expansion of security after 9/11: "significantly increased security and policing expenditures, new security-oriented ministries and agencies, and policies and programs aimed at the expansion, coordination, and integration of all national policing and security activities. Securitized government and governance has also significantly changed public policing in Canada."[9]

As indicated in the previous chapter, the more coercive and assimilationist approaches to newcomer integration that have taken hold in Western Europe are largely absent in the Canadian state. However, one of the statements by interviewees that was highlighted in the last chapter indicates how some very serious concerns over state security practices are present in the wider Canadian Muslim community. Shawkat Hassan, a member of the British Columbia Muslim Association, said, "Look, I tell my children … this is a fearful future, if this trend keeps going, I don't know, sometime the Muslims in the West will be like the Japanese in the concentration camps. Because there is no logic behind such a movement, but it is pushing slowly and encouraged by the government unfortunately."

The fears Shawkat Hassan expressed for his family are stark indications of the level of anxiety among some members of the Canadian Muslim community. By invoking the example of the Japanese community, he draws on local and historical memories of how those deemed to be the dangerous foreigners in the past were treated in Canada: their belonging and loyalty were called into question; their rights of citizenship, property, and personal freedom were stripped away; and they were imprisoned simply because of their racial identity. During an era where Donald Trump has instituted his travel ban and the far right in Europe calls for internment and deportation of Muslims, the sentiments expressed by Shawkat Hassan cannot be seen as alarmist, or far-fetched.[10]

Today, a series of warlike analogies and narratives shape our understanding of domestic security and the place of Western Muslims therein. According to some, Muslim communities are at the centre of a "war of hearts and minds" between radicals and extremists on one side and moderate Muslims on the other. Law enforcement agencies and governments are creating counterterrorism programs and programs to counter violent extremism on the basis of the understanding that "communities defeat terrorism." And of course the seemingly endless "War on Terror" continues, despite a change in rhetoric from former President Obama, as drone strikes and rolling Western interventions make their way from Afghanistan to Iraq, to Libya, to Syria, and back to Iraq. The end result is an atmosphere of fear and suspicion surrounding Muslim communities and the idea that war is not a temporary condition that aims to achieve identifiable goals but rather a permanent condition in which extraordinary measures are constantly required and renewed to ensure national security.

The proposed remedy at the domestic-security level is complex and multifaceted: newly expanded security legislation packages, various community policing strategies, programs to counter violent extremism, and associated assimilationist approaches to integration have emerged in recent years as strategies that aim to address terrorism and prevent "radicalization" in the West. The result in many instances has been hyper-securitized communities that find themselves under a constant cloud of suspicion. As indicated by the opinions of the interviewees and the findings presented below, the no-fly lists, surveillance, and detentions have had predictably negative impacts on Canadian Muslims.

This chapter seeks to understand how complex and rapidly evolving ideas and practices of societal and national security have coalesced over the past decade and a half. Specifically, it asks how securitized public policy has, after 9/11, affected Canadian Muslims. The chapter will examine in detail how security practices that impact Muslim communities have evolved during this period and look to the experiences of Canadian Muslim interviewees with security while exploring what those experiences can tell us about security practices in Canada since 9/11.

SOCIETAL SECURITY

A useful framework of analysis for some of the trends analyzed in this book can be found in the constructivist Copenhagen security school and its understanding of societal security. As outlined in the introduction, constructivist theory reveals that security is not an objective condition but rather a social construct.[11] As Zedner points out, as a vague and often undefined object, security is open to broad interpretation and political manipulation.[12] Given that security is socially constructed, the meaning and parameters of security are dynamic: security is shaped by individuals or "agents" who seek to portray certain issues as requiring a security response entailing extraordinary measures.[13] This has been referred to as a process of securitization where the *perception* of insecurity is established. As Waever contends, "What is essential [to a case of securitization] is the designation of an existential threat … and the acceptance of that designation by a significant audience."[14]

A security issue is established through what Buzan, Waever, and de Wilde refer to as the "speech act," where a securitizing actor presents an issue to an audience in the hopes of legitimizing the issue as a security issue. A securitizing actor declares a referent object to be existentially threatened to a target audience who, by accepting or rejecting the claim, legitimize the issue as a security issue.[15] On this process Buzan, Waever, and de Wilde state, "If by means of an argument about the priority and urgency of an existential threat the securitizing actor has managed to break free of procedures or rules he or she would otherwise be bound by, we are witnessing a case of securitization."[16] Once an issue has entered the realm of security, actors are then free to engage in "emergency politics" that are outside of the normal, everyday politics of a state and its society.[17]

Buzan, Waever, and de Wilde divide security issues into categories including environmental, military, economic, and (the focus of this section) societal security. Here the sector relates to ideas of identity and the ways in which families and individuals conceive of themselves as members of a distinct and sustained community.[18]

Subsequently, the object of societal security is large identity groups that carry sufficient loyalty and devotion from their subjects to create a resonant argument that their "we" identity is threatened through a particular set of circumstances.[19] Thus, the most important referent objects in societal security are groups like tribes, clans, nations, religions, and races.[20]

With security analysts increasingly focused on issues such as "ethnic conflict" in the post-Cold War environment, as Gartner, Hyde-Price, and Reiter point out, "Few problems of contemporary security can be fully comprehended without reference to questions of collective identity."[21] The societal security issues most pertinent to this analysis are what Buzan, Waever, and de Wilde conceive of as cultural competition, such as people being subjected to a project of integration.[22] In the societal security panic reaction, Buzan, Waever, and de Wilde, suggest, as an example, that a majority culture may be threatened by a growing or assertive minority culture. In response the established or "host" culture may through state, educational, media, and other avenues and structures reinforce the established majority society and its view of identity.[23]

Waever et al. identify similar patterns in societal security: "For threatened societies, one obvious line of defensive response is to strengthen societal identity. This can be done through cultural means to reinforce societal cohesion and distinctiveness."[24] Here Buzan, Waever, and de Wilde's description of societal security reflects a subject that was outlined in the previous chapter: coercive approaches to assimilative integration that similarly seek to reinforce a culturally defined national identity by reinforcing "core values" or "cohesion."

The linkage between immigration, integration, and societal security was made as early as the 1990s by Huysmans, who, writing on how immigrant communities were being constructed as a security threat, stated that "thus migration is interpreted as an existential threat, which means that it threatens the survival of the self-identity of the natives. In this struggle, the natives try to survive by distancing themselves from the migrant."[25]

In more severe cases of societal security, securitizing actors may demand deportations (a security strategy currently being proposed by some members of the European far right) or, in more extreme cases, ethnic cleansing. As shown repeatedly in previous chapters, one can find numerous examples of incidences where far-right politicians, and provocateurs from the anti-Islamic social movement, have invoked societal security arguments and identified certain minority groups as the dangerous foreign "other," a threat to the dominant culture and their values, beliefs, and traditions. By identifying an undesirable and dangerous foreign other, these securitized discourses exhibit the ideology of xenoracism. As noted in earlier chapters, identity is a multilayered and relational phenomenon. In cases of societal security, where a particular culture and its values, practices, and characteristics are reified and designated a threat, there are negative markers of otherness assigned to that identity group within a hierarchal understanding of difference.

The concept of societal security captures some of the trends and concepts discussed in the previous chapters and it offers a useful theoretical lens for identifying cases of securitization related to group identities. In the following section the book will identify the political climate in which Muslim communities in the West have been subject to various forms of security.

THE POST-9/11 SECURITIZATION OF IMMIGRATION AND INTEGRATION

During the latter part of the twentieth century, Western states began (re)asserting greater control over immigration and integration policy. In the 1990s international economic organizations like the Organisation for Economic Co-operation and Development (OECD) began warning of the "growth of foreign populations and the problems posed by the social and economic integration of migrants in the main OECD host countries."[26] Rather than being viewed as an economic and social benefit, immigration and newcomer integration were increasingly described as a challenge, as a potential social and economic burden, and integration policy as an area of public policy that required reform. In this sense the late twentieth century is a period when there was an important shift in the public narrative on the value of immigrants in the West. However, it is the events of 9/11 that represent the tipping point, the spark that heralded the securitization of Muslim communities in the 2000s. For Castles and Miller, "the attacks of 9/11 and Madrid and London have had the effect of transforming the decades-old, indeed centuries-old, question of migrant incorporation in Western countries into an important security issue."[27]

In the years after the attacks, security organizations, including the Canadian Security Intelligence Service (CSIS), identified the militant Islamist group al-Qaeda and homegrown terrorism as the primary threat to national security.[28] Terrorism was viewed not only as an external threat, for example the threat coming from groups like al-Qaeda and their splinters like the so-called Islamic State in Afghanistan and Syria, but also as a domestic security threat. Major terrorist attacks in the 2000s, such as those in Madrid in 2004 and London in 2005, added to the perception that homegrown terrorism represented the primary threat to national security in the West. As a result, greater scrutiny was placed on the movements of people, border controls, visas, and immigration. In addition, integration and immigration policy increasingly became interlinked with security policy.

Haverig, articulating how post-9/11 security policy now shapes integration in two European states, namely Germany and Britain, writes, "As an important congruence, both governments now increasingly regard the cultural integration of their migrant populations as of real importance and prioritise achieving an 'integrated' or 'cohesive' society. This re-conceptualisation can be interpreted as a response to the 'threat from within,' as it was shaped by the explicit involvement of European Muslim residents or citizens in violent events since 2001."[29]

During this period some politicians and security services came to believe that unintegrated Muslim communities in the West were a potential hotbed of radicalization. This linkage between radicalization and integration was made in influential policy documents such as a 2007 paper authored by the New York City Police Department entitled "Radicalisation in the West: The Homegrown Threat." In that paper the authors surmised that "living within and as part of a diaspora provides an increased sense of isolation and a desire to bond with others of the same culture and religion. Within diaspora Muslim communities in the West, there is a certain tolerance for the existence of the extremist subculture that enables radicalization."[30]

With little in the way of empirical data to support their claims, the New York City Police Department drew a neat chain of equivalences: spatially concentrated ethnic communities are culturally isolated communities, and isolated communities are breeding grounds for radicalization and violent extremism. When followed to its logical end, this rationale led some to conclude that *all* Muslims were potential extremists and therefore should be treated as suspects.

Contemporary Security Practices
and Suspect Communities

After 9/11 integration became intertwined with security, but more specifically it became intertwined with the priority of preventing radicalization and extremism in Muslim communities living in the West. To conceptualize this, some Western security agencies and governments conceive of the homegrown terrorist threat within a multi-tiered pyramid of risk (a concept imported from public health models and the World Health Organization). At the top of this pyramid of risk, active and engaged terrorists are dealt with by the military, law enforcement agencies, intelligence agencies, and the judiciary. In the middle of the pyramid, individuals who are considered to be vulnerable, at risk, or in the "pre-criminal space" of radicalization are targeted with surveillance and with various counter-radicalization strategies that aim to disengage them from pathways that lead to violence and terrorism. At the bottom of the pyramid, ethnic and religious communities are targeted with multiple integration and engagement strategies in the understanding that segregation and a lack of social cohesion can represent a precondition for radicalization.[31] With this in mind, as Fekete observes, within contemporary security practices, integration policy became an "adjunct" to counterterrorism.[32]

In states like Britain, which had direct experience with al-Qaeda-based terrorist violence during the 7 July 2005 transit bombings, the government prioritized the "cohesion-agenda" as part of a wider strategy called Prevent that sought to address extremism, particularly among British Muslims.[33] Britain represents one of the "first movers" on programs to counter violent extremism and was one of the first states to intermix ideas of integration, social cohesion, and counter-terrorism. As such they represent an important case study for understanding how security has evolved in the west in the 2000s and 2010s. Moreover, the problems that Britain has encountered in these programs provide a cautionary tale for other states, including Canada, which has adopted elements of the British approach and is now developing its own counter-extremism programs through the Office of the Community Outreach and Counter-radicalization Coordinator, which was established in 2016.

The British criminologist Imran Awan notes that when Prime Minister David Cameron began identifying "active muscular liberalism" not only as an approach to address perceived problems with state multiculturalism but also as a means of tackling the root causes of "Islamic extremism" in Britain, he was articulating priorities that were already contained in Britain's Prevent program, which at its core represents a "soft" form of counterterrorism.[34]

In actuality, Prevent is only one element in the larger British counterterrorism model known as CONTEST, a policy framework that was developed in secret in 2003 in response to the 9/11 attacks and released to the public in 2006.[35] While Prevent has evolved as a program over the years it contains several distinct priorities: for example, it seeks to undermine the ideological causes of terrorism; to prevent radicalization and violent extremism at the individual level; and to promote partnerships between the government and community groups around the issue of radicalization and violent extremism.[36]

Prevent has its roots in the City of London's Muslim Contact Unit and practices of community policing that seek to generate more effective counterterrorism by gaining the trust and co-operation of British Muslim communities.[37] Arguably, Prevent's genealogy goes back even further than that of the Muslim Contact Unit, to the British experience with terrorism in Northern Ireland and the idea that "communities defeat terrorism": the idea that communities are a battleground where ideologies and practices related to extremism and terrorism are either encouraged or discouraged by community leaders. For law enforcement and intelligence agencies, practices like community policing hold the promise of generating "human intelligence" while simultaneously undermining support for extremist groups, thereby preventing domestic terrorism.[38]

Thus, it was ideas and priorities related to community policing that helped to shape the City of London's first forays into counterterrorism shortly after 9/11. One obvious problem with employing a community policing approach within a wider counterterrorism strategy is that the former's success is based on the ability to establish a trusting and co-operative relationship with affected communities whereas counterterrorism is a form of intelligence work that has traditionally been conducted through secrecy, surveillance, and the use of "hard" forms of deterrence and prevention.

John Gearson and Hugo Rosemont observe on CONTEST and Prevent, "substantial efforts have been made by police services in particular to work with communities to counter extremism, thereby extending well beyond central government's encouragement of society to enhance its own emergency preparedness through the development of such concepts as 'community resilience.'"[39] Recognizing that a priority of the Prevent program is to undermine the ideologies that promote violent extremism, one of the sub-programs within Prevent that focuses on this specific area is the Channel Program, which offers interventions for individuals who are identified as being at risk of, or engaged with, radicalization.[40] Channel has been touted as a flagship counterterrorism program by the Conservative British government and as an effective approach to countering extremist narratives. Since Channel's inception in the spring of 2007, thousands of cases of suspected radicalization have been referred to the program, with the vast majority of these cases linked to militant Islamism.[41]

However, one potential issue with this particular program is that by using the language of vulnerability and risk it may target individuals who are not necessarily indicating, for example through their behaviour and actions, that they are "radicalized" or, more importantly, that they are committed to violent acts. Rather, through risk assessment some practices of counterterrorism move into what has been called the realm of pre-crime. In the United Kingdom and elsewhere, various tools have been employed for risk assessment related to radicalization and violent extremism, such as VERA and VERA-2 (assessment tools that were created by a Canadian social scientist, Elaine Pressman). Those assessment tools aim to create a predictive methodology that can identify the vulnerabilities of individuals to radicalization, or "radicalization trajectories."[42]

Ostensibly these assessment tools are intended to be used on individuals who are already involved in extremism activities or who have been convicted of terrorist offences, to predict their future propensity for violent behaviour and terrorism. However, a legitimate concern is that with programs like Prevent and Channel and assessment tools like VERA and VERA-2, that risk could be assessed more broadly and arbitrarily among securitized populations and communities, or more specifically among young males within those communities (who have been the primary target group for the Channel program).

Tools like VERA use a checklist system to assess an individual's potential vulnerability to radicalization and violent extremism. A recognized potential problem with these methodologies is that some of the behaviours and risk factors that are identified during an assessment may be associated with normal behaviour, for example among rebellious young people. In other words, the approach risks creating false positives, problematizing common behaviours among young people, and identifying a significant pool of individuals as potential terrorists.[43]

As Western states desperately try to prevent future domestic terrorist attacks they have turned to programs to counter violent extremism like Prevent that focus a significant majority of their resources and efforts on Muslim communities. Understandably, these programs have been viewed with trepidation and suspicion by communities that are already highly securitized. Highlighting some of these concerns, a 2011 study carried out by the Equality and Human Rights Commission in Britain highlighted how the development of counterterrorism programs in British communities had created "parallel lives" for Muslims and non-Muslims living in the same neighbourhood. Muslims in the study believed they were increasingly treated as suspected extremists and terrorists and that counterterrorism policy was contributing to a climate of fear and hostility toward Muslims.[44] According to the study, British Muslims are also increasingly wary of intra-community surveillance through the activities of Covert Human Intelligence Sources, where community informants partner with police and intelligence agencies to identify radicalized and/or violent community members.[45]

As indicated by the commission's study, these programs and counterterrorism techniques have a negative impact on trust between the police and Muslims, and within the wider Muslim communities of Britain. One former senior police officer (Dal Babu) has gone so far as to observe that Prevent "has become a toxic brand and is widely mistrusted."[46] In this sense some of the techniques employed in the name of counterterrorism in Britain may undermine key goals contained in the Prevent program, for example, the goal of establishing effective working partnerships between Muslim communities and law enforcement agencies.[47]

It should be noted that some studies have indicated mixed results in terms of British Muslim perceptions of the Prevent and Channel programs, with young British Muslim males indicating the most dissatisfaction, probably because they are the primary targets.[48] According to Fenwick and Choudhury, young British men are disproportionately targeted by police measures that have been approved in British terrorism legislation since 2000. For example, pre-charge detentions, terrorism charges, and stop-and-search powers have been used overwhelmingly against Muslim communities.[49] Awan also identifies how in some communities, such as Birmingham, local police forces have used counterterrorism funds to install covert and overt closed-circuit TV cameras in predominately British Muslim neighbourhoods.[50] It has also been reported that the same police district infamously sent local police to a nursery school in a British Muslim neighbourhood in 2009 because of fears that the children could be at risk of extremism.[51] Obviously, these actions are highly detrimental to relations between the police and Muslim communities.

In this sense Britain seems to be repeating some of the mistakes of the past with its counterterrorism approaches; for example, similar problems were encountered in Northern Ireland in the 1970s and 1980s. Indeed the notion of "suspect" communities was first used by academics to describe the experience of Northern Ireland with British counterterrorism. Similar to what British Muslims experience today, the Catholic Irish community in Northern Ireland was subject to profiling, stop-and-search techniques, heightened surveillance, and detention without charge.[52] Rather than reducing radicalization and terrorism in the community, arguably these methods only increased support and recruitment for militant Republican groups.

As seen in the British experience there is a fine line between community policing and targeted counterterrorism – between treating communities as partners in public safety and treating them as suspects who are unduly targeted with soft counterterrorism measures.[53] While Britain has been one of the initial movers on counter-extremism and counter-radicalization programs since 9/11, Western states, and indeed states around the world, have been moving toward designing and implementing similar programs. In many cases, returning to the pyramid of risk model, states have targeted their programs to counter violent extremism not only on individuals actively engaged with violent behaviours and ideologies but also on those who are deemed at risk of integrative deficiencies.

For example, in Denmark the government has prioritized social and economic integration as part of its approach to prevent radicalization and violent extremism in the long term. By comparison, the Dutch have focused on the potential threat of radicalization in spatially concentrated neighbourhoods. According to Bartlett at al., "Dutch agencies are concerned with the long-term social threat of groups who preach segregation and withdrawal from Dutch society."[54] Thus, in these particular states the governments have decided (to use another analogy from public health) to target their programming on the "primary" or preventive space rather than targeting actual behaviours and actions.

Schiffauer found similar trends in his study of the experience of Muslims in Germany. According to Schiffauer, the German government prioritized integration policy as part of a broader security strategy. To highlight this priority he cites a report released by the Federal Office for the Protection of the Constitution that identified among immigrant communities problems with "integration into majoritarian society" and "segregated accommodations for immigrants" as stimulating racialization and recruitment of "Islamists."[55] According to Schiffauer, "since September 11th 2001, discussions about the integration of Muslim immigrants into the European societies have been dominated by issues of national security. This is a consequence of the new security policies characterized by an increase of 'repressive measures' complemented by more extensive 'preventive measures.' In the language of security agencies, repressive measures aim at preventing people from committing criminal offences so as to ensure law enforcement in general. Since such measures are generally adopted prior to the acts in question, they are meant to eliminate imminent dangers."[56]

Schiffauer's observation here is important, as it highlights how securitized integration policy operates at a practical level. Once a community has been singled out as a potential threat to national security there is a presumption of guilt, not necessarily among all members; however, the existence of even a tiny minority of violent extremists casts a cloud of doubt over the larger community. As security officials seek to prevent attacks through "repressive measures," the security logic requires more targeted security practices. As Murphy recognizes here,

> The security crisis of 9/11 transformed some urban communities into security problems for local police, changing communities from partners to suspects, from crime problems to security problems, and from communities *at* risk to communities *of* risk. The apparently ordinary domestic lifestyles of either 'imported or home grown' terrorists, and a lack of reliable community information, make all citizens, in some ethnic communities, either potential suspects or informants. The 'community as security problem' thus becomes a legitimate space for security policing operations such as disruptions, surveillance, informants, and various forms of social penetration. This 'enemy within' logic invariably distances local police from the community, increases mutual suspicion, and undermines previous trust-based relationships.[57]

With Murphy's portrait of post-9/11 security in mind, the requirements of community-targeted counterterrorism strategies, combined with the perceived scale of the threat posed by both the external enemy and the enemy within, led to the development of a new kind of security response unlike what had been seen in the past.

After 9/11 broader and more diffuse security practices were normalized and institutionalized as the police, intelligence agencies, and military institutions, once thought to be separate domains, were mobilized to work together with various state ministries and departments to identify and combat threats related to the threat of globalized terrorism.[58] Recognizing these trends, the book now returns to the case study of Canada and poses the question of how post-9/11 security concerns have been addressed by the Canadian state and how Canadian security policy has affected the Canadian Muslim community.

SECURITY AND COUNTER-TERRORISM IN CANADA

As in many other states, immediately after 9/11 there were concerns expressed over vulnerabilities to terrorism in Canada. Some politicians, security experts, and members of the media singled out a number of potential susceptibilities. These included a system of immigration that was perceived of as lax in terms of risk assessment, and even some of the rights and freedoms contained in the Canadian Charter of Rights and Freedoms.[59] Even before 9/11, security critics and some officials had been arguing that the adoption of the Charter in 1982 had restricted police powers in favour of individual rights by putting in place a series of limitations that subjected law enforcement and national security agencies to greater scrutiny from the judiciary.[60] Journalist and security commentator Stewart Bell highlighted many of these concerns in his work *Cold Terror: How Canada Nurtures and Exports Terrorism around the World*, where he warned that progressive reforms to Canadian legal and immigration systems, combined with inadequate security services, had made the country a preferred sanctuary for a host of terrorist groups ranging from the Tamil Tigers to al-Qaeda.[61]

Acquiescing to the concerns of the police, intelligence agencies, and allies like the United States after 9/11, the federal government adopted the Anti-terrorism Act, which mirrored aspects of initiatives seen elsewhere, such as the Patriot Act in the United States. Together the new legislative measures and security climate opened the door to a host of security policies and practices that aimed at establishing greater national security. As a result, Murphy describes what he sees as considerable "security creep": the spreading of security practices and infrastructure to various government ministries and institutions.

> First, the federal government radically reconceptualized and reorganized the governance of all national policing and security in Canada. A national security policy was proclaimed which provided a federal vision of national security that called for more integrated national policing and security. To facilitate this, a new *über* security ministry called 'Public Safety and Emergency Preparedness Canada' (PSEPC) was created to combine and coordinate various existing and newly created agencies and departments involved in security governance. PSEPC manages the Royal Canadian Mounted Police, the Canadian Security Intelligence Service, the Communications Security Establishment, the Canada Border Services Agency, and other agencies with public safety functions, such as Emergency Preparedness Canada and Health Canada. Under the political direction of a powerful new cabinet minister, PSEPC, like its US Homeland Security counterpart, is designed to bring about more effective security governance through more explicit political direction and the central coordination of the diverse activities of various national and local policing and security agencies.[62]

The portrait painted by Murphy is illuminating – it demonstrates the scale of co-operation in the civil service on security and the extent to which security has been integrated into the bureaucratic structure of the state.

Perhaps the most important security reform that has taken place in Canada since 9/11, in terms of its influence on Canadian security policy, is the aforementioned Anti-terrorism Act/Bill C-36, which significantly expanded the security powers of law enforcement and national security agencies, including increased powers of surveillance, arrest, and detention.[63] The Anti-terrorism Act allows detention without charge and the replacement of "reasonable belief" with "reasonable suspicion" as the basis of police action, and it allows for the use of private investigative hearings.[64] Some of these measures drew criticism and concerns from legal experts and civil rights activists over provisions that they believe significantly undermine some of the individual rights contained in constitutional documents like the Canadian Charter of Rights and Freedoms.[65]

Since its introduction there has been considerable political and public debate over the Anti-terrorism Act, with federal political parties like the New Democratic Party and various civil rights advocacy groups actively opposing it. These oppositional forces hoped to derail the efforts of the former Conservative government to renew the legislation (it was first up for renewal in 2007). However, with support from the federal Liberal Party, the Conservative government passed Bill S-7 in April 2013, effectively preventing the sunsetting of provisions contained in the Anti-terrorism Act and allowing for the continuation of controversial measures such as preventive detentions (i.e., allowing individuals to be held without charge for up to 3 days on the basis of suspicion of involvement in terrorism).[66] Bill S-7 also allowed for investigative hearings where suspects who are believed to have knowledge of terrorist activities could be compelled to answer questions. Individuals who refuse to answer those questions can be subject to up to 12 months in prison. Organizations such as the Canadian Council on American-Islamic Relations argued that S-7 continued the extraordinary legal powers that appeared after 9/11, which represent a challenge to "democratic principles."[67]

In June 2015 the powers available to the Canadian government and its security agencies were further expanded through the passing of Bill C-51 in the final year of the Harper Conservative government. Bill C-51 represents the most comprehensive bill of its kind since the passing of the original Anti-terrorism Act in December of 2001. It focuses on expanding the power of law enforcement agencies to engage in preventive detentions, criminalizing the promotion of terrorism offences, increasing areas of information sharing between seventeen government agencies, expanding the mandate of CSIS (allowing it to engage in controversial "disruption" activities), and providing the Public Safety minister with the power to add individuals to the no-fly list. As with past post-9/11 security-based legislative reforms in Canada, C-51 can be seen as somewhat reactive and a response to the homegrown terrorist attacks in Ontario and Quebec in the fall of 2014 and the growing threat posed by groups like the so-called Islamic State and their supporters.

Among some civil liberties advocates the greatest concern related to Bill C-51 is what amounts to a considerable expansion of CSIS's mandate, effectively allowing an agency that was established to collect intelligence to actively disrupt terrorist plots. According to Forcese and Roach, these disruptions could involve, among other activities, stopping Canadian "foreign fighters" from returning to Canada, removing Internet postings that the agency found threatening, and engaging in "disinformation campaigns."[68] Forcese and Roach believe that the primary issue with this expansion of powers is inadequate oversight. The main safeguard in the bill is judicial warrants that CSIS would require when its actions might violate Canadian law and the Canadian Charter of Rights and Freedoms. However, according to Forcese and Roach, "this safeguard is imperfect. CSIS warrant proceedings are secret and one-way: The target of the requested warrant is not represented. Such proceedings always run the serious risk of wrongly penalizing an innocent person." Forcese and Roach also identify the inadequate and outdated nature of Canada's independent security review mechanism, the Security Intelligence Review Committee, which is widely viewed as being understaffed and lacking in budgetary resources.[69]

Since C-51 became law, CSIS has acknowledged that it has used its disruption powers at least two dozen times, although as of the time of writing it has not had to acquire a warrant in these cases because CSIS contends its actions have not yet violated Canadian laws or the Constitution.[70] The Liberal Party, which supported C-51 while it was in opposition, has promised to revise parts of the legislation now that it is in government. Ultimately, C-51 and other iterations of the Anti-terrorism Act have generated concerns not only among civil liberties advocates but also among Canadian Muslim communities and related civil society groups, who point out that Muslims have been disproportionately targeted with the Anti-terrorism Act since it came into law. On the other hand, the supporters of C-51 and the Anti-terrorism Act argue that an evolving global terrorist threat requires adaptive legal frameworks that are able to respond to those threats, to ensure public safety. There is validity in both of these arguments and the Liberal government will face a significant challenge as it attempts to strike a balance between security interests, the rights of religious minorities, and core Canadian values.

The danger here, and what is most relevant to the analysis, is that new powers can further isolate already concerned communities and create sometimes dire results for those who are targeted. Canadian Muslim civil society groups have been expressing concerns that C-51 may further damage relations between the government, law enforcement agencies, and marginalized Muslim communities.[71] In Canada the specter that looms large in these discussions is the Maher Arar case, and similar cases, where issues related to information sharing and oversight have previously led to disastrous consequences for those involved. In the case of Arar this resulted in the rendition and torture of a Canadian citizen in Syrian prisons.

Ultimately the concern of groups such as the Canadian Council on American-Islamic Relations and other Canadian Muslim civil society groups can be traced to what has been seen as the detrimental effects of the legislation and post-9/11 security practices on Canadian Muslims. Helly, in her study of discrimination against Canadian Muslims, argues that counterterrorism measures "are extremely detrimental for Muslims. They create suspicion in people's minds about the presence of Muslim extremists in Canada and the Muslim population's failure to report their existence to the authorities."[72] For Hanniman the overall effect of these security measures is that communities like Canadian Muslims have had their "Canadian-ness" called into question.[73]

While Canada has followed the lead of many Western states in expanding the powers and techniques available to its security services to prevent and combat domestic terrorism, the Canadian government has moved more cautiously in its implementation of programs to counter violent extremism. Similar to their counterparts in states like Britain, Canadian law enforcement and intelligence agencies have used community policing techniques and human intelligence sources. Specifically, in the post-9/11 environment the Royal Canadian Mounted Police (RCMP) has drawn on models established in Western Europe. For example, Spalek notes how the RCMP "has drawn heavily on the model of the MCU [Muslim Contact Unit] in London, adopting community policing within its remit of national security policing. Within this context it has been argued that community-based policing enables trust to be built between the police and communities, particularly those minority communities most affected by national security measures."[74]

Further emulating the British approach to counterterrorism, Public Safety Canada also established a "Prevent" element in Canadian counterterrorism strategy in 2012 and identified goals similar to those of the British model, such as building "resilience" in communities and countering the narratives that support violent extremism.[75] During the tenure of the Conservative government the actual tangible out- comes of this strategy were minimal. Public Safety Canada and the RCMP did engage in some outreach and public engagement activities related to this strategy, for example through the Cross-Cultural Roundtable on Security, which ostensibly sought to gain public input on security measures and strategies through consultation with government-approved community interlocutors. The RCMP also employed a National Security Community Outreach program to engage with and promote local initiatives that seek to address radi- calization and violent extremism.[76] The RCMP's initiative was at least in part a response to the Commission of Inquiry into the Actions of Canadian Officials in Relation to Maher Arar, or the O'Connor inquiry as it became known, which recommended that Canadian security agencies engage more productively with communities that are impacted by security investigations.

Despite the modest efforts to date, the Canadian government, Public Safety Canada and the RCMP have also long identified their desire to develop preventive measures to address "the factors that may motivate individuals to engage in terrorist activities."[77] The Canadian Government has been publicly voicing its intention to establish distinct counter-radicalization programs since at least 2013, a move that can has come in response to the "foreign fighter" phenomenon in Canada, which has seen roughly 180 Canadians leave to join extremist and terrorist movements abroad.[78] However, since that time, perhaps in recognition of the problems encountered by allies like Britain in their own approach to countering violent extremism, the Canadian govern- ment and its security agencies have moved cautiously.

What emerged in late 2015 and early 2016 is a seeming commit- ment to more approaches to counter-radicalization in Canada where municipalities and provinces create tailored responses the problem. In 2016 the federal Liberal government announced the creation of the Office of the Community Outreach and Counter-radicalization Coordinator and pledged $35 million in funding for federal-provincial initiatives, a move that signaled a modicum of support for counter- radicalization efforts. Furthermore, the Liberal government has identi- fied counter-radicalization as one pillar in a reorganized approach to Canadian counterterrorism at home and abroad.

As shown in the British example, there is a fine line between treat- ing communities as partners and treating them as suspects; there is also a fine line between community policing and targeted and indiscriminate counterterrorism. Far too often over the past 15 years, Muslim communities in the West have been subject to the latter. An important question going forward is this: Can the emerging Canadian model of counterterrorism balance the need to ensure public safety with the preservation of the rights and dignity of already highly securitized communities?

SECURITY AND THE EXPERIENCE
OF CANADIAN MUSLIM INTERVIEWEES

A majority of the interviewees from the Canadian Muslim community expressed at least some concern over Canadian security policy and practices, and a number of interviewees described direct contact with Canadian security officials. In some cases, interviewees described these actions in positive terms; For example, Bashir Ahmed, executive director of the Somali Canadian Education and Rural Development Organization, described how CSIS visited him with the Canada Border Services Agency and the RCMP in 2010. Speaking of his organization's relationship with Canadian security services, he remarked, "We have a very good relationship." Imam Sadique Pathan also spoke about how Canadian Muslim communities have a positive relationship with Canadian security agencies and articulated how Muslims were actively policing cases of extremism in their communities: "We have a strong relationship with the RCMP and local police – Muslims work with authorities – Muslims continue to report [problems]. When that guy [Michael Zehaf-Bibeau] went to Vancouver, the imam of the mosque and the congregation, they tried to correct him, they told him to leave, because his views were too extreme, they were un-Islamic." Shawkat Hassan of the British Columbia Muslim Association, despite his significant fears for the future of the Canadian Muslim community, spoke of his dealings with security services in positive terms, "Yes, we have a committee concerning the RCMP, they come here to our schools and our masjid once a year with their equipment like their helicopters and ambulances, et cetera."

However, Shawkat Hassan was quick to qualify his positive dealings with security services with his reservations about the broader security strategy of the former Conservative federal government and issues of profiling: "but the prime ministers and the Jason Kenneys, what they are doing ... We want to be abiding citizens here, we want to be good citizens, we choose this country to live in, and then they point the fingers into the Muslim community, and this is not healthy." The same interviewee also went on to point out the double standards applied to different communities: "We should not label the whole group with one person, like if somebody has done wrong we say that person did wrong. The same thing happened in Oklahoma – we should not say that all of the Christians [are like] Timothy McVeigh, who hates everybody and wants to kill everybody."

Azar Syed, Mr Hassan's associate at the British Columbia Muslim Association, believes that, while it hasn't yet become a major issue for the community, "off and on CSIS have been intruding into different people at times, not in a big way, but still people are on the list, they are monitored, that kind of thing is happening after 9/11." His comments betrayed a view of security practices, such as surveillance, as quite normalized and matter-of-fact. Expressing similar ideas and concerns, community organizer Ahmed Abdulkadir stated that while he has personally not encountered any issues related to security, "I know my brother-in- law and others are continuously going through the process at the airport. For some people, it's becoming the norm and it has been agitating them." After raising the issues that Muslims face related to security practices in Canada in the post-9/11 environment, Ahmed Abdulkadir recognized that there were efforts under the Trudeau government to reform security practices and elements of C-51: "the public safety minister [Ralph Goodale] came for a consultation and talked about how to change the system ... if you are not a terrorist you can remove your name from the database – and this is an idea that is very much welcomed from the community."

Presenting a mixed perspective, an anonymous interviewee, a Somali community leader from Ontario, spoke of some concerns related to security practices but also the responsiveness of specific law enforcement agencies to individual concerns: "You see some members of the community complaining about being stopped at airports and things like that – the no-fly lists. A friend of mine experienced that sort of thing, [but] he went to the RCMP and met with them and they cleared him. They treated him very well, with respect – so I think it's sort of a mixed thing – overall the relationship is good – you just have these incidents."

Another anonymous interviewee, the head of a Muslim cultural association, believed there was a "moderate" level of concern in the Muslim community in Canada over security. Referring specifically to the measures of the Anti-terrorism Act he recounted, "I think overall yes, that is a concern that has been there, and sometimes it has manifested itself in terms of new legislation, in profiling anyone with a Muslim name." Soraya Hafez, a president of the Canadian Council of Muslim Women, also recounted some concerns over security practices: "People are worried because we hear about people being arrested and not charged and they stay in prison for a long time with no respect to civil rights or human rights ... so people worry a lot about that."

Ahmed Shoker, director at the Canadian Islamic Congress, directly experienced security measures when he was denied the right to fly. He remarked in relation to his experience, "It's a problem ... the fear that there are unequal treatments towards Muslims." Yasmeen Nisam, a lawyer, noted that even for Muslims who do not experience security measures directly, they may at least know someone who has: "There's this no-fly list – there are certain names there and if unfortunately you have the same name you'll be detained every single time. And in fact, my brother-in-law was detained once at the airport, until they could figure out that he had no such connections with any terrorist organization. But that's a real major concern, and another concern with the anti-terrorist legislation – on any *reasonable* ground you can be detained – that's very scary because they don't really define 'reasonable.' Civil liberties are a concern as far as our community is concerned."

Shaykh Zak, a Muslim chaplain, also expressed concerns over profiling and the actions of security agencies: "The concerns are still there, and the attitude is still there from the organizations. You hear how names of Canadians are being passed to the United States. The way that CSIS and the RCMP are operating ... everybody is leery about them, and I say rightfully so. The general attitudes of these organizations call for our suspicion for sure." Dalal Daoud, of the Canadian Islamic Congress, expressed a great deal of concern over how the Canadian government had handled security after 9/11:

I feel like in general after September 11 the Muslim community living in the West have been victimized ... when something like this happens – the Charter of Rights and Freedoms exists to support the most vulnerable people – because of 9/11 they are the most vulnerable, and I feel like you should take extra measures to assure them, to guarantee them their rights. But I felt like the government went the opposite way and again that creates that sense of isolation. Muslims are still worried, there is still some fear, and that's unfortunate, because the government should have [undertaken] measures to make them feel safe and secure, and not to make them feel as outsiders, that they don't belong.

Similarly, Soraya Hafez expressed her disappointment that the Canadian government has not done more to protect the civil liberties of Canadian Muslims: "I don't hear about the government doing anything to let the Muslim community know that there is respect for their civil rights."

As indicated by these findings, Canadian Muslims express some concern over being targeted with the security measures that were put into place after 9/11. Furthermore, interviewees expressed a general sentiment that the former Conservative government was not doing enough to protect the civil liberties they are afforded as Canadians. To explore these experiences further, the analysis will turn to some of the most publicized examples of the potentially negative effects of Canadian security practices on Canadian Muslims: the cases of Maher Arar and Omar Khadr.[79]

The Maher Arar Case

The case of Maher Arar offers arguably the most publicized example of the detrimental effects of Canadian security practices on Canadian Muslims. Arar was born in Syria but immigrated to Canada as a teenager; he became a Canadian citizen and later worked as a telecommunications engineer. In 2002, while returning to Canada from a vacation, he was detained in the United States. Subsequently, while in American custody, Arar was deported and transferred to Syrian custody by American law enforcement, at least partially because of information provided by Canadian security officials to American security agencies. He was detained in Syria for more than a year and tortured.[80]

Arar's ordeal has been tied to post-9/11 security practices that resulted in the profiling of Muslim Canadians. In part, this was the findings of a public review of Arar's experience by the O'Connor commission led by the associate chief justice of Ontario, Dennis O'Connor. The report that came out of that inquiry concluded that Arar did not engage in criminal terrorist activities and was therefore innocent, and that Canadian officials had most likely provided incriminating information to US officials, information that helped them to decide to transfer him to Syria where he was subsequently tortured.[81]

Following the recommendations of the commission, Arar received a public apology and CDN$10.5 million in monetary compensation. The apology letter issued by then Prime Minister Stephen Harper read, "On behalf of the Government of Canada, I wish to apologize to you, Monia Mazigh and your family, for any role Canadian officials may have played in the terrible ordeal … please rest assured that this government will do everything in its power to ensure that the issues raised by Commissioner O'Connor are addressed."[82]

The United Nations Committee against Torture also drew attention to the role of security legislation and Canadian security practices in contributing to the violations of Arar's rights as a Canadian citizen; specifically, the committee condemned Canadian government "complicity" in torture and other human rights violations.[83] In addition, the report cited several individual cases of deportation that took place after the Arar case (some individuals were reportedly tortured in the same prison in Syria), including Muayyed Nureddin, Abdullah Almalki, and Ahmad Abou El Maati. The United Nations report cited earlier findings from the public Canadian Iacobucci inquiry, which looked into claims that these individuals had been taken to Syria and tortured and found that Canadian officials had "indirectly" contributed to at least two individuals' detention and torture.[84]

Arar's case provides evidence of the potentially negative ramifications of Canadian security practices and the targeted treatment that Canadian Muslims citizens can receive. The case also draws attention to problems with information sharing and oversight in Canadian security agencies. According to Murphy, "the very public exposure of the role of security and policing in the Maher Arar case graphically illustrated the potential for errors and abuses of unaccountable security-based powers."[85] It is worth noting that similar issues and concerns are still being raised by civil liberties advocates and Muslim civil society groups in relation to the expansion of security powers through Bill C-51.

As Abu-Laban and Nath demonstrate in their analysis of media and state discourse on the Arar case between 2002 and 2007, Arar was dynamically portrayed as both a Syrian/Muslim (foreigner/extremist) and a Canadian citizen in media accounts.[86] As Arar's case moved from his early incarceration to his release and his wrongful detention became more publicly apparent, Arar's identity, his citizenship, shifted from Syrian/Muslim to Canadian citizen in public discourses.[87] As discussed in chapter 3, according to Abu-Laban and Dhamoon, in periods of acute insecurity particular identity groups have been framed as dangerous foreigners, resulting in the blurring of the boundaries of citizenship and belonging.[88]

Arar's experience demonstrates how security practices have resulted in some individuals being framed as dangerous foreigners, much to the detriment of their rights as citizens. From this perspective, the Arar case provides an example of how xenoracism may operate through securitized discourses, policies, and practices. As Fekete observed in the case of Britain, anti-terrorism legislation "set the seal on xenoracism" as security became another institutional channel through which the ideology can operate.[89]

However, the institutional response to the Arar case – the public inquiry and the apology that followed – indicates that some institutional redress is available within the bounds of the Canadian multicultural state. As Abu-Laban and Nath conclude, Arar's experience demonstrates the potentially negative racialization that Canadian Muslims face but also highlights some institutional reflexivity in Canada: "It is meaningful that Maher Arar found an important and particular form of resolution within the bounds of the Canadian liberal democratic multicultural state – this avenue of resort would not necessarily be available in other state formations."[90]

Despite the damage that was inflicted on Arar and his family, the ability of the Canadian government to address the mistake in a way that promoted public inquiry, an apology, and compensation can be viewed as the continued institutional responsiveness of the multicultural state. By comparison, the experience of Omar Khadr provides a quite different example of the responsiveness of the government, where the logic of security overrode any considerations of liberal individual rights and the rights of a Canadian minor.

The Omar Khadr Case

As Drury rightfully observes, "the story of Omar Khadr is a tragedy in the classic Greek sense of the term."[91] Omar is the son Ahmed Khadr and his wife Maha el-Samnah (who had emigrated from Egypt in the 1970s); he was born in 1986 in the Greater Toronto Area. The Khadrs are a highly transnational family who regularly relocated between Afghanistan, Pakistan, and Canada during Omar's child-hood.[92] Members of his family, in particular his deceased father, were actively engaged in terrorist activities. Ahmed Khadr was closely associated with Osama bin Laden and was understood to be a senior member of al-Qaeda.

In 2002, at the age of 15, Omar Khadr was indoctrinated by his family into militant Islamism and subsequently sent for weapons training in Afghanistan.[93] By July of that year, in the context of the US invasion of Afghanistan, Omar Khadr was captured in a firefight where he was accused of killing a US combat army medic and Delta Force member, Sergeant Christopher Speer. Khadr was eventually transferred to the American military prison at Guantanamo Bay and he remained in custody there until September 2012.

During this period, the Canadian government made little effort to repatriate Khadr from Guantanamo (unlike other Western states including Australia and Britain, which actively repatriated their citizens) despite having extraterritorial jurisdiction to prosecute Khadr in domestic courts.[94] Moreover, during this period it has been reported that Khadr was tortured: first at Bagram air base in Afghanistan after his capture and later at Guantanamo. According to Amnesty International, Khadr was subjected to sleep deprivation and disruption under a technique known as the frequent flyer program.[95]

In 2010 Khadr was convicted of a variety of war crimes including the murder of Sergeant Speer and sentenced to 40 years in prison. However, under a bilateral agreement with the United States, Khadr was later repatriated to Canada and his sentence reduced to 8 years.[96] In April 2015 he was granted bail pending the outcome of an appeal in the United States. The former Conservative government appealed the decision to grant Khadr bail, but the Liberal government later dropped that appeal, resulting in his release from prison in Alberta.[97]

According to Knight and McCoy, the detention, arrest, and trial of Khadr represents what can best be described as a highly unorthodox legal proceeding, shaped by the extraordinary legal environment that has followed 9/11, against a minor.[98] The case can be seen as highly unorthodox for several reasons. For instance, Khadr's conviction represents the first prosecution of a child soldier since the Nuremberg Trials after the Second World War and the first case of an individual being tried and convicted of a battlefield murder in Afghanistan.[99] Further, the legal proceedings involving Khadr were in direct violation of a number of international customary and criminal laws related to child soldiers that Canada has signed and ratified: this includes the United Nations Convention on the Rights of the Child and its 2000 Optional Protocol to the Involvement of Children in Armed Conflict.[100]

Despite the Canadian government's responsibilities under international law, the Conservative government failed to advocate for a Canadian citizen who was a minor at the time of his offence and purposely allowed him to remain in detention in the extra-legal environment of Guantanamo Bay. This course of action singled out Canada as the only Western state that has failed to lobby for a citizen's release from the prison. On this point Khadr's lawyer Dennis Edney states, "And do we ever consider why no American charged with a terrorism offence has been sent to Guantanamo Bay? Or why all Western nations except Canada refused to allow their detainees to remain in Guantanamo Bay, and demanded their release from Guantanamo which was granted?"[101]

According to Edney, the trial, plea, and repatriation were heavily influenced by the Canadian government. He believes that the Conservative government "got what it wanted, it wanted to eviscerate the character of Mr Khadr before he arrives in Canada."[102] Recognizing the Conservative government's complicity in what Khadr was subjected to and its unwillingness to advocate for his return, Edney bluntly surmises, "Guantanamo is a place good enough for a young Canadian Muslim who has been there since the age of fifteen."[103]

How do we explain the ignoring of international and domestic norms and laws by the former Conservative government in the case of Omar Khadr? For Edney, part of this answer is clear – "Islamophobia," in both the United States and Canada. On this matter he states, "Anti-Muslim sentiment is not limited solely to the United States but is also alive and well in Canada."[104] Others have attributed the government's actions to Omar's family. For instance, in a 2008 address to the Moynihan Institute of Global Affairs, University of Toronto law professor Audrey Macklin linked the government's actions to the "Khadr effect," by which she was referring to the longstanding public and government distaste for the Khadr family because of a long history of inflammatory rhetoric from family members in the media and controversial dealings between the family and the Canadian government.[105]

There is little doubt that Omar Khadr, who at the time of writing was 30 years old and has spent more than a third of his life in prisons, has suffered from guilt by association with his family. Arguably the Khadr family became the public face of "Muslim extremism" for the

Canadian public much in the same way that the infamous, hook-handed cleric Abu Hamza took on a similar role in Britain. However, these associations should not have influenced his treatment or led to the violation of his individual rights as a Canadian citizen and minor.

As a citizen and as a minor, Khadr was abandoned by the state, his rights were stripped away under domestic and international law, and he was vilified by the government through guilt by association with his family. The Canadian state ignored not only his domestic rights (such as chapter 15 of the Charter, which promises equal treatment under Canadian law) but also international legal conventions such as the United Nations Convention on the Rights of the Child.[106] The Canadian government's decision to allow Khadr to remain in the extra-legal space of Guantanamo Bay as an "alien" and to actively undermine public perceptions of a juvenile is a clear example of xenoracism in Canada.

Edney is particularly condemning on this point and casts the blame for Khadr's plight beyond the government to the failure of civil society as a whole: "The story of Omar and Guantanamo Bay reflects the failure of civil society, its institutions, and its people to speak out in ensuring our shared values of a just society are carried out. When we cave in to fear and apathy, when we fear to speak out in opposition, there are no longer boundaries between state action and impermissible behavior."[107] For one interviewee the Khadr case was an example of the double standards that the Canadian government employs when dealing with Canadian Muslims. Ali Maher Shawwa, a retired Muslim chaplain, had this to say about Khadr: "The Canadian reaction at the government level is really unacceptable. This is a Canadian citizen; [Canada] should stand by him." Speaking in the context of the Arar and Khadr cases, other outstanding cases related to the treatment of Canadian citizens abroad, and the Canadian government's inconsistent advocacy for Canadian Muslims, Ahmed Abdulkadir observed, "The perception of the communities – both Somali and Muslim communities – is that if a Somali or Muslim individual is being arrested outside of Canada – they do not receive the same advocacy as a white person – case and point is Bashir Makhtal who has been in Ethiopian prison for over 10 years. By comparison when two white Canadians were arrested in an African country they were released in 24 hours – there was a lot of media attention."

As Nesbitt-Larking has pointed out, while cases like those of Arar and Khadr may be relatively rare, the effects of these cases can be quite detrimental on the Canadian Muslim community: "They have exerted a powerful impact, and rendered the task of sustaining inter-community communication, trust, and respect more challenging than it otherwise would have been."[108]

In the summer of 2017 a new chapter was written in the Omar Khadr saga as the Liberal government under Justin Trudeau contro-versially offered Khadr a $10.5 million settlement, thereby matching the payout received by Arar. Tapping into the resulting public anger over the settlement, the Conservative Party, under its new leader, Andrew Scheer, was quick to condemn the payout, stating that "Canadians know this is wrong."[109] The settlement was accompanied by a public apology that recognized the violation of Khadr's rights under the Canadian Charter of Rights and Freedoms. For some, these actions will bring a sense of closure, but the resulting public anger over the settlement and the Conservative Party's indication that they will probably use it as a point of contention in future politicking demonstrates how the "Khadr effect" remains as pertinent now as it was in the 2000s.

SECURITIZATION AND THE SOCIETAL SECURITY FEEDBACK LOOP

The cultural anthropologist Talal Asad has aptly described how Muslims have been portrayed in the contemporary security climate: "In the contemporary era, where the politics of unease explicitly imbricates state security with integration governance and immigra-tion control, the Muslim is a figure of fluid transnationality and potential 'disloyalty,' neither entirely alien but alienating and dis-integrated, fusing the past failures of multiculturalism with the current exigencies and anxieties of immigration politics. It is not just that future 'Muslim migration' can be designated a security threat, but that the Muslim is a metonymy for undesirable non-Western migra-tion, for bad diversity.[110]

Asad's comment draws out many of the key themes of this book. He identifies how at the centre of the failure of multiculturalism nar-rative, at the centre of calls for the assimilation of the non-integrated "other," and at the centre of societal security speech acts are targeted Muslim communities.

Peripherally, some analyses from immigration and integration stud-ies have identified the negative effects of securitized immigration and integration policy on Muslim communities. For example Cesari, in her research on the experience of French Muslims, identified what she saw as a counter-reaction to securitized public policy: "These policies are not only compounding the negative feelings of many Western Europeans towards Muslims but are also reinforcing a tendency for Muslims to use Islam in a defensive or reactive way."[111] Similarly, as Eisenberg and Kymlicka note, in the context of identity politics, when groups are not accommodated or are faced with demands to reform cultural practices, "identity politics can trigger a cultural defensiveness or reactivism, which also reinforces the power of conservative elites who will encourage group members to strictly adhere to traditional markers of identity to shield the group from pressures exerted on it from outsiders."[112]

The suggestion here is that discrimination and targeted public policy related to security and integration are driving Muslim communities into "defensive" and "reactive" religious identities and that such measures strengthen conservative and isolationist religious identity groups. This idea was explored briefly earlier in the book in relation to the idea of Muslim communities and diasporic tendencies in the post-9/11 environment.

To explore this idea further we can return to some of the observations of race and racism theorists. As found in this area of study, individuals who are subject to racism may adopt and use ideas of race to organize strategies for resistance. For example, this phenomenon was identified by Miles in historical movements such as Black Power, and associated groups like the Black Panthers, in the United States, where racialized minorities turned a marker of difference employed in racist narratives, as assigned by the majority culture, into an identity of empowerment and militancy.[113] Fellow race and racism scholar David Goldberg believes that racialized groups may begin to internalize stereotypes "to act against the stereotyping ascriptions as to act on them, to act them out."[114] Relating this idea to religious identity, Eid has highlighted how Muslims in Quebec who are struggling with discrimination find it difficult to dissociate experiences with discrimination from their Muslim identity.[115]

In a case of societal security, one culture, for example a cultural or national community, designates another culture as a threat to their continued existence as a culturally distinct nation – as a threat to the nation's ability to maintain a certain set of values, practices, and characteristics. Such a threat is framed by elites (e.g., politicians and community leaders) as a crisis requiring emergency measures to address it. This atmosphere of crisis may exacerbate societal divisions as identity groups fall back on narrower symbolic conceptions of national, religious, and cultural identity, further fragmenting already divided societies.

Of course this scenario can be inversed as minority communities, and their elites, may portray coercive projects of integration as a threat to their ability to maintain a certain set of values and practices. Such claims, or "speech acts," gain greater resonance in an atmosphere of crisis. And, of course, since 2001 the West has experienced the War on Terror, homegrown terrorism, the most severe economic crisis since the Great Depression, what has been portrayed as a demographic crisis in some European states (for instance, by the European far right and the anti-Islamic social movement), and the emergence of a significant new terrorist threat emanating from the aftermath of American interventionism, the Arab Spring, the Syrian Civil War, and the emergence of the so-called Islamic State. With these multiple crises and events in mind, it should be of no surprise that some individuals . and groups are falling back on more exclusivist and "traditional" forms of social identity.

Moreover, today another influence may be stimulating the development of more reactive and essentialist identities: globalization, a trend that is driven by increasing economic interconnectedness and that generates more diffuse patterns of migration. Globalization has helped to bring about increasingly multicultural societies and has made us more aware of similarities and differences related to culture and other forms of identity. Sociologist Stuart Hall points out that globalization can "have the effect of contesting and dislocating the centered and 'closed' identities of national culture. It does have a pluralizing impact on identities, producing a variety of possibilities and new positions of identifications, and making identities more positional, more political, more plural and diverse."[116] Here Hall is speaking of globalization stimulating the emergence of hybrid and transnational identities.

At the same time, globalization may have the opposite effect. Some identities have gravitated toward what Robins calls "tradition ... attempting to restore their former purity and recover the unities and certainties which are felt as being lost."[117] In this sense globalization can be seen as producing contradictory social forces: the emergence of multicultural societies and transnational identities but also exclusive and "essentialist" traditions. Writing in 1996, Hall identified resurgent Eastern European nationalism and religious fundamentalism as examples of the essentialist reaction to globalization.[118] Therefore, what Hall identified at the time, years before these social forces were to make their full weight known on the world stage, are the reactionary forces generated by globalization: exclusivist social movements associated with the far right and militant religious-political groups.

Religious identities may display diasporic impulses that are said to be a response to experiences with discrimination.[119] These larger forms of identity offer solidarity and unity during times of crisis and when other avenues, identities, and ideas of belonging are blocked. According to Baha Abu-Laban, a professor of sociology and a member of the Canadian Muslims sample group, "When the going gets tough, when the community is under attack ... even if they don't know very much about Islam, they become protective and they retreat and they feel alienated from the larger community ... this is a case of loyalty resurfacing ... Take the pressure away – it dissipates."

An example of one of these defensive identity reactions may be found in some variants of political Islam. Indeed, this identity can be seen as one of the few available counter-hegemonic identities available to individuals today. As Sivanandan notes, Today there are no great working-class movements, no Third World revolutions. There is no cohering ideology that transcends national boundaries, like socialism. Hence the struggles against immiseration, against dictatorships, against foreign occupation, grow up around religion, 'the sigh of the oppressed'... And in the interstices of these movements arise their distortions: fundamentalism."[120]

Certain literalist variants of Islam, for example those related to Salafism and Wahhabism, offer empowered identities that may attract young marginalized Muslims and disaffected religious converts who feel as though the interpretation's clear and resolute religious message promotes a sense of confidence.[121]

Faced with xenoracism and associated alienation and marginalization from the host society, a minority of Western Muslims seek the insularity and protection of these exclusivist religious communities. Young Muslims in the West today have experienced their formative years in the post-9/11 environment with its attendant War on Terror, numerous Western interventions in the Muslim world, and a steady stream of global terrorist attacks in the name of Islam. In this environment, their identity has been shaped by some of the political and media narratives that shape our understanding of conflict and global politics.[122]

Feelings of alienation can be particularly resonant for some second-generation Western Muslims who occupy a challenged space in terms of national and social belonging, where they do not quite fit in with the cultural identity of their parents and grandparents and, because of experiences with discrimination and xenoracism, do not quite fit into the society in which they were born, raised, and educated. Transnational social identity movements, such as what can be found in some militant Islamist groups, can offer alternative identities, alternative belongings for these dislocated individuals. In one recent review of radicalization literature, Hafez and Mullins identified how the "reactive religiosity" of some second- and third-generation European Muslims, and their experiences with discrimination and isolation in European societies, can explain why some "have found a home in the global jihadist movement, including becoming foreign fighters."[123]

Thus, there is a reinforcing relationship between exclusivist social identity movements as far-right political parties and the anti-Islamic social movement stimulate isolationist tendencies and strengthen conservative and militant Islamist identity groups. In turn, the growth of conservative and isolationist religious movements legitimizes the narratives, the raison d'être for the reactionary forces of the right. Thus, in short, this relationship represents a societal security feedback loop.

Moreover, there may be a catch-22 in some Western security policies. Preventing an attack may be essential to avoiding the more egregious forms of societal and national security, yet the preventive measures ascribed to under current security practices may drive some individuals closer to the margins of society: for example, the assimilative and securitized integration approaches that only serve to further marginalize transnationally situated Muslim communities.

The profiling and targeting of communities in current national security policies directly calls into question the belonging and loyalty of Muslim communities, challenging their status as residents and citizens. On this vicious circle Van Munster observes, "As a result, the work of securing a community must constantly secure itself anew, as reassuring practices may generate new insecurities. Hence, from a political perspective, the management of fear and misgivings through security practices is not necessarily a strategy for success."[124]

This idea of a security feedback loop is not unlike the security dilemma as understood in the sub-discipline of international relations. According to Jervis, a security dilemma exists when one state's attempt to increase its own security – for instance, through the acquisition of armaments – causes another state to question its own security and take actions to increase its security in kind. The state that first sought to increase its own security, for example for purely defensive reasons, may want to consider that other state actors may view such actions as aggressive and respond in kind, a response that promotes conflict and fails to achieve the original goal of the state: security.[125]

Roe has directly applied the idea of the security dilemma to societal security, noting that in projects of nation building that seek to establish a more culturally homogenous or unifying concept of national identity, for example within a culturally plural state, the result of such policies can be the stimulation of increasingly adversarial cultural identities.[126] The majority culture that sought to reassert its identity in the face of perceived threats from "competitors" fails to achieve a sense of security: instead, social fragmentation and conflicts only worsen. From this understanding, approaches to societal security found in some European states today are not only problematic but also self-defeating.

CONCLUDING REMARKS

This chapter has shown how in the post-9/11 era, issues of societal and national security have coalesced around Muslim communities in the West. Fears over homegrown terrorism, over the domestic enemy within, have combined with fears of unintegrated communities. The findings discussed in this chapter and the previous one indicate that immigration and integration policies in Canada have not experienced the kind of securitization seen in some Western European states. There is no compelling societal security narrative or speech act in Canada related to Muslim communities. Outside of some of the narratives that surrounded the 2015 federal election, there are few detectable societal security speech acts. It is noteworthy that security policy has not been explicitly intertwined with newcomer integration in Canada; this is another box that can be checked in the list of trends that Canada has dodged in the crisis of multiculturalism.

But, and this is a significant *but*, Canadian governments have adopted certain national security practices in the post-9/11 environment that may be harmful to Canadian Muslim communities. In relation to national security, the preventive logic of contemporary counterterrorism generates surveillance, profiling, and security measures that challenge the civil liberties of Canadian Muslims. The former Conservative government established a new normal when it comes to security. The renewal and expansion of measures contained in Bill S-7 and the considerably expanded scope of counterterrorism powers under Bill C-51 signal the Canadian government's willingness to deal with the threat of terrorism in Canada, despite the costs and challenges to Canadian values and individual rights.

Since 9/11 Muslims have been disproportionately targeted with these measures as they face differential treatment on the basis of religious identity. As indicated by the comments of the interviewees, Canadian Muslims experience considerable anxiety over Canadian security practices. Several interviewees expressed their disappointment that the Canadian government had not protected the constitutional rights to which they are entitled as Canadian citizens in a multicultural state. The glaring injustices suffered by Omar Khadr and Maher Arar most clearly challenge the perception among Canadian Muslims that Canada is a fair and just state for all Canadians.

The events of October 2014 generated a reactive security response that culminated not only in the passing of C-51 but also the creation of more developed approaches to counter-radicalization. While the Canadian government and the RCMP have moved slowly and cautiously on these programs, only time will tell if these efforts can avoid some of the issues seen in other states, in particular in Britain. After 15 years of post-9/11 security, bonds of trust have been strained and sometimes broken between Canadian Muslim communities and the Canadian government and its security agencies. These bonds will have to be carefully and slowly rebuilt, and there are legitimate questions about whether this can be accomplished without reforms to the Anti-terrorism Act, improved dialogue between securitized communities and the government, and greater independent oversight of national security practices.

Co-operation and reciprocity and some quid pro quo between Canadian Muslim communities and security agencies will be essential for the success of Canadian counterterrorism efforts. For example, municipal, provincial, and federal law enforcement should be more responsive to complaints of hate crimes and xenoracism in Canadian Muslim communities. In the inherently secretive world of counterterrorism it is difficult to create a balance between positive community policing and more blatantly targeted, exploitative, and uncooperative practices. As Spalek recognizes, on contemporary approaches to counterterrorism, "communities may perceive and experience police and community engagement as intelligence gathering exercises with little sense of dialogue and exchange; communities may perceive themselves to be the targets of state control, reinforcing them as 'suspect communities.'"[127] In the current social and political climate, contemporary security practices and community policing can easily reach an oversaturation point where trust-building efforts are overwhelmed by feelings of mutual suspicion. At this point, community policing becomes intrusive, unethical, and often counterproductive.

Furthermore, what has been identified here as the societal security feedback loop is of particular concern to those engaged with security in Canada, and indeed in much of the Western world. Marginalization and alienation caused by current security practices have been combined with the fragmenting tendencies of globalization to create oppositional social identity movements that sit at the heart of the crisis of multiculturalism: the anti-Islamic social movement and conservative/isolationist religious groups. In the former's calls for assimilation or deportation of a minority deemed to be problematically and dangerously foreign to the national ideal, the latter finds good reason to pursue further isolationism, only furthering the logic of exclusion.

A small minority of conservative religious communities and far-right groups may espouse extremist and even violent rhetoric as they seek alternative ideas and identities that can challenge the perceived hostility of their defined enemy. For militant Islamists in particular, in movements like the so-called Islamic State and al-Qaeda, which have defined themselves through experiences of invasion, prosecution, torture, and injustice, this rationale is particularly resonant.[128] A relative handful of these individuals have turned to violence and terrorism, resulting in the conformation of the anti-Islamic social movement's worst fears, legitimizing their calls for urgent action to address the societal and national threat to security, with expediency.

What is increasingly clear is that states such as Canada need to rethink security strategies in a way that maintains the successful elements of its systems of multiculturalism, integration, and immigration – policies that, despite all the damage wrought over the past decade, continue to hold appeal for a majority of Canadians. There should be recognition that some of the current security strategies are by their very nature self-defeating. As argued by this author, "In the end, security concerns should be left to the security services and the judiciary. For those who use Canada as a safe haven for extremist activity, or for those who have chosen to advocate violence, the answer is not changing our traditions of accommodation or dismantling multiculturalism. Rather, it is law enforcement carried out under the banner of a just and fair society."[129]

8

Conclusion

This book started with a question: Has Canada bucked the trend in relation to the crisis of multiculturalism? By focusing on xenoracism and specific areas of public policy where the crisis is most apparent in the Western world, it sought to unearth the potential vulnerabilities and failings of the Canadian model. Prior scholarship has looked at outcomes and experiences of Canadian Muslims in specific policy areas: for example, in relation to immigration and settlement. By comparison, this work took a more holistic approach and examined the concomitant and overlapping impacts within different policy spheres, especially integration and security. This approach allowed for a more robust assessment of Canadian multiculturalism and the experience of Muslims therein. Ultimately, this is what makes this book unique.

It drew on the experiences and opinions of a diverse array of leaders in the Canadian Muslim community, allowing them to inform the reader about their perspectives, concerns, hopes, and ideas. Through this exercise the author cut to the heart of the crisis of the politics of diversity in the West and in Canada and to the heart of what is being presented publicly by some politicians, alarmists, and the media as a primary reason for the so-called demise of multiculturalism. What was exposed in the narrative of the failure of multiculturalism is that Muslim communities are taking much of the blame for the policy's failure. When the layers are peeled off the crisis, what is revealed is a very particular form of racism.

From outward appearances, Canada, the original multicultural state, may appear to be the exception to the crisis. Among the political mainstream there is no "failure of multiculturalism" narrative. The far right, which is threatening to ascend to political power in countries across Europe and holds sway in the United States under the Trump administration, is relegated to the fringes of Canadian party politics, civil society, and online forums. An increasingly diverse Canadian society remains largely supportive of immigration and multicultural- ism and, perhaps most importantly in terms of the future of the policy, young Canadians express high levels of support for multiculturalism and demonstrate a degree of comfort with cultural and ethnic diversity that has not been previously known in the country.

Critically for this analysis, despite some negative experiences, Canadian Muslim communities remain remarkably resilient in the face of numerous manifestations of xenoracism; they have responded positively to numerous incidents and adversities and report high levels of belonging to Canada. In Canada, the rapid expansion of post-9/11 security has not yet overshadowed the priorities of settlement and civic, linguistic, and economic integration that have for decades defined the Canadian model of diversity and immigration. Thus, when com- pared with its peers in Western Europe and elsewhere, Canada stands apart. Canada *is* the exception.

Some will think this assessment optimistic, even wildly so. Pessimists, sceptics, and some eternally critical scholars will point to the divisive legacy of the Harper years and the 2015 election campaign, the con- troversies around Shari'a law and the niqab, and some of the vitriolic debate surrounding the admission of refugees from the Syrian Civil War. They will point to the symbolic manipulation of Canadian citi- zenship under the Harper Conservatives, the post-9/11 security prac- tices, and the obvious xenoracism that exists in segments of Canadian society, civil society, and politics. They will point to the direct experi- ence of a sizable minority of Canadian Muslims with discrimination and xenoracism. They will point to the antagonistic rhetoric found on Facebook, Twitter, and other social media platforms and "feeds" around discussions of terrorism, refugees, and accommodation. They will point to some of the struggles of second-generation Canadians to find belonging in the Canadian cultural milieu, the spatial concen- tration of cultural groups around major urban centres, and anxieties over the growth in non-official languages in those neighborhoods. Some will point to the obvious economic priorities that have clearly shaped Canadian immigration and integration policy for decades.

Many of these are legitimate concerns. The challenges are many in an era of pronounced cultural and economic globalization. Here it is argued that the greatest challenge to the success that Canada has enjoyed in its approach to multiculturalism and integration thus far lies in the balancing of interests related to national security and liberal-multicultural rights. Furthermore, in an era where social and alternative media sources are increasingly supplanting traditional media, and individuals are often as connected to communities online as they are offline, Canadian borders do not represent a hard barrier to the hyperbole of a growing anti-Islamic social movement – a movement that is present, growing, and increasingly militant in Canada.

When we get down to brass tacks it is security, specifically the securitization of Muslim communities, that is the driving force behind the assimilationism and failure of the multiculturalism narrative in Western Europe. It is the language of national security, with its attendant expediency and extra-normality, that allows politicians and others to justify and advocate for the more dramatic reorganizations of immigration, integration, and multiculturalism policies witnessed on the other side of the Atlantic. It is the language of security and the perception of societal insecurity that has driven the growth of the far right, the anti-Islamic social movement, and its increasingly militant rhetoric and actions. In the end, to elucidate what differentiates the Canadian experience from these international trends it was necessary to employ the theoretical and conceptual lenses used by European and other international scholars, to see how they applied (or not) to the Canadian state.

These are the broad strokes and assertions of the book; they are assertions that rest on the evidence presented in the preceding chapters. The book will conclude with a brief examination of some key findings as it pulls the threads of the analysis together and draws out some modest policy recommendations.

UNDERSTANDING XENORACISM

The first priority for the book was to provide a better understanding of xenoracism, specifically the variant that targets Muslim communities. A review of the race and racism literature acted as a starting point for a more developed and nuanced understanding of a growing and increasingly resonant form of racism in the West. Among the key findings of this section were that racism is an ideology – one that is shaped by political power and priorities and one that is tempered by historical knowledge. In particular, racist ideologies have been shaped by colonial practices and the development of European national identities.

While racism and nationalism are not synonymous, certain variants and forms of nationalism, by their very nature, contain the foundations of a racist ideology. When defined in terms of biological uniqueness and/or cultural exclusivity, nationalism may be imbued with ideas of superiority – a hierarchical and relational idea of difference that is juxtaposed with other nations, cultures, and peoples. Indeed, highly exclusivist and exclusionary ideologies of ultra-nationalism and fascism have shaped our understandings of race and racism today. These ideologies are framed around ideas of "pure" and "superior" races, and when fascists used those ideas to justify acts like the Genocide of European Jews (and others) during the Second World War, the potential destructiveness of racist ideologies was demonstrated to the world. As Europe and emergent international organizations like the United Nations sought to prevent future conflict during the post-war period, they focused on creating norms and conventions that were specifically opposed to biological racism. For example, by the mid-1960s the United Nations had established its Convention on the Elimination of All Forms of Racial Discrimination to specifically target this form of racism.

In the first section of the book, the dynamic nature of racism and its interconnection with political power were borne out by a review of what Barker termed new racism, what has also been referred to in the race and racism literature as cultural racism. Barker most especially associated this form of racism with the divisive politics of the Thatcher era in Britain.[1] The key point here is this that by reframing the language of difference and diversity, by speaking in terms of cultural incompatibility rather than of race and racial superiority and inferiority, politicians were able to sanitize the language of racism. In turn, sanitized racism became a tool to justify immigration controls and limit the access of newcomers to the post-war welfare state, without specifically using the taboo language of biological racism.

The ideas outlined above were useful as they allowed for a better understanding of xenoracism that targets Muslims in Western states. As a dynamic and socially constructed ideology, racism does not necessarily have to be framed by the idea of race; racism can just as readily be mobilized through the language of cultural difference and dangers. Additionally, these findings demonstrate the distinctly institutional nature of racism – how the ideology could be framed and driven by political projects and discourse.

With this outline in mind, the book built on the pre-existing work of Liz Fekete and Ambalavaner Sivanandan and their understanding of xenoracism. Here xenoracism was identified as an institutionalized ideology that is not necessarily colour coded but instead constructed around ideas of foreignness. Drawing on Fekete's interpretation of xenoracism, the analysis focused on the variant that targets Muslim communities (including newcomers and long-standing residents) in the West.[2] For Fekete, Muslim communities had been caught up in the "expanding loop" of xenoracism as they joined asylum seekers, the Roma, and Eastern European economic migrants as the undesirable foreign "other" of Western Europe.

An essential point here is that xenoracism that targets Muslims is inseparable from the emergence of post-9/11 security policy – from both national and societal forms of security. Under the logic of preventive security, whole communities deemed to be at risk of radicalization and/or non-integration may be designated as the potential site of homegrown terrorism. This kind of threat assessment can then be used to justify a host of security practices from coercive "integration" policies, to expanded police powers, to enhanced surveillance, and, more recently, state-led counter-radicalization programs, like Prevent in the United Kingdom. As Fekete bluntly states, many of these security practices can be "shot through" with xenoracism.[3]

Then there are trends, related to the anti-Islamic social movement, that are often overlooked, underestimated, or misunderstood by scholars. Stimulated by the fears over cultural practices, extremism, and militancy among Muslim communities in the West, a growing anti-Islamic social movement has emerged and proliferated throughout the Western world, including in Canada. The fears and conspiracy theories that define that movement are horizontally dispersed via social media and vertically dispersed through the political parties and platforms of the far right: from the National Front in France to the Party for Freedom in the Netherlands. They are embedded in grassroots and vigilante cross-Atlantic movements like Patriotic Europeans against the Islamization of the West and the Soldiers of Odin.

Thus, as we see in its many reinforcing and overlapping layers, xenoracism is now firmly rooted in the West. It is apparent in the tweets and campaign-style speeches of President Donald Trump and others and in social and mainstream media. It is clear that these sentiments and narratives are not confined to the European continent. While xenoracism is an ideology that is increasingly part of contemporary politics, it is also an ideology that draws on historical experience and knowledge. Xenoracism that is centred on Muslim communities draws on a deep and centuries-old body of knowledge of the other – it draws on Orientalism. The key observance here is that contemporary representations contained in xenoracism are ultimately the product of historically situated knowledge that is mediated by contemporary frames of reference. According to Said's theory of Orientalism, historical portrayals of Islam in the West have been shaped by oppositional, coercive, and reductive narratives and representations. In the works of Orientalists, Islam became representative of a counter-response to European modernity that is regressive and anti-democratic in nature: it became representative of the archetypal foreign other.[4]

In this sense, ideologies like xenoracism are legitimized by historical knowledge that assigns a timeless quality to social relations between Islam and the West. Today's updated form of Orientalism can, not surprisingly, be most commonly found among the works of Western security critics and professional anti-Islamic provocateurs. Individuals like Daniel Pipes, Bruce Bawer, Peder Nøstvold, and Robert and Richard Spencer present a range of societal and national security "speech acts" that problematize the position of Muslims and Islam in the West. These alarmists exist alongside a vast array of more nuanced writers and academics who are situated in security-, immigration-, and integration-related fields – those who work in universities and think tanks and are critical, at least in some form, of the presence of Islam and Muslims in the West.

Taken together, these observations lead to the conclusion that studies seeking to understand xenoracism in a particular setting must also be attuned to the ideology's genealogy and how knowledge related to Islam is replicated and (re)produced. In the end, the conceptual development of xenoracism in the book provides a more nuanced understanding of the ideology than what has been presented to date: a form of racism that has demonstrated significant influence over public policy in the early twenty-first century. With this understanding in mind, the book went on to examine Canadian Muslim communities and their often diverse experiences in Canada.

CANADIAN MUSLIM COMMUNITIES AND THEIR
EXPERIENCES WITH XENORACISM

A long-standing criticism of Western scholarship on Islam and Muslim communities has been that academics tend to portray Islam and Muslims as homogenous. However, building on a growing body of literature that is mindful of the heterogeneity of religious communities, the book presents a multifarious understanding of Canadian Muslims. In short, Canadian Muslims exhibit multiple belongings and varying degrees of religiosity and are members of culturally and linguistically diverse ethnic communities. This understanding runs counter to the facile generations of the anti-Islamic social movement. Even the most basic of analyses reveals that there is, of course, no one essential experience within *any* religious community, let alone a global religion with more than a billion-and-a-half members.

As revealed in the unpacking of the concept of diaspora, the idea of a Muslim diaspora is problematic on a number of levels. As Canadian Muslims come from no single territory there is no communal preference for any one homeland. Moreover, as indicated by the opinions of the interviewees, many Canadian Muslims view Canada as home, not a temporary place of residence: they define themselves as Canadian first. In today's day and age, ideas of transnationalism more aptly describe the Canadian Muslim experience, in that, like other minority communities with ties to outside cultures, to the cultures of their parents and grandparents, they operate between multiple countries and exhibit multiple belongings. Knight has referred to this as the experience of the sojourner.[5] For all of these reasons, "Muslim diaspora" is a problematic description of the community.

There is a qualification here, since as shown in the book some experiences *can* drive identity groups into broader and traditional camps of identity, such as a religion. Within a "diasporic impulse," individuals from varying ethnic communities may seek out others who share a religious identity and experiences with marginalization and alienation. When belonging to a host culture is challenged, when bridges between communities are blockaded, for example through experiences with discrimination, religion can become a defensive marker of identity where individuals seek empowerment and community. In this sense xenoracism can drive these diasporic impulses.

As the research findings reveal, 78 per cent of the Canadian Muslim sample group expressed concerns over racism and 47 per cent reported direct personal experience with some form of racism in Canada. Interviewees identified what they saw as a variety of potential reasons for their experience; some believed it was based on religion and others attributed it to racial factors. Unsurprisingly, interviewees believed that racism toward Muslims had grown as a source of discrimination in Canada since 9/11 and waxed and waned with local and international events (e.g., the Second Gulf War, the Maher Arar affair, the Shari'a law debate, the Toronto 18 plot, the 2015 federal election and associated political wedge issues surrounding Muslims, and the Syrian Civil War and the associated rise of the so-called Islamic State and Syrian refugee crisis).

According to the EDS and SMC data, which measured opinions and attitudes shortly after the 9/11 attacks, around the time of the Shari'a law debate in 2005, and around the time of the 2015 federal election, roughly one-third of Canadian Muslims experienced discrimination, and according to the EDS 37.5 per cent of Muslims "felt out of place" in Canada. Thus, both the sample group and statistical data revealed that a sizeable minority of Canadian Muslims experienced some form of racism (or discrimination as defined by the EDS and SMC).

A pertinent finding from the interview data was that while the Canadian Muslim interviewees viewed societal-level discrimination as an issue, it was generally viewed as a secondary problem; Canadian society was seen, on the whole, as a welcoming multicultural society. By comparison, especially during the Harper years, Canadian politicians, the Canadian government, and the media were viewed as being hostile toward Canadian Muslim communities, and many interviewees expressed the opinion that the government was purposely sowing societal discord and discrimination against Muslim communities. One caveat here is that in more recent years, with the growth of the anti-Islamic social movement in Canada and concerning trends like a significant increase in hate crimes and incidents targeting Muslims, there are some signs of heightened xenoracism among the Canadian public. The answer to the question of what is driving this trend is complex. However, the growth in hate-based activity online and the emergence of powerful political advocates for xenoracism internationally has undoubtedly had a knock-on effect in Canada.

Supporting an understanding of xenoracism as an ideology that is heavily politicized and institutionalized, the portrait of xenoracism that emerges in Canada, at least the one that is painted by the interviewees, is a form of racism that is driven from the top down. With this realization in mind, the book explored various institutions and policy areas previously implicated in the crisis of multiculturalism: it sought out possible manifestations of xenoracism in multicultural, newcomer integration, and security policy. Through exploring these areas of policy and the experience of Muslim communities therein, the book sought to answer the question of whether Canada represented an exception to the crisis.

MULTICULTURALISM AND MUSLIMS IN CANADA: THE OPTIMIST'S PERSPECTIVE

State multiculturalism in Canada can be seen as a successful model for a number of reasons. One point in favour of this view can be related to what Eisenberg and Kymlicka have called the Canadian state's "deep institutional memory."[6] After more than 40 years of official multiculturalism in Canada, the framework has become deeply embedded in the legal and political structures of the state, most especially through the Canadian Charter of Rights and Freedoms and the Canadian Multiculturalism Act. This constitutional and institutional entrenchment offers some protection from the crisis of multiculturalism, in that repeal would represent a daunting task for any government that might wish to oppose the policy framework on ideological grounds.

In addition, as was found in chapter 5, public support for multiculturalism is of particular importance to its success, as it encourages the longevity of the policy and offers another defence against hostile political forces. Indeed, the findings from the Environics surveys and most especially the 2012 survey by the Mosaic Institute and the Association of Canadian Studies (which found that 74 per cent of respondents between the ages of 18 and 24 years hold a positive view of multiculturalism) are noteworthy, as they suggest that Canadian multiculturalism enjoys considerable public support and will most probably continue to enjoy that support in the future.[7] Furthermore, the identified association between multiculturalism and national identity (as shown by Environics surveys) is also of importance, indicating that Canadian nationhood is tied to a vision of respect for cultural diversity.[8]

Another point in favour of multiculturalism in Canada is the fact that the policy was in part a response to the agency of what has been called the third force – minority communities that lobbied the Royal Commission on Bilingualism and Biculturalism in the 1960s to be recognized as part of the Canadian national mosaic. Therefore, multiculturalism in Canada was not just a strategy of the Liberal elite to manage bicultural conflict (although that was a significant part of it), it was also the result of conflict and compromise between Canada's established host cultures and an emerging alliance of minority communities. The multicultural framework offered these minorities an avenue to political recognition and resources that were previously unavailable.

Importantly, for this study, Canadian Muslim interviewees overwhelmingly expressed a favourable view of state multiculturalism in Canada. They viewed it as a defining and attractive part of the national identify that drew them in as immigrants and citizens. In terms of levels of social integration (which was primarily measured through EDS, SMC, and interview data and a sense of national belonging) Canadian Muslims compared favourably even with mainstream religious groups, with roughly 70 per cent expressing a strong sense of attachment to Canada.

In part, the strong sense of belonging felt by Canadian Muslims to the Canadian state may be explained by the Canadian approach to integrating newcomers. As a multicultural model of integration that has not adopted the assimiliationist approach now seen in states like the Netherlands, the Canadian approach to integration reinforces cultural pluralism and creates a space where newcomer and minority communities can maintain a nostalgic connection to the culture of their homeland, parents, and grandparents. Broad public support for multiculturalism and immigration in Canadian society not only presents a more welcoming vision of Canada, it also allows for more flexible standards for assessing newcomer integration; it is easier for newcomers to meet an acceptable threshold of integration. Furthermore, Canada's targeted approach to assimilation (in areas of language and civic participation) is viewed as consistent with a functional approach to inclusion that aims to further access to the civic, social, and economic life of the country.[9]

The positive observations related to the Canadian public's identification with multiculturalism as a defining part of national identity point to another reason for viewing state multiculturalism as a success. As an imagined community, to borrow Anderson's concept, a nation need not be imagined in exclusivist terms; rather, nations can be conceived in a way that reflects and embraces cultural differences.[10] This is of course the idea that is at the heart of official multiculturalism: the idea that the nation can be tied to a symbolic vision of cultural diversity. National identities can be inward or outward looking: they can be revisionist, seeking a return to a golden age, a restoration of prior imagined identity, or they can contain more pluralistic ideals. Hall recognizes this when he writes, "The discourse of national culture is thus not as modern as it may appear to be. It constructs identities which are ambiguously placed between past and future. It straddles the temptation to return to former glories and the drive to go forwards."[11]

Nationalism, as conceived of in Canada, is both "thinner," in that it is less defined and historically tied to any one cultural group, and more open, in that the multicultural identity of the state engenders a wider conception of identity in which newcomers from a diverse array of cultures can find symbolic meaning and belonging. As indicated by the findings on sense of national belonging and the enthusiasm shown by the Canadian Muslim sample group for multiculturalism, this vision of national identity is attractive to Canadian Muslim communities. A more open and welcoming conception of national identity has also been linked to higher levels of citizenship acquisition among immigrants. This was, for example, the conclusion of Bloemraad in her comparative study of citizenship in the United States and Canada.[12] Additionally, within a more open and welcoming vision of Canadian nationalism, an ideology like xenoracism, which targets its victims on the basis of the quality of foreignness, finds less fertile soil. As Foster has put it, multiculturalism has created a state where "the future is in the hands of the foreigners."[13]

Finally, the deep institutionalization of multiculturalism, the public support for multiculturalism, and the interlinkages between cultural pluralism and Canadian national identity have helped the Canadian state to avoid some of the more egregious forms of securitization of Muslim communities seen elsewhere. Critically, the blending of policy priorities related to newcomer integration and societal and national security has not taken place in Canada. Newcomer integration policy remains focused on priorities of initial settlement and linguistic and civic integration. Unlike what is found among the far right and anti-Islamic social movement in Western Europe and the United States, there is no societal security narrative or speech act in Canada, at least not one that has been able to mobilize the kind of public support that would be required to justify a crisis narrative on multiculturalism and Muslims. However, symptoms of these trends can be detected, especially in the final years of the Harper government and the 2015 federal election. These issues should give pause to any overly enthusiastic triumphalism related to Canadian multiculturalism.

MULTICULTURALISM AND MUSLIMS IN CANADA: THE PESSIMISTIC ASSESSMENT

At the beginning of the last section it was suggested that state multiculturalism benefits from institutional memory and the long-standing constitutional protection that the policy has enjoyed. However, as revealed by the former Conservative government's efforts to undermine aspects of the policy from within, these protections may be in some ways insufficient. Bureaucratic channels, in particular through the former Citizenship and Immigration Canada, offered an avenue for micromanaging ministers to tighten immigration and refugee requirements and dismantle or interrupt established aspects of the multiculturalism program, such as the anti-racism policy.

Lentin and Titley have used the idea of "rehabilitative action" to describe measures that have been presented by conservative politicians as necessary fixes to the social damage wrought by multiculturalism.[14] The former Conservative government's rehabilitative approach to immigration and multiculturalism policies was operationalized through the considerable powers afforded to the Conservatives through the offices of the Privy Council Office, the Prime Minister's Office, and a handful of trusted cabinet ministers. These observations indicate that a crisis narrative may not be necessary for governments to pursue an agenda that seeks to undermine aspects of state multiculturalism.

Another area of concern is the implications and long-term effects of the Conservative Party's nation-building project that began in 2011 and engaged in the symbolic manipulation of Canadian nationhood and national identity. That strategy promoted symbols of English Canadian identity, for example, the increased display of the Queen's portrait in government buildings and Royal designations for the military. Further, this vision of identity found its way into Canadian citizenship documents and examinations. In Bill C-24, which aimed to strip convicted dual-citizen terrorists of their citizenship, and through the mobilization of the niqab wedge issue around debates over citizenship (e.g., the Zunera Ishaq case), the Conservatives played on public anxieties over the accommodation of Muslims and fears over "Islamic extremism." Thus, they mobilized xenoracist rhetoric and policy.

Ultimately those wedge issues failed spectacularly as the Conservatives were routed by their traditional political foe – the Liberals, under the leadership of a Trudeau, no less. But it would be ill-advised to underestimate the impacts of these divisive initiatives on societal attitudes. Some will dismiss the Conservative strategy as largely symbolic. However, as shown in this book, when it comes to nationalism, symbolism is imperative – nations are constructed from symbols, myths, and legends. The symbolism fostered by the Conservatives was not the stuff of pure invention, rather it was grounded in Canada's British colonial heritage and history of conservative loyalism.

Therefore, it will take years, if not decades, to fully measure the impact of the Harper legacy on Canadian multiculturalism and Canadian Muslims, but there are already some grounds for concern. For example, as demonstrated by EKOS polling, the number of Canadians who believe there are "too many immigrants" in the country nearly doubled during the time the Conservatives were in power. The distressing 253 per cent increase in police-reported hate crimes against Muslims from 2012 to 2015 is also indicative of burgeoning xenoracist sentiment at the societal level.

The growth of the anti-Islamic social movement in Canada and the appearance of a host of explicitly anti-Islamic online and offline groups (e.g., Patriotic Europeans against the Islamization of the West, Soldiers of Odin, and numerous social media hate forums) provide further grounds for concern. A steady stream of mainstream and online news stories highlighting, among other things, fears over Syrians and other refugees from Muslim-majority states are constantly recycled and amplified through electronic mediums. With these trends in mind, it can be observed that xenoracism is buttressed from the top – from the populism and fearmongering of explicitly anti-Muslim politicians – and reinforced from the bottom by grassroots and civil society groups that replicate misinformed and inflated fears that have long coloured Western discourse on the Islamic other.

There is little doubt that in the contemporary environment, debates over the accommodation of religious minorities and values that may be opposed to liberal rights traditions in Canada will also continue to be an area of tension between Canadian Muslim communities, the host culture, and a variety of civil society groups. As evidenced by the Shari'a law debate in Ontario in 2005, the ongoing discussion of these issues, within the larger debates over social inclusion and integration, will take place in Canada much like they have taken place in Western Europe.

However, arguably the greatest test for Canadian multiculturalism policy will be around the issue of security and the ability or inability of the Canadian government to balance issues surrounding public safety with the responsibility to create an equitable and fair state for all Canadians. Canadian Muslim interviewees expressed a number of concerns over security practices that they believed negatively impacted their civil liberties. They expressed disappointment that the Canadian government had not granted them protection under the Charter rights to which they are entitled as Canadian citizens. As the cases of Maher Arar, Omar Khadr, and others reveal, once Canadian Muslims are suspected of extremist activity, no matter what their legal status as a citizen or as a minor, their rights can be rendered null and void: they become the dangerous foreigner and are subject to the extraordinary legal space of the War on Terror.

Several interviewees recounted direct or vicarious experiences with post-9/11 security practices in Canada: for example, through no-fly lists and surveillance. There were concerns that expanded powers under the various iterations of the *Canadian Anti-terrorism Act* were being unevenly applied to Canadian Muslim communities, resulting in the erosion of their rights. For many Canadian Muslims, national security practices had become, disturbingly, a fact of life – a normalized part of being a Muslim in Canada. The events of October 2014 and global trends in violent extremism related to the emergence of the so-called Islamic State in the failed states of the Middle East have only exacerbated these trends.

Furthermore, as suggested in the analysis of the negative feedback loop, some of the current security measures deployed in Western states may be self-defeating, producing a cycle of marginalization, extremism, violence, and renewed security measures. To an extent, security practices that exhibit xenoracism may be creating a self-fulfilling process. By isolating and vilifying certain religious groups, religion becomes a rallying call for the marginalized – most especially young people who are born and bred in Western societies yet do not feel as though they are given the same acceptance and access to resources as those born into "mainstream" communities.

In the end, there are persuasive cases to be made on both sides; optimists and pessimists on Canadian multiculturalism can draw on compelling arguments. However, in the next section the book will reiterate the case for viewing Canada as the exception to the crisis of multiculturalism.

FINAL THOUGHTS ON MULTICULTURALISM

In one of his many scholarly works on multiculturalism, Kymlicka explored two potential dangers to Canada's official policy. Writing in the early 2000s, he asked what would happen if the anti-multiculturalism then Canadian Alliance Party, now Conservative Party, came into power. Kymlicka believed that because of the multiculturalism policy's constitutional foundations and support in "deeper social forces" the model would remain robust.[15] To a large extent this prediction seems accurate. In particular, the importance of popular support cannot be underestimated in terms of the defence it offers. The kind of nation-building efforts put forward by Harper's Conservatives have failed, thus far, to find a receptive audience with the wider population, which supports a multicultural vision of the state. As long as the image of Canada as a nation of immigrants remains resonant with the Canadian public and its young people, the public repudiation of multiculturalism by democratically elected politicians seems highly unlikely.

A critical advantage that has protected the policy during the crisis of multiculturalism has been the Canadian vision of national identity, and although there is no papering over some of the deficiencies of the policy, at least as it stands today, and the historical legacies related to Indigenous rights and affairs, the shift from the bicultural to the multicultural vision has left Canada less encumbered by the pitfalls of ethnic nationalism. At the same time, it cannot be denied that Canada enjoys a number of advantages when it comes to its approach to its immigration and cultural diversity, some of which are not enjoyed by European countries: for example, geographic isolation from politically and socially unstable regions and the introduction of multiple generations of affluent and educated migrants under the selective points system. In this sense, the Canadian case is both exceptional and unique.

Simply put, there are considerable ramparts for the populists and anti-Islamic demagogues to overcome in Canada. However, a second hazard that Kymlicka identified in his writing is potentially far more destructive to state multiculturalism. In 2004 he predicted that societal securitization represents a major threat to Canada's accommodative policies: "If ethnic relations become securitized, then all bets are off, and the progress we have seen towards accommodating diversity may be reversed."[16] To date, societal securitization, with its associated adoption of coercive and assimilationist approaches to integration and blending of integration and security policy, has thankfully been largely absent in Canada. Whatever the trials and tribulations of the Canadian settlement and integration system (credential recognition certainly leaps to mind), there is little denying the efficacy of many of its programs, especially in comparison with those of Canada's Western peers.

Where it will be much more difficult to strike a balance between liberal multicultural rights and security is in the arena of public safety and counterterrorism. There is already an unfortunate legacy in this area. Yet, there is still an opportunity for Canada to avoid the mistakes witnessed elsewhere, such as in Britain, with its particularly fraught approach to counterterrorism and "radicalization." It is national security with its qualities of exceptionality and urgency where the Canadian state, its politicians, its bureaucrats, and civil society must tread most carefully or risk undermining the welcoming environment that Muslim newcomers and established citizens continue to enjoy. In particular it is imperative that Canadian policy-makers and bureaucrats avoid the blending of integration and security policy. Integration policy should be about promoting belonging, bridge building between ethnic and religious communities, and inclusion in the political and economic life of the country. Integration should not be about the prevention of radicalization and other security problems. For one thing, the latter approach makes highly problematic assumptions about the root causes of violent extremism and domestic terrorism.

Thus, in the end, it must be recognized that, in many meaningful ways, Canada has bucked important features of the crisis of multiculturalism. Viewed alongside the policies currently being employed in other states in the West and the current political and societal strife being experienced from Sweden to Britain to the United States, the criticisms of state multiculturalism must be put in the context of the alternatives. Canadian multiculturalism has withstood a stress test within the crisis of multiculturalism.

At the same time it would be naive to state that the continued success of that model is assured. It is vital that the supportive elements of Canadian civil society and ordinary Canadians who value multiculturalism, who view it as an essential aspect of Canadian identity, sound the alarm over policies and societal trends that threaten the continued success of the made-in-Canada policy. As witnessed in social media feeds and shifting public polls on the accommodation of newcomers, the voices of the anti-Islamic social movement are increasingly loud, assertive, and resonant among the Canadian public. With all of this in mind, perhaps the greatest danger is that in Canada, our world-famous civility and our somewhat smug comfort over our own success will lead us to take something extraordinary for granted.

MULTICULTURALISM AND MUSLIMS IN CANADA: THE WAY FORWARD

In the final section of the book some modest suggestions will be put forward for how states can better address issues related to xenoracism and how state multiculturalism can move forward with an ever-changing Canadian society. These suggestions and policy prescriptions are not new or unique, rather they are generally supportive of what has been said (arguably better) elsewhere.

Throughout the book, the voices of Canadian Muslims, their opinions and experiences, were used to explore multiculturalism in Canada. By placing the experiences of Muslims at the centre of the analysis, the book tested Canadian multiculturalism on grounds where other multicultural states had struggled and failed. Continuing with this approach, the final segment of the book will draw on the opinions of the Canadian Muslim interviewees and look to their vision of a better and more just multicultural state.

At the beginning of this book a quote from Edward Said was juxtaposed with a quote from a man who represents the most extreme manifestation of xenoracism and the anti-Islamic social movement, Anders Breivik. Said laid out his hope that by drawing on the contemporary "rise to political and historical awareness of so many of the earth's peoples," the more divisive legacies of the past – the racism and Orientalism that had for so long defined the relationship between East and West, Orient and Occident – could be challenged and re-articulated into something else.[17] Canada is a nation that can benefit from the awareness of "so many of the earth's peoples" as it represents a rare example of a successful multicultural state in an era of crisis, conflict, and social fragmentation. But the continued success of multiculturalism in Canada will depend on the ability of politicians and Canadian civil society to adapt to an increasingly culturally diverse society and the inevitable conflicts that will emerge within it.

Political scientists like Mojtaba Mahdavi and W. Andy Knight have suggested that one way forward, not only for Canada but also for culturally plural states around the world experiencing political and societal discord, is to adopt the idea of the "dignity of difference." Mahdavi and Knight contrast this vision of dignity with Huntington's Clash of Civilization thesis – an idea of cultural relations stuck in the reductive and oppositional logic of Orientalism. By comparison, Mahdavi and Knight see intercultural dialogue and exchange as essential to overcoming the conflicts we encounter in a post-9/11 world and suggest that multiculturalism may offer one potential path to the dignity of difference.[18]

But how can multiculturalism go forward? How do we as Canadians go beyond merely tolerating and accommodating the other, to finding dignity and value in our differences? How can multiculturalism evolve with the multiple generations of immigrants and their children and grandchildren who now make up the young state of Canada and define themselves as Canadian first? The answer provided in this text is that these goals must be pursued, first and foremost, through education and nation building. Canadian society has changed since 1971, 1988, and 1994: it needs to draw on the successes of the past and adapt the multicultural framework to contemporary and future social realities.

As one interviewee, Amyn Sajoo, an instructor at Simon Fraser University, points out, the priority in the 1970s was a departure from the failed assimilative vision of the past: "You keep it thin [conditions], you let them in and you let them relax, and that is the mosaic, we don't want the melting pot since assimilation has failed." In introducing multiculturalism to Parliament, Trudeau stated, "National unity, if it is to mean anything in the deeply personal sense, must be founded on the confidence in one's own individual identity; out of this can grow respect for that of others and a willingness to share ideas, attitudes and assumptions."[19] Trudeau's comment presents an important idea – that state multiculturalism was originally built around the concept of liberal individualism and the expression and mediation of cultural identity at that level.

Balancing Individual and Group Identity Rights in the Constitution and the Judiciary

As recognized in this study, individuals contain complex identities: they exhibit multiple belongings and affinities. Said argues that the conception of the Orient as a "constituted entity" where inhabitants "can be defined on the basis of some religion, culture, or racial essence proper to that geographical space is ... a highly debatable idea."[20] The failure of Orientalism, the failure of those who bought into a vision of Islam as a static site of conservative tradition, is the failure to recognize the complexity of individual experiences. While undoubtedly situated in a social context, individuals should be allowed to express what identity means to them, rather than having elites from within the community or from outside of the community decide what it means to belong to a religious or racial identity group.

This idea is consistent with findings from studies on the Muslim community in Canada. For example, Karim found that Muslims in general do not blindly follow religious dogma or authority but rather they bring a subjective approach to religious faith – they define what Islam means to them, they define what it means to be Muslim.[21] Importantly, ideas of subjective religious identity and individual rights are contained in the existing constitutional and multicultural framework of Canada. For example, under the Canadian Charter of Rights and Freedoms and the Canadian Multiculturalism Act individuals can advocate for their religious rights, such as the right to pray at work, through the courts.[22]

By the use of the "sincerity criterion" the courts have examined identity claims through the subjective experience of the individual by offering the court's judgment on the sincerity of those claims. Within this legal framework, judges balance the sincerity of individual claimants and their rights against the imposition those calls for accommodation would cause: for instance, the imposition on a business when the claimant seeks a space for prayer.[23] This process operates through the Oakes test (which measures whether or not it is justified to limit individual rights in consideration of the greater good of society); this is a "test" that follows section 1 of the Charter, also known as the reasonable limits clause.[24] Judgment of sincerity is based not only on a claimant's individual assertions related to identity but also on assertions that such practices fit within the larger context of the faith and consistency of religious practice.[25] Beaman points out that accommodation in this area is applied at the individual level, but it also recognizes group rights and identity by acknowledging "the individual believer as a key component in the conceptualization of religious freedom and, second, the possibility of group rights or acknowledgments of the link between the individual and institutional religion. The mention of a personal component supports the notion that religious frames of reference are always mediated by the individual and thus are lived, fluid, and changing."[26]

At the same time, according to Eisenberg and Kymlicka, "the adoption of the sincerity criterion aims to privilege more subjective and lived understandings of religion while undercutting the legal sanctity of canonical interpretations of the faith (and hence of the religious elites who define the canon)."[27] Considering the complexities of individual identity, and the need to balance individual rights with the greater good of society, such an approach is appropriate in that it allows individuals to offer a personal interpretation of religious belief while mediating potential conflicts and negative impacts of religious practice on the rights of other Canadians.

There are recent examples where these legal and constitutional principles have been put into action in support of the rights of Canadian Muslims. For example, in 2012 this process was used to examine the rights of testifying witnesses to wear the niqab. The Supreme Court of Canada granted the right to wear the niqab in certain incidences, depending on the nature of the trial itself and the effects that wearing the niqab might have on the rights of relevant parties. Chief Justice Beverley McLachlin highlighted the balancing of rights in the court's statement on the matter: "The answer lies in a just and proportionate balance between freedom of religion and trial fairness, based on the particular case before the court ... A witness who for sincere religious reasons wishes to wear the niqab while testifying in a criminal proceeding will be required to remove it if (a) this is necessary to prevent a serious risk to the fairness of the trial, because reasonably available alternative measures will not prevent the risk; and (b) the salutary effects of requiring her to remove the niqab outweigh the deleterious effects of doing so."[28]

Thus, rather than an outright ban, the court balanced liberal individual rights with the sincerity of the woman's religious claim and her identity rights in a multicultural society. It is noteworthy that the decision drew support from Canadian Muslim advocacy groups such as the Canadian Council on American-Islamic Relations, now known as the National Council of Canadian Muslims, and the Muslim Canadian Congress.[29] Some of the interviewees, like community organizer Ahmed Abdulkadir, specifically cited these kinds of rights as providing protection for Canadian Muslims: "The advantage of being a Canadian Muslim is that you have the Charter of Rights, it protects you, it doesn't allow the abuse of your human rights – there is a remedy against the hate that you face."

A critical point here is that the judiciary will remain an essential instrument for maintaining, interpreting, and protecting the framework of state multiculturalism (as contained in the Charter and the Act) as Canadian society evolves. It is the courts that will act as the final line of defence for the individual and multicultural rights of Canadians and mediate conflicts within a changing multicultural society. As seen during the years that the Harper government was in power, the courts were successful in upholding the rights of the individual to express his or her cultural and religious beliefs in the public sphere even around the most controversial of issues. In the case referenced above, and in the Zunera Ishaq case, where the government sought to uphold its ban on the niqab in citizenship ceremonies, the courts were successful in maintaining individual rights in the face of ideologically driven political initiatives. Moving forward, these traditions and institutions will continue to serve as effective enforcers of liberal multiculturalism in Canada.

Recognizing the Importance of Religion and Religious Identity in Canada

As the Canadian population becomes increasingly religiously diverse, calls for accommodation of religious beliefs and practices will only grow. How these claims are assessed and addressed will have important ramifications for the success of multiculturalism going forward. Accommodating religious difference represents an important evolutionary step in state multiculturalism, because as Bramadat notes, despite past commitments to multicultural principles, "the virtual exclusion of religion from public discourse (including the absence from, or awkward presence in, national ceremonies, media coverage, and in most public schools) has produced a kind of religious illiteracy, the result of which is that Canadians are increasingly ignorant about world religions, including Christianity."[30]

As interviewee Amyn Sajoo notes, based on the re-emergence of more assertive forms of religious identity over the past decades, religion can no longer be ignored in contemporary identity politics: "In the 1990s religion came out of the woodwork, and post 9/11 it's in your face. Multiculturalism can no longer contain Sikh religious, or Muslim religious, or Hindu religious, or Catholic religious, or

Evangelical religious militants. Culture is no longer a sufficient con-
tainer for that ... if multiculturalism was an engagement of cultural
categories – *only* that – and left out religion, in the hope of the old
modernist dream that religion would just fade away and we would
all become objective and scientific ... it's not happening – it's *back
with a bang*."

Eisenberg and Kymlicka note that when multicultural states over-
look religious identity and prioritize ideas and accommodation around
other conceptions of group identity, public agencies are less likely to
have institutional memory, best practices, or documented experiences
to draw on in assessing and addressing religious rights claims.[31] Within
the crisis of multiculturalism, state approaches to multiculturalism
have struggled to respond to what Amyn Sajoo describes as the return
of religion with a bang. Religion can no longer be neglected in the
public sphere. The lack of awareness related to religion and religious
identity in Canadian society leaves the door open to ideologies like
xenoracism, the narratives of the anti-Islamic social movement, and
even, arguably, fundamentalist and militant strains of religious belief.
Thus, not only is intercultural dialogue important but so too is awareness of religious and non-religious belief systems, including atheism,
both at the institutional and societal level.

As multiculturalism continues to evolve in Canada, at both the state
and societal level, as multiple generations of minority communities
establish themselves in Canadian society, that society will need to be
more accommodative to complex religious communities. Canadian
multiculturalism will need to move beyond what some have derisively
referred to as the song-and-dance model of multiculturalism, which
involves the celebration of static folkloric identities at cultural festivals
and other venues. Authentic intercultural dialogue and true respect
and dignity in difference will require changing how we think about
inclusion and integration. It is argued below that part of the answer
to addressing the current blind spot in Canadian multiculturalism
toward religion and religious identity groups is developing awareness
through public education.

Improving Our Understanding of, and Approach to, Social Integration

As indicated in chapter 6, newcomers to Canada have a lower bar or
threshold to meet in terms of social integration. In part, this lower

threshold exists because of the long-standing multicultural heritage of the state, a "thinner" form of Canadian national identity, and the value that is placed in Canada on immigrants and their contributions to Canadian society. In terms of social integration, a sense of belonging to the state has been identified by scholars as an important barometer for social integration and inclusion. The acquisition of citizenship, political participation, and general life satisfaction among newcomers have also been identified by Canadian immigration and integration scholars as important aspects of integration. But when it comes to generating deeper forms of inclusion and the kind of intercultural dialogue and exchange that is necessary to establish true dignity in difference in Canada, these standards may be inadequate. Given these kinds of concerns, some Canadian scholars have been advocating for a more developed and complex understanding of social integration.

The more established analogy for integration in Canada is the two-way street, where newcomers and the host culture mutually adapt to each other's presence in the state and society and meet somewhere in the middle of the integration paradigm. However, according to Dib, Donaldson, and Turcotte, in this analogy there is "no consideration of where people actually live together, where they meet, and where the two-way street would end up."[32] As an alternative, Dib, Donaldson, and Turcotte have suggested the idea of integration taking place within "common spaces." Here they present an image of a town square where "people mix in space and time and together produce a new, shared identity for themselves as a community."[33]

Building on this alternative vision of social integration within common spaces, Enns, Kirova, and Connolly have introduced the idea of social capital and "bonding" and "bridging" behaviours as a means of conceptualizing more meaningful interactions within and between individuals and identity groups in Canada. The work of Robert Putnam and of Alastair Ager and Alison Strang has defined bonding as social behaviours within a social identity group and bridging as "efforts to extend relationships beyond one's group [that] can have positive effects on expressed feelings of safety, and provide social and economic benefits if successful, but may undermine subsequent efforts at integration if rebuffed."[34]

According to Enns, Kirova, and Conolly, these kinds of intra- and inter-community activities are "valuable not only because they may facilitate material outcomes, or reduce conflict through the creation of common spaces, but because they contribute to less objective but equally important notions of social connection and trust in the integration process."[35] Employing data from the Ethnic Diversity Survey, their study found that "bonding and bridging activities exhibited primarily positive effects on the likelihood that participants expressed trust in people at work or school."[36] Ultimately the authors settled on expressed levels of generalized community trust and a sense of belonging to Canada as barometers for social integration in Canada, and they found that bonding and bridging activities were positively associated with social integration.[37]

The expanded conception of social integration offered by these scholars is a useful means of identifying the modalities through which deeper and more meaningful forms of social integration can be achieved in Canada and where government resources are best placed to further integration and social cohesion. Future studies and integration initiatives through the government, civil society, and settlement agencies can benefit from understanding these more complex and meaningful concepts of social integration.

Reforming National Security Practices

An impediment to the integration of Muslim communities in Canada is not only the barrier of xenoracism but also negative experiences related to national security practices. Concerns over homegrown terrorism related to groups such as al-Qaeda and the so-called Islamic State, and more recently the phenomenon of "foreign fighters" travelling to the Middle East and North Africa region, are shaping the priorities and policies of the Canadian government and its security agencies. These priorities have directed law enforcement and intelligence agencies to focus on Muslim communities in the West as a potential site of extremism and militancy.

In a multicultural society, it is critical that Canadian policy-makers and security officials actively seek to moderate the negative impact of security practices on Muslim communities while addressing some of the societal divisions between Muslim and non-Muslim communities that are generated not only by security practices but also by global political events, terrorism, the media, and social media. As indicated above, this is the greatest challenge that Canadian multiculturalism and Canadian Muslims face now and most likely in the foreseeable future. However, there are a number of potential approaches to counterterrorism and security that can help to reduce these impacts.

For example, at the level of national security, preventive counter-terrorism should be limited to cases where there is clear evidence of behaviour that indicates violent extremism and criminality at the individual level. Government-run security agencies must avoid assessing risk and vulnerability at the community level and among those who have not engaged in criminal behaviours; rather, these are activities that must be addressed within communities, families, non-governmental organizations, and civil society groups. The most ethical and arguably efficient response to the threat of domestic terrorism rests in a combination of traditional law enforcement and community-driven measures. It does not rest in the logic of the seemingly endless War on Terror.

Moreover, to rebuild trust between the government and securitized communities, which has been so negatively affected during the past decade and a half of post-9/11 security practices, the government and law enforcement agencies must be more responsive to the concerns of Canadian Muslim communities over security legislation, hate crimes, discrimination, and xenoracism.[38] Generating partnerships with communities rather than treating communities as potential suspects or informants will not only help to regenerate lost trust but will also improve national security outcomes.[39]

Furthermore, recognizing the startling growth in far-right extremism and militancy in the Western world in recent years, which has manifested itself in a deadly terrorist attack on a mosque in Quebec City in 2017, security agencies and the government must seek to address all forms of violent extremism and recognize that domestic terrorism is not a "Muslim issue" – it is a societal issue. States and agencies must do this not only to avoid the perception of unfair community targeting but also because of the mutually reinforcing tendencies of these hate groups, a pattern that was outlined in part in the section of the book on the societal security feedback loop.

So too is it a mistake to equate radicalism with violent extremism in communities. In states like Britain the government has linked non-violent radicalism to violent extremism and has targeted those whom they view as radical.[40] Through targeting and prosecuting ideas and those deemed to be radical, not only do some governments potentially become "thought police" but so too can they shut down alternative paths of political advocacy and foment alienation among at-risk groups.

Drawing these ideas together, it should be recognized that, in the current social and political climate, contemporary security practices can easily reach an over-saturation point where trust-building efforts are overwhelmed by feelings of mutual suspicion between securitized communities and security agencies. When community policing becomes community targeting, security becomes not only intrusive but also unethical and counter-productive.

Developing "softer" alternative models of counterterrorism that moderate these problems will represent a significant challenge for the Canadian government as it seeks to prevent domestic terrorism while protecting the civil liberties of all Canadians. Addressing these issues will require reforms to Bill C-51 and the Anti-terrorism Act, it will require more open and less secretive dialogue between securitized communities and the government, and it will require greater independent oversight of national security practices. The implementation of reforms that promote accountability and fairness in security practices must include an enhanced and better funded Security and Intelligence Review Committee, or version thereof, that can provide independent oversight of a considerably expanded Canadian security apparatus. These reforms are necessary to ensure that the experiences of individuals like Maher Arar do not reoccur.

Harnessing the Energy of Civil Society in a Renewed and Reconceived Anti-Racism Campaign

In many of the fears expressed in Canada over multiculturalism, for example, concerns over "ethnic enclaves" that are seen as the site of cultural values and practices that may be opposed to the norms and values of the host culture, we find that many of these fears rest on ideas of deficient intercultural interaction, awareness, and understanding. Establishing bridges, establishing avenues and channels for intercultural exchange, will be essential to addressing not only a lack of social integration in some communities but also the ignorance, stereotyping, and (xeno)racism that exist in Canadian society. These represent societal-level barriers to integration for newcomers and longer term minority resident communities. An important question here is who will drive these kinds of activities? Will it be the state, or civil society, or do authentic intercultural bridge-building interactions need to take place at the grassroots level: do they need to form organically?

Recognizing the limitations of past efforts in terms of social engineering, and indeed some of the more divisive approaches such as coercive assimilation that have appeared in recent years, some have suggested that states should develop an approach of "letting be," allowing people to simply get "on with their lives."[41] But the complete disengagement of the state from this area of policy contains an underlying assumption that, once left alone, individuals and communities will naturally develop their own networks, affinities, and bonds that can lead to a more cohesive society. Moreover, this approach contains underlying assumptions about human nature and behavior. Such assumptions may be problematic, since as Amyn Sajoo points out, "I think there are too many examples around the world including Sudan, Somalia, et cetera, where it seems that the more you know your neighbour, the more you hate them. This comfortable assumption that you know we are alike and in the end we're all going to be friends, I don't think the record bears that out – and I think when economic times get tough that's the test. How are people going to behave when they compete for jobs?"

Additionally, "letting be" also means that the state abdicates its responsibilities to address underlying historical inequalities and inequities in social relations. It means ignoring the legacies of the past that continue to shape contemporary social relations. Ideologies of racism reflect and contain these historical narratives and events and continue to produce negative social effects in Canadian society. Following from these observations, strategies such as anti-racism and awareness remain important tools for multicultural states to address the disadvantages and divisions caused by racist ideologies. The looming remaining question is how to best shape this controversial area of policy and who should deliver anti-racism programming.

Chapter 2 identified how ideas of race are fluid and how ideologies of racism are subject to change and contestation. They are not as they are presented – as timeless and immutable hierarchical understandings of social relations. According to Lentin, "the fact that racialization and racism are repeated, affecting different groups over time, does not mean that racism is inevitable. Rather, it shows that considerable transformations of our political systems, our social and cultural infrastructure, and our discourse – the very way in which language is used – need to change if racism in Western societies is to be overcome."[42]

Here it is argued that critical to the development of effective anti-racism strategy will be including the insights and opinions of those who are most vulnerable to racist ideologies and understanding how to best approach target audiences. As Van Munster points out, more inclusive societies can only be created when minorities and newcomers, their struggles and successes, are viewed as constitutive of the community.[43]

After 9/11 a series of coalitions, intra- and inter-community civil society groups, have emerged to combat ignorance and racism while building bridges between communities. The experiences, opinions, and pre-existing outreach activities of these bodies offer a valuable resource for states seeking to develop more effective approaches to anti-racism. As Baha Abu-Laban observes, "What is also important to remember is that coalition building helps the community a great deal ... so Muslim groups built coalitions with various other groups, advocate for human rights, anti-racism, et cetera. This coalition building was in progress shortly after 9/11 ... and egalitarian Canadians also rose up to defend the communities that were attacked."

Harnessing the experience and energy of these engaged organizations and ad hoc coalitions, and the pre-existing bridging initiatives with which they are engaged, is an important step in furthering not only an anti-racism agenda but also promoting deeper forms of social integration. Governments, with their mixed record of delivering top-down social engineering programs, can harness and support the activities of the best equipped civil society groups. Academics and practitioners engaged with immigration, settlement, integration, and multiculturalism can also play a role in these activities through offering ideas and material resources to allow grassroots approaches to grow into larger scale local programs.

Prior iterations of anti-racism programs operating through departments such as the former Citizenship and Immigration Canada, for example, *Racism, Stop It!* have focused on media campaigns. While public awareness may represent an important aspect of anti-racism campaigns, a far more comprehensive and nuanced approach is required. Anti-racism campaigns can't just "speak to the converted," in other words, use language and resources that appeal to already progressive segments of society. Rather, such programming must be framed and designed in such a manner that it reaches those engaged with ideas and language rooted in cultural ignorance and prejudice. This represents a considerable challenge, and the individuals who implement this kind of programming must look to other areas of public awareness that have had success in altering attitudes and behaviours.

For example, successful public awareness initiatives led by the public health sector around smoking arguably provide some exportable knowledge and ideas. The most efficacious public awareness campaigns related to smoking induced positive rather than negative emotions, which increased the likelihood that the target audience (smokers or prospective smokers) would alter their behaviour.[44] The success of these campaigns can be linked in part to an ability to convey messages that non-smokers were, for lack of a better word, "cool" and the willingness of government health agencies to use non-governmental groups and advertising agencies to craft the public health message. It was recognized, quite rightly, that government actors tend to not produce the most efficacious and credible public awareness materials. In the United States it has been estimated that anti-smoking awareness campaigns helped to prevent 1.6 million smoking related deaths from 1964 to 1992 and additional 4.1 million deaths from 1993 to 2015.[45]

Therefore, reaching out to non-governmental groups around anti-racism is in keeping with best practices related to public awareness. But the framing and delivery of anti-racism programs is critical to their success. As shown by the experience of public health campaigns, simply highlighting the undesirability or ignorance of ideas and behaviours will not produce the desired result. Rather, a positive message must be crafted that challenges the binary-like thinking that tends to define racism. Campaigns must subtly introduce plausible grey areas that challenge individuals to re-examine their belief systems and world views. Given its relative success, awareness and education in this area may be able to mine some of the positive aspects of the Canadian multicultural experience.

Multicultural Education Programs as Nation Building

The final recommendation of this book relates to education and awareness. As Bramadat points out, the exclusion of religion from public life has led to the development of an increasingly religiously illiterate generation.[46] In addition, as shown by Said, Orientalism has left the West with a legacy of misinformed knowledge of the other, particularly in relation to Islam.[47] The past decade has seen a renewal of these stereotypes in the discourses of national and societal security that permeate political, media, and online narratives. Recognizing that multicultural education represents an important area of reform, this final recommendation was drawn out by a number of interviewees from the Canadian Muslim sample group. For

example, for Ahmed Abdulkadir the way forward for multiculturalism and Canada is clear: "Promote multiculturalism through public
education, promote diversity within the media, and promote diversity
in Cabinet and in elected politics." Shaykh Zak, a Muslim chaplain,
notes the considerable progress Canada has made as a more culturally sensitive society but suggests that there is still a great deal of
ignorance about religion and cultural difference: "So I would say
generally speaking [society] has come a long way, but we're not there
yet. So, whether based on religion or ethnicity … I would say ignorance is a major factor … people don't take the time to know anything
and the only way really you can have a dialogue with the Muslims
is to understand their religion, because you can find a lot of pitfalls.
If you can distinguish between what is cultural and religious you can
have a reasonable understanding."

Similarly, Dalal Daoud of the Canadian Islamic Congress points to
the level of ignorance and misunderstanding of Islam in Canadian
society: "The average Canadian citizen does not have a lot of knowledge on Muslims and Islam, and I feel like extra measures should be
taken from schools to universities to workplaces, and it doesn't just
stop at 'we respect your diversity.' … I think people are eager and
would like to learn. Like more than one time I have had people [come
to me] and ask, you know, 'Why do you wear the hijab?' And I think
people do want to learn."

For Sohail Quadri, a former M LA and member of the Muslim
interviewee sample group, education is key to the success of multiculturalism: "It can't be forced – it's not about legislation. We create
awareness and tolerance – it is about education … it all comes down
to the individual."

But more than its ability to address religious illiteracy or ignorance
related to cultural difference, multicultural education represents a
powerful tool for nation building. Education can be used to promote
ideas of cultural exclusivity and competition, or it can be used to
encourage respect and dignity in difference.

Recognizing the established success of state multicultural policy
in developing a generation that views multiculturalism not only as
an important part of Canadian identity but also as an essential aspect
of social relations, education represents a tool for continuing to
develop these perspectives among successive generations. Supporting
this view, Amyn Sajoo states, "I think most people would have great
difficulties disagreeing that if universities and schools take pluralism

seriously then in the long term you are going to produce a generation that is much more at home with it."

To develop a truly progressive vision of education would require including minorities and their stories in the curriculum development stage. It would require a re-imagination of a history of social relations that wouldn't involve forgetting or glossing over exploitation and injustice but rather would involve unpacking that history and re-articulating it in what is undoubtedly a richer picture of social relations – one marked by both conflict and co-operation, by both exploitation and exchange. It would mean highlighting not only Canada's important military history but also its history of colonialism and its decidedly mixed record in addressing Indigenous and minority rights. It would have to include cultural and religious studies in a way that can address the ignorance and misunderstandings that have developed in Canadian society. It would have to start with those who have no pre-existing familial and socially engrained prejudices by focusing on early childhood development and education.

Yasmeen Nisam of the Canadian Muslim interviewee sample group spoke of how developing this approach to education, especially one that can properly represent religious identities, will be not easy, but it is necessary "because the Muslim community is so diverse it would really be a difficult task for government to do." Soraya Hafez, a interviewee from the Canadian Muslim community who has previously worked in education, spoke to what she sees as an important starting point in developing this form of education: "I feel as though we have to spend the money in curriculum at schools from kindergarten to universities ... they should have some lessons, some training in other cultures – teaching about other cultures, equality and human rights, it should start really in kindergarten ... we have teachers coming to the classroom with no ideas about the background of the students." Interviewee Azim Jeraj also suggested that, at the post-secondary level, religious studies and interfaith dialogue initiatives can play an important role in promoting dialogue: "The government money can also be spent on interfaith, and I believe we need to start interfaith chapters at universities. You know why we need them? Because this is the place you can ask difficult questions."

In the final analysis, bringing state multicultural policy into the twenty-first century will mean adapting to ever-changing societies that are situated both locally and transnationally in an increasingly globalized world, with all the benefits and hazards that implies.

Maintaining a successful multicultural state will mean harnessing the forces of cultural hybridity contained in globalization and multicultural societies while actively mediating the forces of fragmentation. Conflict and cultural difference are part of the human condition that cannot be erased or glossed over. What is important is how conflicts are mediated: how difference is accommodated, respected, and treated with dignity in the institutions of the state. Moving forward will require changes.

Will Canada submit to the devolutionary forces of divisiveness, of false promises of return to monoculturalism, or will it embrace the promise of a collective future in a rejuvenated multicultural state? If the normative ideal of the latter is achieved, Canada will continue to offer an example of how multicultural societies can succeed, when so many have succumbed to the crisis of multiculturalism.

Notes

CHAPTER ONE

1 See, for example: Kymlicka, *Finding Our Way*; Day, *Multiculturalism and the History of Canadian Diversity*; Bannerji, *Dark Side of the Nation*; Fleras and Kunz, *Media and Minorities*; Abu-Laban and Gabriel, *Selling Diversity*; Bissoondath, *Selling Illusions*; Adams, *Unlikely Utopia*; Kymlicka, "Testing the Liberal Multiculturalist Hypothesis"; Ryan, *Multicultiphobia*; Haque, *Multiculturalism within a Bilingual Framework*; and Foster, *Genuine Multiculturalism*.
2 Breivik, "2083: A European Declaration of Independence."
3 Berntzen and Sandberg, "Collective Nature of Lone Wolf Terrorism," 761–2.
4 *The Economist*, "Reticent Populists"; and McCoy and Knight, "Refugee Crisis."
5 Spencer, *Stealth Jihad*, 5.
6 Chrisafis, "Marine Le Pen Goes on Trial."
7 Fekete, *Suitable Enemy*, 44.
8 Critics of multiculturalism have used the concept of parallel communities to describe segregated cultural and religious communities that voluntarily establish spatially separate neighbourhoods and social services leading to a lack of integration into mainstream society.
9 McCoy and Knight, "Attack on Multiculturalism."
10 BBC News, "Merkel."
11 Dempsey, "Difficult Choice for Turks."
12 Lentin, *Racism and Ethnic Discrimination*, 115.
13 Ryan, *Multicultiphobia*, 4.
14 Lentin and Titley, *Crises of Multiculturalism*.

15 Ibid.

16 Breivik, "European Declaration," 16.

17 Pipes, "Trump: Ban Islamists."

18 Caldwell, *Reflections on the Revolution Europe*, 131–2.

19 *The Economist*, "Europe's Populist Insurgents."

20 Castles and Miller, *Age of Migration*, 15.

21 Biles, Burnstein, and Frideres, "Conclusion: Canadian," 269.

22 Adams, *Unlikely Utopia*, x.

23 Reitz, "Multiculturalism Policies," 120.

24 Adams, *Unlikely Utopia*, 41.

25 Reitz, "Assessing Multiculturalism," 9.

26 Moghissi, Rahnema, and Goodman, *Diaspora by Design*.

27 Williamson, "Introduction."

28 McCoy and Knight, "National Identity Overhauled."

29 Keenan, "When Stephen Harper Refers to 'Barbaric Culture.'"

30 Ibid.

31 Graves, "The EKOS poll."

32 McRoberts, *Misconceiving Canada*.

33 Ibid., 124.

34 Kymlicka, "Comment on Meer and Modood."

35 Ibid., 214.

36 Miles, *Racism after "Race Relations*," 60.

37 Lentin, *Racism and Ethnic Discrimination*, viii.

38 Sivanandan quoted in Fekete, *Suitable Enemy*, 20.

39 Fekete, *Suitable Enemy*.

40 Sivanandan, "Race, Terror and Civil Society," 2.

41 Said, *Orientalism*.

42 Ibid., 27.

43 Pitcher, *Politics of Multiculturalism*, 23.

44 Fleras and Elliott, *Unequal Relations*.

45 Friedman, *The World Is Flat*.

46 Keohane and Nye, *Power and Interdependence*.

47 Knight, "Conceptualizing Transnational Community Formation," 22.

48 Castles and Miller, *Age of Migration*, 262.

49 Kymlicka, "Ethnocultural Diversity in a Liberal State," 62–3.

50 Fleras and Kunz, *Media and Minorities*, 12.

51 McRoberts, *Misconceiving Canada*.

52 Fekete, *Suitable Enemy*, 1.

53 Lentin, *Racism and Ethnic Discrimination*, 114.

54 Fekete, *Suitable Enemy*, 44.

55 Asad, *Formations of the Secular*, 160.
56 Lepinard, "From Immigrants to Muslims," 10.
57 Wilkinson, "Introduction," 1.
58 Castles and Miller, *Age of Migration*, 247.
59 Krause and Williams, "Broadening the Agenda," 242.
60 Waever, "Securitization and Desecuritization," 4.
61 Van Munster, *Securitizing Immigration*, 36.
62 Ibid.
63 Fekete, "Anti-Muslim Racism," 5.
64 CBC News, "Canadians Who Have 'Fallen Prey.'"
65 Ayoob, "Political Islam."
66 Abu-Laban and Dhamoon, "Dangerous (Internal) Foreigners," 179–80.
67 Fekete, *A Suitable Enemy*, 61.
68 Burnham, "Comparative Methodology."
69 Peters, *Comparative Politics*.
70 Ruane, *Essentials of Research Methods*, 76.
71 Ebbinghaus, "When Less Is More," 134.
72 Ruane, *Essentials of Research Methods*, 89.
73 For example, see Denzin, *Reflexive Interview*; Smaling, "The Pragmatic Dimension"; and Oleinik, "Mixing Quantitative and Qualitative Content Analysis."
74 Erzberger and Prein, "Triangulation," 142.
75 Flick, *Introduction to Qualitative Research*, 265.
76 Enns, Kirova, and Connolly, "Examining Bonding and Bridging Activities."
77 Flick, *Introduction to Qualitative Research*, 64.
78 Denzin, "Reflexive Interview," 43.
79 Leech, "Asking Questions," 665.
80 Leech, "Interview Methods," 663.
81 Leech, "Asking Questions," 665.
82 Goldstein, "Getting in the Door," 669.
83 Ruane, *Essentials of Research Methods*, 118.
84 Walford, "Classification and Framing of Interviews," 147–8.
85 Flick, *Introduction to Qualitative Research*, 69.
86 Ibid., 70.
87 Said, *Orientalism*, 328.
88 Knight, "Conceptualizing Transnational Community Formation."

CHAPTER TWO

1 Lentin, *Racism and Ethnic Discrimination*, v.

2 See, for example, Balibar and Wallerstein, *Race Nation, Class*; Miles, *Racism after "Race Relations"*; Omi and Winant, *Racial Formation*; Banton, *Racial Theories*; Taguieff, Force of Prejudice"; Miles and Brown, *Racism*; and Goldberg, *Threat of Race*.

3 Lasswell, *Politics. Who Gets What, When, How.*

4 Miles, *Racism after "Race Relations,"* 59.

5 Shih et al., "Social Construction of Race"; Harris and Sim, "Who Is Multiracial?"; and Spickard, "Illogic."

6 Shih et al., "Social Construction of Race," 125.

7 Harris and Sim, "Who Is Multiracial?" 625.

8 Lentin, *Racism and Ethnic Discrimination*, 14.

9 Miles and Brown, *Racism*, 58.

10 Duffield, "Racism, Migration and Development," 71.

11 Miles and Brown, *Racism*, 66.

12 Ibid., 44.

13 By racial idiom, Banton is referring to what he sees as a "whole family of expressions centred upon the conception of race, including racial discrimination, racial group, racial prejudice, racial segregation and racism" (Banton, *Racial Theories*, 2).

14 Banton, *Racial Theories*, 235.

15 Ibid., 199.

16 Ibid., 208.

17 Goldberg, *Threat of Race*, 157.

18 Sefa Dei, "Speaking Race," 54.

19 Omi and Winant, *Racial Formation*, 54.

20 Ibid., 55.

21 Ibid., 55.

22 On this point Shih et al. state, "It is important to keep in mind that although it may be argued that race may have no biological basis, race plays an important role in our social world, and the impact that race has on social experiences should not be trivialized" (Shih et al., "Social Construction of Race," 132).

23 Balibar and Wallerstein, *Race, Nation, Class*, 17–18.

24 Barker, *New Racism*, 28–9.

25 Memmi, *Racism*, 5–6.

26 Goldberg, *Threat of Race*, 4.

27 Miles, *Racism after "Race Relations,"* 60.

28 Ibid., 60.

29 Miles and Brown, *Racism*, 83.

30 Barker, *New Racism*, 1.

31 Balibar and Wallerstein, *Race, Nation, Class*, 17–19.

32 Essed, *Understanding Everyday Racism*, 2.

33 Gramsci, *Selections from the Notebooks*.

34 Gramsci, *Prison Notebooks*.

35 Ibid.

36 Omi and Winant, *Racial Formation*, 67.

37 Balibar and Wallerstein, *Race, Nation, Class*, 17–18.

38 Barker, *New Racism*, 23–24.

39 Modood, "'Difference' Cultural Racism."

40 Barker, *New Racism*, 10–11.

41 Ibid., 3.

42 Lentin, *Racism and Ethnic Discrimination*, 110.

43 Barker, *New Racism*, 20.

44 Balibar and Wallerstein, *Race, Nation, Class*, 217–18.

45 Omi and Winant, *Racial Formation*, 14–24.

46 Chanock, "'Culture' and Human Rights," 18.

47 Mac an Ghaill, *Contemporary Racisms and Ethnicities*, 7.

48 Omi and Winant, *Racial Formation*, 12.

49 Mac an Ghaill, *Contemporary Racisms and Ethnicities*, 5.

50 Chanock "'Culture' and Human Rights," 18.

51 Miles, *Racism after "Race Relations,"* 3.

52 Omi and Winant, *Racial Formation*, 71.

53 Balibar and Wallerstein, *Race, Nation, Class*, 45.

54 Lentin, *Racism and Ethnic Discrimination*, viii.

55 Anderson, *Imagined Communities*, 6–7.

56 Said, *Reflections on Exile and Other Essays*, 582.

57 Goldberg, *Threat of Race*, 38.

58 Harrison, "Cultural Difference," 343.

59 Hall, "Question of Cultural Identity," 612.

60 Ibid.

61 Anderson, *Imagined Communities*, 4.

62 Gellner, *Nationalism*, viii.

63 Ibid., 31.

64 Ibid., 94.

65 Ibid., 108.

66 Buzan and Segal, *Anticipating the Future*, 122.

67 Miles, *Racism after "Race Relations,"* 56.

68 Lentin, *Racism and Ethnic Discrimination*, 107.

69 Miles, *Racism after "Race Relations,"* 78.

70 Lentin, *Racism and Ethnic Discrimination*, x.

71 Miles, *Racism after "Race Relations,"* 60.

CHAPTER THREE

1 Buzan, Waever, and de Wilde, *Security*.
2 Mac an Ghaill, *Contemporary Racisms and Ethnicities*, 11.
3 Lentin, *Racism and Ethnic Discrimination*, 99.
4 Fekete, *Suitable Enemy*.
5 Sciutto, *Against Us*, xiii.
6 Fekete, *Suitable Enemy*, 44.
7 Sajid, "Islamophobia," 31.
8 Miles, *Racism after "Race Relations,"* 14.
9 Sivanandan, "Race, Terror and Civil Society," 2.
10 Sivanandan, "Poverty Is the New Black," 2.
11 Lentin, *Racism and Ethnic Discrimination*, 113.
12 Cole, "A Plethora of 'Suitable Enemies.'"
13 Lentin, *Racism and Ethnic Discrimination*, ix.
14 Mills, "Critical Race Theory."
15 Cole, "A Response to Charles Mills."
16 Fekete, "Anti-Muslim Racism," 4.
17 Balibar and Wallerstein, *Race, Nation, Class*, 23.
18 Goldberg, *Threat of Race*, 3.
19 Mills, "Critical Race Theory," 9.
20 Gottschalk and Greenberg, *Islamophobia*, 5.
21 Sajid, "Islamophobia," 31.
22 Lentin, *Racism and Ethnic Discrimination*, ix.
23 Fekete, "Anti-Muslim Racism," 4.
24 Sivanandan, "Poverty Is the New Black," 5.
25 Barker, *The New Racism*.
26 Fekete, *Suitable Enemy*, 20.
27 Ibid., 20.
28 Abu-Laban and Dhamoon, "Dangerous (Internal) Foreigners," 164.
29 Ibid., 163.
30 Ibid., 166.
31 Fekete, *Suitable Enemy*, 41.
32 Fekete, "Anti-Muslim Racism," 8.
33 Ibid.
34 Miles and Brown, *Racism*, 24.
35 Ibid., 51.
36 Said, *Covering Islam*, 55.

37 Elgamri, *Islam in the British Broadsheets*, 17.
38 Said, *Orientalism*, xlix.
39 Ibid., 2–3.
40 Ibid., 3.
41 Elgamri, *Islam in the British Broadsheets*, 23.
42 Said, *Culture and Imperialism*, 9.
43 Barsamian and Said, *Culture and Resistance*, 122.
44 Said, *Orientalism*, 328.
45 Farris, "'Ideal Type,'" 268.
46 Sajid, "Islamophobia," 35.
47 Elgamri, *Islam in the British Broadsheets*, 18.
48 Lewis, *What Went Wrong?*
49 Said, *Covering Islam*, xxx.
50 Ibid., xvi.
51 Said, *Orientalism*, 26–7.
52 Ibid., 43.
53 Werbner, *Imagined Diasporas*, 257.
54 Said, *Covering Islam*, xlviii.
55 Goldberg, *Threat of Race*, 33.
56 Ayoob, "Political Islam," 1.
57 Ibid., 12.
58 Gerges, *Far Enemy*.
59 Fekete, *Suitable Enemy*, 63.
60 McCoy and Knight, "Refugee Crisis"
61 Farris, "'Ideal Type,'" 282.
62 Said, *Orientalism*, 322.
63 Ibid., 325.
64 Said, *Culture and Imperialism*, xx.
65 Brown, "Aga Khan Hails Canada."

CHAPTER FOUR

1 Bawer, *While Europe Slept*.
2 Cesari, "Islam, Immigration, and France," 202.
3 Bramadat, "Beyond Christian Canada," 18.
4 Ramadan, *What I Believe*, 42.
5 Moghissi, Rahnema, and Goodman, *Diaspora by Design*.
6 Said, *Covering Islam*, xvi.
7 Werbner, *Imagined Diasporas*, 271.
8 Ramadan, *What I Believe*, 46.

9 Ibid., 46–7.
10 Rahnema, "Contradictions," 395.
11 Reitz, "Assessing Multiculturalism," 29.
12 McDonough and Hoodfar, "Muslims in Canada," 136.
13 Ibid., 133.
14 Ibid.
15 Siddiqui, "Canada's Flawed National Census."
16 Hanniman, "Canadian Muslims," 272.
17 Ibid., 273.
18 Ibid.
19 Moghissi, Rahnema, and Goodman, *Diaspora by Design.*
20 Bramadat, "Beyond Christian Canada," 16.
21 Knight, "Conceptualizing Transnational Community Formation," 14.
22 Ibid., 15.
23 Ibid., 14.
24 Bramadat, "Beyond Christian Canada," 16.
25 Ibid., 15.
26 Ibid., 16–17.
27 Knight, "Conceptualizing Transnational Community Formation," 4.
28 McDonough and Hoodfar, "Muslims in Canada," 136.
29 Moghissi, Rahnema, and Goodman, *Diaspora by Design*, 12.
30 Ibid., 14.
31 Knight, "Conceptualizing Transnational Community Formation," 15.
32 Ramadan, *What I Believe*, 27.
33 Ibid., 28.
34 Werbner, *Imagined Diasporas.*
35 Cesari, "Islam, Immigration, and France," 202.
36 Essed, *Understanding Everyday Racism*, 3.
37 Foster, *Where Race Does Not Matter.*
38 McLaren, "Stemming the Flood," 190.
39 Ibid., 190.
40 Satzewich, *Racism in Canada*, 38.
41 Walker, *History of Immigration*, 237.
42 Ibid., 237.
43 Backhouse, *Colour-Coded.*
44 Satzewich, *Racism in Canada*, 91.
45 Wortley and Julian, "Data, Denials, and Confusion," 371.
46 Creese and Ngene Kambere, "What Colour Is Your English?" 565.
47 Satzewich, *Racism in Canada*, 91.
48 Seljak et al., "Challenge of Religious Intolerance," 9.

49 Bahdi, "No Exit."

50 Korteweg, "Sharia Debate in Ontario," 435–6.

51 Khan, "Ontario Sharia Debate," 475–6.

52 CBC News, "Ontario Premier."

53 CBC News, "Shariah Law: FAQs."

54 Government of Canada, *Constitution Act, 1982 Part I.*

55 Jimenez and El Akkad, "Values."

56 Siddiqui, "Sharia Is Gone."

57 McCoy and Jones, "Anti-Muslim Hatred."

58 Perry and Scrivens, "Uneasy Alliances," 820.

59 Harris, "Hate Crimes."

60 Ethnic Diversity Survey Public Use Metafile, 2002 [computer file].

61 Ibid.

62 Ibid.

63 Environics, "Muslims and Multiculturalism."

64 Environics, *Survey of Muslims,* 6.

65 Ibid., 22.

66 Ibid., 38.

67 Jedwab and Al-Yassini, "Canadians."

68 Eid, *Being Arab,* 52.

69 Hanniman, "Canadian Muslims," 273.

70 European Union Agency for Fundamental Rights, *Experience of Discrimination.*

71 Ibid.

72 Pew Research Center, "Muslims in Europe."

73 Essed, *Understanding Everyday Racism,* 3.

CHAPTER FIVE

1 Malik, "Assimilation's Failure, Terrorism's Rise."

2 McCoy and Knight, "Refugee Crisis."

3 Lentin and Titley, *Crises of Multiculturalism,* 2.

4 Ibid., 3.

5 Lepinard, "From Immigrants to Muslims," 191.

6 Pitcher, *Politics of Multiculturalism,* 2.

7 Abu-Laban and Gabriel, *Selling Diversity,* 121.

8 Fleras and Kunz, *Media and Minorities,* 12.

9 Castles and Miller, *Age of Migration,* 262.

10 Kymlicka, quoted in Milot, "Modus Co-Vivendi," 111.

11 Abu-Laban and Gabriel, *Selling Diversity,* 121.

12 Castles and Miller, *Age of Migration*, 248–9.

13 Dallmayr, *Beyond Orientalism*, 211.

14 Quoted in Reitz, "Assessing Multiculturalism," 9.

15 Biles and Ibrahim, "Religion and Public Policy," 154.

16 Vermeulen and Penninx, "Introduction," 1.

17 Biles and Ibrahim, "Religion and Public Policy," 157.

18 Anderson and Black, "Political Integration of Newcomers," 45.

19 McRoberts, *Misconceiving Canada*, 122–3.

20 Abu-Laban and Gabriel, *Selling Diversity*, 108.

21 Winter, "Trajectories of Multiculturalism," 177.

22 Dupré, "Intercultural Citizenship," 228.

23 Garcea, Kirova, and Wong, "Introduction," 3.

24 Kymlicka, "Comment on Meer and Modood," 211–12.

25 Gangnon and Iacovino, *Federalism, Citizenship, and Quebec*, 151.

26 Montpetit, "Will Interculturalism Replace Multiculturalism?"

27 Dupré, "Intercultural Citizenship."

28 Ibid., 243.

29 Ibid., 235.

30 Ibid., 236–40.

31 Canadian Press, "Marois."

32 Sugunasiri, *Towards Multicultural Growth*, 116.

33 Milot, "Modus Co-Vivendi, 111.

34 Biles and Ibrahim, "Religion and Public Policy," 163.

35 Fleras and Kunz, *Media and Minorities*, 15–16.

36 Ibid., 15.

37 Citizenship and Immigration Canada, "Evaluation."

38 Ibid.

39 Bicker and Ibbitson, *Big Shift*, 156.

40 McLaren, "Stemming the Flood," 190.

41 Walker, *History of Immigration*, 238.

42 Ibid., 238.

43 Joppke, "Through the European Looking Glass," 3.

44 Ibid., 3.

45 Ibid.

46 Galabuzi, "Economic Exclusion," 279–85.

47 Samuel and Basavarajappa, "Visible Minority Population," 8–11.

48 Ibid., 11.

49 Pendakur and Pendakur, "Colour of Money."

50 Trumper and Wong, "Canada's Guest Workers."

51 Stasiulis and Bakan "Marginalized and Dissident Non-Citizens," 276.

52 Boyd, "Educational Attainments."
53 Picot and Hou, Preparing for Success.
54 Ibid.
55 Kazemipur and Halli, *New Poverty in Canada*, 155.
56 Balakrishnan and Gyimah, "Spatial Residential Patterns."
57 Walks and Bourne, "Ghettos in Canada's Cities?"
58 Ibid.
59 Li, *Destination Canada*.
60 Bramadat, "Toward a New Story," 224.
61 Adams, *Unlikely Utopia*, 20.
62 Ibid.
63 Association for Canadian Studies and the Mosaic Institute, *Younger Canadians*.
64 Ibid.
65 Kymlicka, "Testing," 263.
66 Fleras and Kunz, *Media and Minorities*, 11.
67 Esses et al., "Perceptions of National Identity," 660.
68 Soroka, Helliwell, and Johnston, "Measuring and Modelling."
69 Bloemraad, *Becoming a Citizen*.
70 Ibid.
71 Banting, Courchene and Seidle, "Conclusion," 662–3.
72 Howe, "Political Engagement."
73 Adams, *Unlikely Utopia*, 70–4.
74 Keung, "Parliament's Lack of Diversity."
75 Government of Canada, *Constitution Act, 1982 Part I*.
76 Government of Canada, *Canadian Multiculturalism Act R.S.C., 1985*.
77 Ryan, *Multicultiphobia*, 4.
78 Milot, "Modus Co-Vivendi," 119.
79 Drury, "Omar Khadr," 414.
80 Ibid., 414–15.
81 Bissoondath, *Selling Illusions*.
82 Bannerji, *Dark Side of the Nation*, 5.
83 Ibid., 9.
84 Reitz et al., "Race," 702.
85 Malik, "Assimilation's Failure, Terrorism's Rise."
86 Lentin and Titley, *Crises of Multiculturalism*, 14.
87 Ibid., 15.
88 Ibid., 3.
89 Ibid., 8.
90 Ryan, *Multicultiphobia*, 122.

91 Elliott, "Immigrant Visas."
92 Wilkinson, "Introduction."
93 Woods, "Doctors, Lawyers."
94 Ryan, *Multicultiphobia*, 202.
95 Ibid., 203.
96 McCoy and Knight, "Attack on Multiculturalism."
97 McKay and Swift, *Warrior Nation*.
98 McCoy and Knight, "National Identity Overhauled."
99 Mahoney and Bailey, "New Immigration Guide."
100 Beeby, "Massive Failure Rates."
101 Tolley et al., "Introduction," 7.
102 Abu-Laban, "Reform by Stealth," 150.
103 Ibid., 150.
104 Kymlicka, "Ethnocultural Diversity," 78.
105 Kymlicka, "Testing," 260.
106 Elke, "Trajectories of Multiculturalism," 180.
107 Bramadat, "Beyond Christian Canada," 10.
108 Fekete, "Anti-Muslim Racism," 18.
109 Blanchfield and Bronskill, "Documents."
110 Payton, "Ethnic Riding Targeting."
111 Ryan, *Multicultiphobia*, 199.

CHAPTER SIX

1 Huntington, *Clash of Civilizations*.
2 Banting and Soroka, "Minority Nationalism," 156.
3 Vasta, "Do We Need Social Cohesion?" 199.
4 Vermeulen and Penninx, "Introduction," 1.
5 Castles and Miller, *Age of Migration*, 240.
6 Rich, "It Depends on How You Define Integrated," 830.
7 Wong and Tézli, "Measuring," 10.
8 Gordon, *Assimilation in American Life*.
9 Ibid.
10 Wilkinson, "Introduction."
11 Jurkova, "Role of Ethno-Cultural Organizations," 24.
12 Wilkinson, "Introduction."
13 Banting and Soroka, "Minority Nationalism," 156.
14 Doerschler and Jackson, "Do Muslims in Germany Really Fail to Integrate?" 505.
15 Ley, "Does Transnationalism Trump Immigrant Integration?" 923.

16 Jurkova, "Role of Ethno-Cultural Organizations."
17 Reitz, "Assessing Multiculturalism," 21.
18 Bawer, *Surrender*.
19 Tayob, "Muslim Responses," 75.
20 Joppke, "Europe and Islam," 1314.
21 Quoted in Joppke, "Europe and Islam," 1321–2.
22 Jacobson and Deckard, "Surveying the Landscape," 118.
23 Joppke, "Europe and Islam," 1331.
24 Tayob, "Muslim Responses," 73.
25 Joppke, 1331–2.
26 Banting, "Transatlantic Convergence?" 67.
27 Ibid., 81–2.
28 Fekete, *Suitable Enemy*, 67.
29 Ibid., 67.
30 Portes, "Migration and Social Change."
31 Banting, "Transatlantic Convergence?" 81.
32 Kymlicka, *Finding Our Way*.
33 Haque, "Multiculturalism," 204.
34 Reitz et al., "Race," 696.
35 Castles and Miller, *Age of Migration*, 247.
36 Ibid., 246.
37 Cesari, "Islam, Immigration, and France," 206.
38 Vermeulen and Penninx, "Introduction."
39 Wilkinson, "Introduction."
40 Kymlicka, *Multicultural Citizenship*, 96.
41 Castles and Miller, *Age of Migration*, 274.
42 Fekete, *Suitable Enemy*, 63.
43 Lentin and Titley, *Crises of Multiculturalism*, 14.
44 Miles, *Racism after "Race Relations,"* 175.
45 Ibid., 180.
46 Balibar and Wallerstein, *Race, Nation, Class*, 222–3.
47 Banting, Courchene, and Seidle, "Conclusion," 648.
48 Omi and Winant, *Racial Formation*, 16.
49 Bolt, Özüekren, and Phillips, "Linking Integration."
50 Richmond, "Immigration and Pluralism."
51 Ley, "Does Transnationalism Trump Immigrant Integration?" 923.
52 Wilkinson, "Introduction," 1.
53 Bolt, Özüekren, and Phillips, "Linking Integration."
54 Reitz, "Canada: Immigration and Nation-Building," 100.
55 Canadian Press, "Canada's Foreign-Born Population."

56 Banting, "Canada," 82.
57 Kymlicka, "Ethnocultural Diversity," 44.
58 Joppke, "Europe and Islam," 1315.
59 Reitz, "Assessing Multiculturalism," 15.
60 Millar, "Interdiscursive Analysis," 20.
61 Banting, "Canada," 85.
62 Ibid., 99.
63 Millar, "Interdiscursive Analysis," 21.
64 Ibid., 29.
65 Jurkova, "Role of Ethno-Cultural Organizations," 27.
66 Elke, "Trajectories of Multiculturalism," 184.
67 Banting, Courchene, and Seidle, "Conclusion," 654.
68 Biles and Ibrahim, "Religion and Public Policy," 160.
69 Anderson and Black, "Political Integration of Newcomers," 45.
70 Biles and Ibrahim, "Religion and Public Policy," 160.
71 Reitz et al., "Race," 698.
72 Biles and Ibrahim, "Religion and Public Policy," 160.
73 Banting, Courchene, and Seidle, "Conclusion," 645.
74 Li, quoted in Anderson and Black, "Political Integration of Newcomers,"
   46.
75 Reitz, "Assessing Multiculturalism," 21.
76 Banting, Courchene, and Seidle, "Introduction," 2.
77 Kazemipur, *Social Capital and Diversity*.
78 Reitz and Banerjee, "Racial Inequality."
79 Banting and Soroka, "Minority Nationalism."
80 Ibid., 163.
81 Miles, *Racism after "Race Relations,"* 175–6.
82 Wong and Tézli, "Integration in Canada," 20.
83 Seidle and Joppke. "Introduction," 7.
84 Kelly, "Who Needs a Theory?"
85 Joppke "Transformation of Citizenship."
86 Brodie, "Three Stories."
87 Ignatieff, *Blood and Belonging*.
88 Joppke, "Transformation of Citizenship," 3.
89 Ibid., 2.
90 Levesque, "Rethinking Citizenship Education," 137.
91 Gangnon and Iacovino, *Federalism, Citizenship, and Quebec*, 123–4.
92 Keenan, "Stephen Harper."
93 Joppke, "Through the European Looking Glass," 9.
94 Ibid., 8.

95 Keenan, "Stephen Harper."
96 Parry, "Liberals Move to Overhaul Rules."
97 Wong, "Transnationalism."
98 Vasta, "Do We Need Social Cohesion?" 198.
99 Ibid., 198.
100 Ibid., 210–11.
101 Hussain and Bagguley, "Citizenship, Ethnicity and Identity," 415.
102 De Haas, "International Migration," 26.
103 Yuval-Davis, Kannabiran, and Vieten, "Introduction."
104 Vasta, "Do We Need Social Cohesion?" 211.
105 Hussain and Bagguley, "Citizenship, Ethnicity and Identity," 416.
106 Wilcox, "Culture," 576.
107 Modood, *Multiculturalism*, 148–50.
108 Ghorashi and Vieten, "Female Narratives," 737.
109 Reitz, "Assessing Multiculturalism," 41.
110 Ethnic Diversity Survey Public Use Metafile.
111 Ibid.
112 Environics, *Survey of Muslims*.
113 Ibid., 9.
114 Ibid.
115 Ibid., 12.
116 Millar, "Interdiscursive Analysis," 29.
117 Reitz, "Multiculturalism Policies," 105.
118 Ibid., 108.
119 Ibid., 114–20.
120 Graves, "The EKOS poll."
121 See Haque, "Multiculturalism"; and Reitz et al., "Race."
122 Ramadan, *What I Believe*, 68.
123 Banting, "Transatlantic Convergence?" 73.

CHAPTER SEVEN

1 Vidino, "Islamism and the West."
2 Erlanger, "Amid Rise of Multiculturalism."
3 McCoy and Knight, "Twisted Motives in Europe."
4 Scott and De Vogue, "Trump Says He's Calling It a Travel Ban."
5 McCoy and Knight, "Europe's 'Xenoracism.'"
6 Gollom and Lindeman, "Who is Martin Couture-Rouleau?"
7 CBC News, "Ottawa Shooting."
8 CBC News, "Canadians Who Have 'Fallen Prey.'"

9 Murphy, "'Securitizing' Canadian Policing," 469–70.
10 Holpuch, "Trump."
11 Krause and Williams, "Broadening the Agenda," 242.
12 Zedner, "Too Much Security."
13 Taureck, "Securitization Theory."
14 Waever, "Securitization and Desecuritization," 4.
15 Buzan, Waever, and de Wilde, *Security*, 34.
16 Ibid., 25.
17 Taureck, "Securitization Theory," 55.
18 Buzan, Waever, and de Wilde, *Security*, 119.
19 Ibid., 123.
20 Ibid.
21 Gartner, Hyde-Price, and Reiter, *Europe's New Security Challenges*, 39.
22 Buzan, Waever, and de Wilde, *Security*, 121.
23 Ibid., 122.
24 Waever et al. (1993), quoted in Swimelar, "Education in Post-War Bosnia."
25 Huysmans, "Migrants as a Security Problem," 60.
26 Miles, *Racism after "Race Relations,"* 173.
27 Castles and Miller, *Age of Migration,* 217.
28 Freeze, "Canadian Extremists."
29 Haverig, "Managing Integration," 358.
30 Silber and Bhatt, *Radicalisation in the West*, 22.
31 Bartlett, Birdwell, and King, "Edge of Violence," 21–2.
32 Fekete, "Anti-Muslim Racism," 3.
33 Haverig, "Managing Integration," 358.
34 Awan, "'I Am a Muslim," 1160–2.
35 Gearson and Rosemont, "CONTEST as Strategy," 1038.
36 Awan, "I Am a Muslim," 1161.
37 Spalek, "Community Engagement," 828.
38 Ibid.
39 Gearson and Rosemont, "CONTEST as Strategy," 1045.
40 Ibid., 1049.
41 Travis, "Hundreds of Young People."
42 Klausen, et al., "Toward a Behavioral Model," 69–70.
43 Ibid., 69–70.
44 Spalek, "Community Engagement," 830.
45 Ibid., 830.
46 Halliday and Dodd, "UK Anti-Radicalisation Prevent Strategy."
47 Awan, "I Am a Muslim," 1161.
48 Ibid., 1172.

49 Fenwick and Choudhury, "The Impact of Counter-Terrorism."
50 Awan, "I Am a Muslim," 1167–8.
51 Ibid., 1172.
52 Ibid., 1166.
53 Spalek and O'Rawe, "Researching Counterterrorism," 154–5.
54 Bartlett et al., "Edge of Violence," 22.
55 Schiffauer, "Before the Law."
56 Ibid.
57 Murphy, "'Securitizing' Canadian Policing," 461.
58 Duffield, "Racism, Migration and Development," 68.
59 Murphy, "'Securitizing' Canadian Policing," 451.
60 Ibid., 455.
61 Bell, *Cold Terror*.
62 Murphy, "'Securitizing' Canadian Policing," 460.
63 Macklem, Daniels, and Roach, *Security of Freedom*.
64 Murphy, "'Securitizing' Canadian Policing," 455.
65 Macklem, Daniels, and Roach, *Security of Freedom*.
66 Campion-Smith, "Ottawa."
67 Ibid.
68 Forcese and Roach, "Canada's Anti-Terror Gamble."
69 Ibid.
70 McCharles, "CSIS Used Bill C-51 Powers."
71 Robertson, "Never a Tougher Time."
72 Helly, "Are Muslims Discriminated Against?"
73 Hanniman, "Canadian Muslims," 273.
74 Spalek, "Community Engagement," 829.
75 Public Safety Canada, "Building Resilience against Terrorism."
76 Ibid., 16.
77 Ibid, 2.
78 Bell, "RCMP."
79 Williamson, "Introduction."
80 Privy Council, *Report of the Events*.
81 Ibid.
82 Prime Minister of Canada, "Prime Minister Releases Letter."
83 Milewski, "Canada Accused of 'Complicity'."
84 McCharles, "Canada's Role."
85 Murphy, "'Securitizing' Canadian Policing," 453.
86 Abu-Laban and Nath, "From Deportation to Apology," 86.
87 Ibid.
88 Abu-Laban and Dhamoon, "Dangerous (Internal) Foreigners."

89 Fekete, *A Suitable Enemy*, 41.
90 Abu-Laban and Nath, "From Deportation to Apology," 94.
91 Drury, "Omar Khadr," 412.
92 Williamson, "Introduction," 9.
93 Ibid., 9.
94 Hyndman, "Question of 'The Political,'" 252.
95 Amnesty International, "Military Commission Proceedings."
96 CBC News, "Khadr Eligible for Parole."
97 CBC News, "Omar Khadr to Stay Out."
98 Knight and McCoy, "International Law," 285.
99 Hyndman, "Question of 'The Political,'" 252.
100 Park, "Child Soldiers and Distributive Justice," 331.
101 Edney, "Politics of Fear," 274.
102 Koring, "Guantanamo Bay."
103 Edney, "Politics of Fear," 274.
104 Ibid., 273.
105 Hyndman, "Question of 'The Political,'" 252.
106 Government of Canada, *Constitution Act, 1982 Part I*.
107 Edney, "Politics of Fear," 275.
108 Nesbitt-Larking, "Canadian Muslims," 12.
109 Ibbitson, "Omar Khadr Settlement."
110 Asad, *Formations of the Secular*, 35.
111 Cesari, "Islam, Immigration, and France," 217–18.
112 Eisenberg and Kymlicka, "Bringing Institutions Back In," 4.
113 Miles, *Racism after "Race Relations,"* 57–8.
114 Goldberg, *Threat of Race*, 16.
115 Eid, *Being Arab*.
116 Hall, "Question of Cultural Identity," 628.
117 Ibid., 628.
118 Ibid., 630–1.
119 Moghissi, Rahnema, and Goodman, *Diaspora by Design*.
120 Sivanandan, "Race, Terror and Civil Society," 8.
121 Ramadan, *What I Believe*, 49.
122 Spalek, "Community Engagement," 832.
123 Hafez and Mullins, "Radicalization Puzzle," 962–4.
124 Van Munster, *Securitizing Immigration*, 93.
125 Jervis, "Cooperation."
126 Roe, *Ethnic Violence*, 67.
127 Spalek, "Community Engagement," 830.
128 Gerges, *Far Enemy*.

129 McCoy, "Our Values Sacrificed."

CHAPTER EIGHT

1   Barker, *New Racism.*
2   Fekete, "Anti-Muslim Racism."
3   Ibid.
4   Said, *Covering Islam,* 55.
5   Knight, "Conceptualizing Transnational Community Formation," 22.
6   Eisenberg and Kymlicka, "Bringing Institutions Back In," 26.
7   Association for Canadian Studies and the Mosaic Institute, *Younger Canadians.*
8   Adams, *Unlikely Utopia,* 20.
9   Millar, "Interdiscursive Analysis of Language," 29.
10 Anderson, *Imagined Communities.*
11 Hall, "Question of Cultural Identity," 615.
12 Bloemraad, *Becoming a Citizen.*
13 Foster, *Where Race Does Not Matter,* 52.
14 Lentin and Titley, *Crises of Multiculturalism,* 3.
15 Kymlicka, "Canadian Multiculturalism," 165.
16 Ibid., 170.
17 Said, *Orientalism,* 328.
18 Mahdavi and Knight, "Towards 'the Dignity of Difference?'"
19 Reitz, "Assessing Multiculturalism," 19.
20 Said, *Orientalism,* 322.
21 Karim, *Changing Perceptions.*
22 Beaman, "Assessing Religious Identity," 239.
23 Lepinard, "From Immigrants to Muslims," 208.
24 Beaman, "Assessing Religious Identity," 248.
25 Maclure, "Reasonable Accommodation," 274.
26 Beaman, "Assessing Religious Identity," 242.
27 Eisenberg and Kymlicka, "Bringing Institutions Back In," 25.
28 Makin, "Witness."
29 Ibid.
30 Bramadat, "Beyond Christian Canada," 5.
31 Eisenberg and Kymlicka, "Bringing Institutions Back In," 26.
32 Dib, Donaldson, and Turcotte, "Integration and Identity," 163.
33 Ibid., 164.
34 Enns, Kirova, and Connolly, "Examining," 43–4.
35 Ibid., 43–4.

36 Ibid., 51.
37 Ibid., 58.
38 Bartlett, Birdwell, and King, "Edge of Violence."
39 Spalek, "Community Engagement for Counterterrorism," 828.
40 Gearson and Rosemont, "CONTEST as Strategy," 1051.
41 Kostakopoulou, "Matters of Control," 838.
42 Lentin, *Racism and Ethnic Discrimination*, x
43 Van Munster, *Securitizing Immigration*, 13.
44 Favat and Price, "Truth Campaign."
45 Ibid.
46 Bramadat, "Beyond Christian Canada," 5.
47 Said, *Orientalism*.

Bibliography

Abu-Laban, Yasmeen. "Reform by Stealth: the Harper Conservatives and Canadian Multiculturalism." In *The Multiculturalism Question: Debating Identity in 21st-Century Canada*, edited by Jack Jedwab, 148–72. Montreal: McGill-Queen's University Press, 2014.

Abu-Laban, Yasmeen, and Rita Dhamoon. "Dangerous (Internal) Foreigners and Nation-Building: The Case of Canada." *International Political Science Review* 30, no. 2 (2009): 201–11.

Abu-Laban, Yasmeen, and Christina Gabriel. *Selling Diversity: Immigration, Multiculturalism, Employment Equity and Globalization*. Peterborough: Broadview Press, 2002.

Abu-Laban, Yasmeen, and Nisha Nath. "From Deportation to Apology: The Case of Maher Arar and the Canadian State." *Canadian Ethnic Studies* 39, no. 3 (2007): 71–97.

Adams, Michael. *Unlikely Utopia: The Surprising Triumph of Canadian Pluralism*. Toronto: Viking Canada, 2007.

Amnesty International. "Military Commission Proceedings against Omar Khadr Resume, as USA Disregards Its International Human Rights Obligations." Accessed 5 October 2011. http://www.amnesty.org/en/ library/asset/AMR51/029/2010/en/7b1d3e2c-9824-4c80-9657- 4392d18dfff3/amr510292010en.pdf

Anderson, Benedict. *Imagined Communities: Reflections on the Origin and Spread of Nationalism*. London: Verso Books, 2006.

Anderson, Christopher, and Jerome Black. "The Political Integration of Newcomers, Minorities, and the Canadian-Born: Perspectives on Naturalization, Participation, and Representation." In *Immigration and Integration in Canada in the Twenty-First Century*, edited by John Biles, Meyer Burnstein, and James Frideres, 45–76. Montreal: McGill-Queen's University Press, 2008.

Asad, Talal. *Formations of the Secular: Christianity, Islam and Modernity*. Stanford: Stanford University Press, 2003.

Association for Canadian Studies and the Mosaic Institute. *Younger Canadians Believe Multiculturalism Works; Older Canadians, Not So Sure*. Toronto: Association for Canadian Studies and the Mosaic Institute, 2012.

Awan, Imran. "'I Am a Muslim Not an Extremist': How the Prevent Strategy Has Constructed a 'Suspect' Community." *Politics & Policy* 40, no. 6 (2012): 1158–85.

Ayoob, Mohammed. "Political Islam: Image and Reality," *World Policy Journal* 21, no. 3 (2004): 1–14.

Backhouse, Constance. *Colour-Coded: A Legal History of Racism in Canada, 1900–1950*. Toronto: University of Toronto Press, 1999.

Bahdi, Reem. "No Exit: Racial Profiling and Canada's War against Terrorism." *Osgoode Hall Law Journal* 41 no. 2–3 (2003): 293–317.

Balakrishnan, T.R., and Stephen Gyimah. "Spatial Residential Patterns of Selected Ethnic Groups: Significance and Policy Implications." *Canadian Ethnic Studies* 35, no. 1 (2003): 113–34.

Balibar, Etienne, and Immanuel Wallerstein. *Race, Nation, Class: Ambiguous Identities*. London: Verso, 1991.

Bannerji, Himani. *The Dark Side of the Nation: Essays on Multiculturalism, Nationalism and Gender*. Toronto: Canadian Scholars' Press, 2000.

Banting, Keith. "Canada." In *Immigrant Integration in Federal Countries*, edited by Christian Joppke and F. Leslie Seidle, 79–112. Montreal: McGill-Queen's University Press, 2012.

– "Transatlantic Convergence? The Archaeology of Immigrant Integration in Canada and Europe." *International Journal* 69, no. 1 (2014): 66–84.

Banting, Keith, Thomas Courchene, and F. Leslie Seidle. "Conclusion: Diversity, Belonging and Shared Citizenship." In *Belonging? Diversity, Recognition and Shared Citizenship in Canada*, edited by Keith Banting, Thomas Courchene, and F. Leslie Seidle, 647–87. Montreal: Institute for Research on Public Policy, 2007.

– "Introduction." In *Belonging? Diversity, Recognition and Shared Citizenship in Canada*, edited by Keith Banting, Thomas Courchene, and F. Leslie Seidle, 1–6. Montreal: Institute for Research on Public Policy, 2007.

Banting, Keith, and Stuart Soroka. "Minority Nationalism and Immigrant Integration in Canada." *Nations and Nationalism* 18, no. 1 (2012): 156–76.

Banton, Michael. *Racial Theories*. Cambridge: Cambridge University Press, 1998.

Barker, Martin. *The New Racism: Conservatives and the Ideology of the Tribe*. London: Junction Books, 1981.

Barsamian, David, and Edward Said. *Culture and Resistance: Conversations with Edward W. Said*. Cambridge: South End Press, 2003.

Bartlett, Jaime, Jonathan Birdwell, and Michael King. "The Edge of Violence: A Radical Approach to Extremism." London: Demos, 2010.

Bawer, Bruce. *Surrender: Appeasing Islam, Sacrificing Freedom*. New York, NY: Anchor Books, 2010.

– *While Europe Slept: How Radical Islam Is Destroying the West from Within*. New York, NY: Broadway Books, 2006.

BBC News. "Merkel Says German Multicultural Society Has Failed." 17 October 2010. Accessed 15 May 2011. http://www.bbc.co.uk/news/world-europe-11559451

Beaman, Lori. "Assessing Religious Identity in Law: Sincerity, Accommodation, and Harm." In *Identity Politics in the Public Realm: Bringing Institutions Back In*, edited by Avigail Eisenberg and Will Kymlicka, 238–59. Vancouver: UBC Press, 2011.

Beeby, Dean. "Massive Failure Rates Follow New, Tougher Citizenship Tests." *Toronto Star*, 29 November 2010. Accessed 15 May 2013. http://www.thestar.com/news/canada/2010/11/29/massive_failure_rates_follow_new_tougher_canadian_citizenship_tests.html

Berntzen, Lars, and Sveinung Sandberg. "The Collective Nature of Lone Wolf Terrorism: Anders Behring Breivik and the Anti-Islamic Social Movement." *Terrorism and Political Violence*, 26, no. 5 (2014): 759–79.

Bell, Stewart. *Cold Terror: How Canada Nurtures and Exports Terrorism around the World*. Etobicoke, ON: Wiley, 2004.

– "RCMP Set to Tackle Extremism at Home with Program to Curb Radicalization of Canadian Youth." *National Post*, 4 March 2014. Accessed 25 March 2016, http://news.nationalpost.com/news/canada/rcmp-set-to-tackle-extremism-at-home-with-program-to-curb-radicalization-of-canadian-youth

Bicker, Darrell, and John Ibbitson, *The Big Shift*. Toronto: HarperCollins Publishing, 2013.

Biles, John, Meyer Burnstein, and James Frideres. "Conclusion: Canadian." In *Immigration and Integration in Canada in the Twenty-First Century*, edited by John Biles, Meyer Burnstein, and James Frideres, 269–77. Montreal: McGill-Queen's University Press, 2008.

Biles, John, and Humera Ibrahim. "Religion and Public Policy: Immigration, Citizenship, and Multiculturalism – Guess Who's Coming to Dinner." In *Religion and Ethnicity in Canada*, edited by Paul Bramadat and David Seljak, 154–77. Toronto: University of Toronto Press, 2009.

Bissoondath, Neil. *Selling Illusions: The Cult of Multiculturalism in Canada*. Toronto: Penguin, 2002.

Blanchfield, Mike, and Jim Bronskill. "Documents Expose Harper's Obsession with Control." *Toronto Star*, 10 July 2010. Accessed 20 May 2013. http://www.thestar.com/news/canada/2010/06/06/documents_expose_harpers_obsession_with_control.html

Bloemraad, Irene. *Becoming a Citizen: Incorporating Immigrants and Refugees in the United States and Canada*. Berkeley: University of California Press, 2006.

Bolt, Gideom, A. Sule Özüekren, and Deborah Phillips. "Linking Integration and Residential Segregation." *Journal of Ethnic and Migration Studies* 36, no. 2 (2010): 169–86.

Boyd, Monica. "Educational Attainments of Immigrant Offspring: Success or Segmented Assimilation?" *International Migration Review* 36, no. 4 (2002): 1037–60.

Bramadat, Paul. "Beyond Christian Canada: Religion and Ethnicity in a Multicultural Society." In *Religion and Ethnicity in Canada*, edited by Paul Bramadat and David Seljak, 1–29. Toronto: University of Toronto Press, 2009.

– "Toward a New Story about Religion and Ethnicity in Canada." In *Religion and Ethnicity in Canada*, edited by Paul Bramadat and David Seljak, 222–34. Toronto: University of Toronto Press, 2009.

Breivik, Anders. "2083: A European Declaration of Independence." https://fas.org/programs/tap/_docs/2083_-_A_European_Declaration_of_Independence.pdf

Brodie, Janine. "The Three Stories of Canadian Citizenship." In *Constructing Canadian Citizenship: Historical Readings*, edited by Robert Adamoski, Dorothy Chunn, and Robert Menzies, 43–68. Peterborough, ON: Broadview Press, 2002.

Brown, Louise. "Aga Khan Hails Canada for Getting Pluralism Right." *Toronto Star*, 15 October 2010. Accessed 23 May 2013. http://www.thestar.com/news/gta/2010/10/15/aga_khan_hails_canada_for_getting_pluralism_right.html

Burnham, Peter. "Comparative Methodology." In *Research and Methods in Politics*, edited by Peter Burnham, Karin Lutz, Wyn Grant, and Zig Layton-Henry, 83–101. New York: Palgrave MacMillan, 2004.

Buzan, Barry and Gerald Segal. *Anticipating the Future*. London: Simon and Schuster, 1998.

Buzan, Barry, Ole Waever, and Jaap de Wilde. *Security: A New Framework of Analysis*. London: Lynne Rienner, 1998.

Caldwell, Christopher. *Reflections on the Revolution Europe: Immigration, Islam and the West*. New York: Anchor Books, 2010.

Campion-Smith, Bruce. "Ottawa Gives Security Agencies 'Exceptional' Powers to Probe Terror Plots." *Toronto Star*, 24 April 2013. Accessed 1 June 2013. http://www.thestar.com/news/canada/2013/04/24/ottawa_gives_security_agencies_exceptional_powers_to_probe_terror_plots.html

Canadian Press. "Marois Says She Didn't Mean to Offend with England Comments." *Globe and Mail*, 7 September 2013. Accessed 15 October 2013. http://www.theglobeandmail.com/news/national/marois-says-she-didnt-mean-to-offend-with-england-comments/article14177440/

Canadian Press. "Canada's Foreign-Born Population Soars to 6.8 Million." *CBC News*, 8 May 2013. Accessed 28 May 2013. http://www.cbc.ca/news/canada/story/2013/05/08/census-statistics-canada-household-survey.html

Castles, Stephen, and Mark Miller. *The Age of Migration: International Population Movements in the Modern World*. 4th ed. London: The Guilford Press, 2009.

CBC News. "Canadians Who Have 'Fallen Prey' to Islamic Extremism: Homegrown Radicals Represent a Broad Cross-Section of Community." 2 April 2013. Accessed 27 May 2013. http://www.cbc.ca/news/canada/story/2013/04/02/canada-canadians-al-qaeda.html

– "Khadr Eligible for Parole Next Summer, Lawyers Say." 29 September 2012. Accessed 20 May 2013. http://www.cbc.ca/news/politics/story/2012/09/29/pol-omar-khadr-in-canada-next-steps.html

– "Omar Khadr to Stay Out on Bail after Federal Government Drops Appeal." 16 February 2016. Accessed 5 April 2016. http://www.cbc.ca/news/politics/omar-khadr-bail-fight-1.3454278

– "Ontario Premier Rejects Use of Shariah." 11 September 2005. Accessed 20 May 2013. http://www.cbc.ca/news/canada/story/2005/09/09/sharia-protests-20050909.html

– "Ottawa Shooting: Michael Zehaf-Bibeau Made Video, Police Say." 26 October 2014. Accessed 9 December 2016. http://www.cbc.ca/news/politics/ottawa-shooting-michael-zehaf-bibeau-made-video-police-say-1.2813798

– "Shariah Law: FAQs." 26 May 2005. Accessed 5 March 2010. http://www.cbc.ca/news/background/islam/shariah-law.html

Cesari, Jocelyne. "Islam, Immigration, and France." In *International Migration and the Governance of Religious Diversity*, edited by Paul Bramadat and Matthias Koenig, 195–224. Montreal: McGill-Queen's University Press, 2009.

Chanock, Martin. "'Culture' and Human Rights: Orientalising, Occidentalising and Authenticity." In *Beyond Rights Talk and Culture Talk: Comparative Essays on the Politics of Rights and Culture*, edited by Mahmood Mamdani, 15–36. New York: St Martin's Press, 2000.

Chrisafis, Angelique. "Marine Le Pen Goes on Trial Charged with Anti-Muslim Speech." *The Guardian*, 20 October 2015. Accessed 22 November 2017. https://www.theguardian.com/world/2015/oct/20/marine-le-pen-trial-charged-anti-muslims-hate-speech

Citizenship and Immigration Canada. "Evaluation of the Multiculturalism Program." Accessed 22 July 2012. http://www.cic.gc.ca/english/resources/evaluation/multi/section1.asp

Cole, Mike. "A Plethora of 'Suitable Enemies': British Racism at the Dawn of the Twenty-First Century." *Ethnic and Racial Studies* 32, no. 9 (2009): 1671–85.

– "A Response to Charles Mills." *Ethnicities* 9 (2009): 281–4.

Creese, Gillian, and Edith Ngene Kambere. "What Colour Is Your English?" *Canadian Review of Sociology and Anthropology* 40, no. 5 (2002): 565–73.

Dallmayr, Fred. *Beyond Orientalism: Essays on Cross-Cultural Encounter*. Albany: State University of New York Press, 1996.

Day, Richard. *Multiculturalism and the History of Canadian Diversity*. Toronto: University of Toronto Press, 1998.

De Haas, Hein. "International Migration, Remittances and Development: Myths and Facts." *Third World Quarterly* 26 (2005): 1269–84.

Dempsey, Judy. "A Difficult Choice for Turks in Germany." *New York Times*, 15 April 2013. Accessed 29 April 2013. http://www.nytimes.com/2013/04/16/world/europe/16iht-letter16.html?_r=0

Denzin, Norman. "The Reflexive Interview and a Performative Social Science," *Qualitative Research* 1, no. 1 (2001): 23–46.

Dib, Kamal, Ian Donaldson, and Brittany Turcotte. "Integration and Identity in Canada: The Importance of Multicultural Common Spaces." *Canadian Ethnic Studies* 40, no. 1 (2008): 161–87.

Doerschler, Peter, and Pamela Jackson. "Do Muslims in Germany Really Fail to Integrate? Muslim Integration and Trust in Public Institutions." *International Migration & Integration* 13, no. 4 (2012): 503–23.

Drury, Shadia. "Omar Khadr and the Perils of Canadian Multiculturalism." In *Omar Khadr, Oh Canada,* edited by Janice Williamson, 412–24. Montreal: McGill-Queen's University Press, 2012.

Duffield, Mark. "Racism, Migration and Development: The Foundations of Planetary Order." *Progress in Development Studies* 6, no. 1 (2006): 68–79.

Dupré, Jean François. "Intercultural Citizenship, Civic Nationalism, and Nation Building in Québec: From Common Public Language to Laïcité." *Studies in Ethnicity and Nationalism* 12, no. 2 (2012): 227–48.

Ebbinghaus, Bernhard. "When Less Is More: Selection Problems in Large-N and Small-N Cross-National Comparisons." *International Sociology* 20, no. 2 (2005): 133–52.

The Economist. "Europe's Populist Insurgents: Turning Right." 2 January 2014. Accessed 15 November 2016. https://www.economist.com/news/briefing/21592666-parties-nationalist-right-are-changing-terms-european-political-debate-does

Edney, Dennis. "The Politics of Fear." In *Omar Khadr, Oh Canada*, edited by Janice Williamson, 270–8. Montreal: McGill-Queen's University Press, 2012.

Eid, Paul. *Being Arab: Ethnic and Religious Identity Building among Second Generation Youth in Montreal.* Montreal: McGill-Queen's University Press, 2007.

Eisenberg, Avigail, and Will Kymlicka. "Bringing Institutions Back In: How Public Institutions Assess Identity." In *Identity Politics in the Public Realm: Bringing Institutions Back In*, edited by Avigail Eisenberg and Will Kymlicka, 1–30. Vancouver: UBC Press, 2011.

Elgamri, Elzain. *Islam in the British Broadsheets: The Impact of Orientalism on Representations of Islam in the British Press.* Reading: Ithaca Press, 2008.

Elke, Winter. "Trajectories of Multiculturalism in Germany, the Netherlands and Canada: In Search of Common Patterns." *Government and Opposition* 45, no. 2 (2010): 166–86.

Elliott, Louise. "Immigrant Visas to Drop 5%: Records." *CBC News*, 13 February 2011. Accessed 15 May 2013. http://www.cbc.ca/news/politics/story/2011/02/12/canada-immigration-rates.html

Enns, Richard, Anna Kirova, and David Connolly. "Examining Bonding and Bridging Activities in the Context of a Common Spaces Approach to Integration." *Canadian Ethnic Studies* 45, no. 3 (2013): 39–63.

Environics. "Muslims and Multiculturalism in Canada." Toronto: Environics Research Group, 2007. Accessed 1 November 2011. http://

www.environicsinstitute.org/PDF-MuslimsandMulticulturalisminCanada-
LiftingtheVeil.pdf

Environics. *Survey of Muslims in Canada 2016*. Toronto: The Environics
Institute, 2016.

Erlanger, Steven. "Amid Rise of Multiculturalism, Dutch Confront Their
Questions of Identity." *New York Times*, 13 August 2011. Accessed
2 May 2012. http://www.nytimes.com/2011/08/14/world/europe/
14dutch.html?pagewanted=all&_r=0

Erzberger, Christian, and Gerald Prein. "Triangulation: Validity and
Empirically-Based Hypothesis Construction." *Quality and Quantity* 31,
no. 2 (1997): 141–54.

Essed, Philomena. *Understanding Everyday Racism: An Interdisciplinary
Theory*. London: Sage, 1991.

Esses, Victoria, Ulrich Wagner, Carina Wolf, Matthias Preiser, and
Christopher Wilbur. "Perceptions of National Identity and Attitudes
toward Immigrants and Immigration in Canada and Germany."
International Journal of Intercultural Relations 30 (2006): 653–9.

Ethnic Diversity Survey Public Use Metafile 2002 [computer file]. Ottawa:
Statistics Canada. Data Liberation Initiative [distributor], 2005.
Catalogue no. 89M0019GPE.

European Union Agency for Fundamental Rights. *Experience of Discrimination, Social Marginalisation and Violence: A Comparative Study of
Muslim and Non-Muslim Youth in Three EU Member States*. 2010.
Accessed 15 May 2012. http://fra.europa.eu/sites/default/files/fra_
uploads/1202-Pub-racism-marginalisation_en.pdf

Farris, Sara. "An 'Ideal Type' Called Orientalism." *Interventions* 12, no. 2
(2010): 265–84.

Favat, Pete, and Bryan Price. "The Truth Campaign and the War of Ideas."
CTC Sentinel 8, no. 7 (2015): 9–15.

Fekete, Liz. "Anti-Muslim Racism and the European Security State." *Race
& Class* 46, no. 1 (2004): 3–29.

– *A Suitable Enemy: Racism, Migration and Islamophobia in Europe*.
London: Pluto Press, 2009.

Fenwick, Helen, and Tufyal Choudhury. "The Impact of Counter-
Terrorism Measures on Muslim Communities." Manchester, UK:
Equality and Human Rights Commission, 2011. Accessed 5 April 2016.
http://www.equalityhumanrights.com/sites/default/files/documents/
research/counter-terrorism_research_report_72.pdf

Fleras, Augie, and Jean Elliott. *Unequal Relations: An Introduction to Race,
Ethnic and Aboriginal Dynamics*. Scarborough, ON: Pearson, 1999.

Fleras, Augie, and Jean Kunz. *Media and Minorities: Representing Diversity in a Multicultural Canada.* Toronto: Thompson Educational Publishing, 2001.

Flick, Uwe. *An Introduction to Qualitative Research.* London: Sage, 2002.

Forcese, Craig, and Kent Roach. "Canada's Anti-terror Gamble." *New York Times*, 11 March 2015. Accessed 2 April 2016. http://www.nytimes.com/2015/03/12/opinion/canadas-antiterror-gamble.html

Foster, Cecil. *Where Race Does Not Matter: The New Spirit of Modernity.* Toronto: Penguin Canada, 2005.

Foster, Cecil. *Genuine Multiculturalism: The Tragedy and Comedy of Diversity.* Montreal: McGill-Queen's University Press, 2014.

Freeze, Collin. "Canadian Extremists More Likely Homegrown: 'Secret' CSIS Report." *Globe and Mail*, 2 February 2013. Accessed 29 May 2013. http://www.theglobeandmail.com/news/national/canadian-extremists-more-likely-homegrown-secret-csis-report/article8149887/

Friedman, Thomas. *The World Is Flat: A Brief History of the Twenty-First Century.* New York: Farrar, Straus and Giroux, 2005.

Galabuzi, Grace-Edward. "The Economic Exclusion of Racialized Communities – a Statistical Profile." In *The History of Immigration and Racism in Canada*, edited by Barrington Walker. Toronto: Canadian Scholars' Press, 2008.

Gangnon, Alain, and Raffaele Iacovino. *Federalism, Citizenship, and Quebec: Debating Multiculturalism.* Toronto: University of Toronto Press, 2007.

Garcea, Joseph, Anna Kirova, and Lloyd Wong. "Introduction: Multiculturalism Discourses in Canada." *Canadian Ethnic Studies* 40, no. 1 (2008): 1–10.

Gartner, Heinz, Adrian Hyde-Price, and Erich Reiter. *Europe's New Security Challenges.* London: Lynne Rienner, 2001.

Gearson, John, and Hugo Rosemont. "CONTEST as Strategy: Reassessing Britain's Counterterrorism Approach." *Studies in Conflict and Terrorism* 38, no. 12 (2015): 1038–64.

Gellner, Ernest. *Nationalism.* New York: New York University Press, 1997.

Gerges, Fawaz. *The Far Enemy: Why Jihad Went Global.* Cambridge: Cambridge University Press, 2009.

Ghorashi, Halleh, and Ulrike Vieten. "Female Narratives of 'New' Citizens' Belonging(s) and Identities in Europe: Case Studies from the Netherlands and Britain." *Identities: Global Studies in Culture and Power* 19, no. 6 (2012): 725–41.

Goldberg, David. *The Threat of Race: Reflections on Racial Neoliberalism.*
Oxford: Wiley-Blackwell, 2009.

Goldstein, Kenneth. "Getting in the Door: Sampling and Completing Elite
Interviews." *PS: Political Science and Politics* 35, no. 4 (2002): 669–72.

Gollum, Mark, and Tracey Lindeman. "Who Is Martin Couture-Rouleau?"
CBC News, 21 October 2014. Accessed 10 December 2016. http://www.
cbc.ca/news/canada/who-is-martin-couture-rouleau-1.2807285

Gordon, Milton. *Assimilation in American Life.* New York: Oxford
University Press, 1964.

Gottschalk, Peter, and Gabriel Greenberg. *Islamophobia: Making Muslims
the Enemy.* New York: Rowman and Littlefield, 2008.

Government of Canada. *Constitution Act, 1982 Part I: Canadian Charter
of Rights and Freedoms.* Accessed 14 April 2011. http://laws-lois.justice.
gc.ca/eng/charter/CHART_E.PDF

Government of Canada. *Canadian Multiculturalism Act R.S.C., 1985,
c. 24 (4th Supp.).* Accessed 10 April 2011. http://laws-lois.justice.gc.ca/
PDF/C-18.7.pdf

Gramsci, Antonio. *Selections from the Notebooks of Antonio Gramsci,*
edited and translated by Qunitin Hoare and Geoffrey Smith. New York:
International Publishers, 2003.

Graves, Frank. "The EKOS Poll: Are Canadians Getting More Racist."
iPolitics, 12 March 2015. Accessed 15 December 2016. https://ipolitics.
ca/2015/03/12/the-ekos-poll-are-canadians-getting-more-racist/

Hafez, Mohammed, and Creighton Mullins. "The Radicalization Puzzle:
A Theoretical Synthesis of Empirical Approaches to Homegrown
Extremism." *Studies in Conflict and Terrorism* 38, no. 11 (2015):
958–75.

Hall, Stuart. "The Question of Cultural Identity." In *Modernity: An
Introduction to Modern Societies,* edited by Stuart Hall, David Held,
Don Huebert, and Kenneth Thompson, 595–634. Cambridge:
Blackwell, 1996.

Halliday, Josh, and Vikram Dodd. "UK Anti-Radicalisation Prevent
Strategy a 'Toxic Brand.'" *Guardian,* 9 March 2015. Accessed 30 March
2016. http://www.theguardian.com/uk-news/2015/mar/09/anti-
radicalisation-prevent-strategy-a-toxic-brand

Hanniman, Wayne. "Canadian Muslims, Islamophobia and National
Security." *International Journal of Law, Crime and Justice* 36, no. 4
(2008): 271–85.

Haque, Eve. "Multiculturalism, Language, and Immigrant Integration." In
The Multiculturalism Question: Debating Identity in 21st-century

Canada, edited by Jack Jebwab, 204–23. Montreal: McGill-Queen's University Press, 2014.

Haque, Eve. *Multiculturalism within a Bilingual Framework: Language, Race and Belonging in Canada*. Toronto: University of Toronto Press, 2012.

Harris, David, and Jeremiah Sim. "Who Is Multiracial? Assessing the Complexity of Lived Race." *American Sociological Review* 67, no. 4 (2002): 614–27.

Harris, Kathleen. "Hate Crimes against Muslims in Canada up 60%, StatsCan Reports." *CBC News*, 13 June 2017. Accessed 7 July 2017. http://www.cbc.ca/news/politics/hate-crimes-muslims-statscan-1.4158042

Harrison, Simon. "Cultural Difference as Denied Resemblance: Reconsidering Nationalism and Ethnicity.," *Comparative Studies in Society and History* 45, no. 2 (2003): 343–61.

Haverig, Anika. "Managing Integration: German and British Policy Responses to the 'Threat from Within' Post-2001." *International Migration and Integration* 14 (2013): 345–62.

Helly, Denise. "Are Muslims Discriminated Against in Canada since September 2001?" *Canadian Ethnic Studies* 36, no. 1 (2004): 24–47.

Holpuch, Amanda. "Trump Re-ups Controversial Muslim Ban and Mexico Wall in First Campaign Ad." *Guardian*, 4 January 2016. Accessed 20 February 2016. http://www.theguardian.com/us-news/2016/jan/04/donald-trump-great-again-first-campaign-ad-isis-mexico-wall-muslim-ban.

Howe, Paul. "The Political Engagement of New Canadians: A Comparative Perspective." In *Belonging? Diversity, Recognition and Shared Citizenship in Canada*, edited by Keith Banting, Thomas Courchene, and F. Leslie Seidle. Montreal: Institute for Research on Public Policy, 2007.

Huntington, Samuel. *The Clash of Civilizations: Remaking of World Order*. New York: Touchstone, 1996.

Hussain, Yasmin, and Paul Bagguley. "Citizenship, Ethnicity and Identity: British Pakistanis after the 2001 'Riots.'" *Sociology* 39, no. 3 (2005): 407–25.

Huysmans, Jus. "Migrants as a Security Problem: Dangers of 'Securitizing' Societal Issues." In *Migration and European Integration: The Dynamics of Inclusion and Exclusion*, edited by Robert Miles and Dietrich Thranhardt, 53–72. London: Pinter Publishers, 1995.

Hyndman, Jennifer. "The Question of 'The Political' in Critical Geopolitics: Querying the 'Child Soldier' in the 'War on Terror.'" *Political Geography* 29, no. 5 (2010): 247–55.

Ibbitson, John. "The Omar Khadr Settlement Will Be a Political Albatross
    for Trudeau." *Globe and Mail*, 5 July 2017. Accessed 29 July 2017.
    https://www.theglobeandmail.com/news/politics/omar-khadr-settlement-
    will-be-a-political-albatross-for-trudeau/article35554383/
Ignatieff, Michael. *Blood and Belonging: Journeys in the New Nationalism.*
    Toronto: Penguin, 1992.
Jacobson, David, and Natalie Delia Deckard. "Surveying the Landscape of
    Integration: Muslim Immigrants in the United Kingdom and France."
    Democracy and Security 10, no. 2 (2014): 113–31.
Jedwab, Jack, and Ayman Al-Yassini. "Canadians Regard the Internet as
    the Place Where Racism Is Most Prevalent." Association for Canadian
    Studies and Canadian Race Relations Foundation, 21 March 2012.
    Accessed 1 June 2012. http://www.crr.ca/images/stories/pdf/Racism_
    and_Prejudice_Sources_Trust_and_Blame.pdf
Jervis, Robert. "Cooperation under the Security Dilemma." *World Politics*
    30 (1978): 167–214.
Jimenez, Marina, and Omar El Akkad. "Values at Heart of Islamic
    Tensions." *Globe and Mail*, 8 November 2005.
Joppke, Christian. "Europe and Islam: Alarmists, Victimists, and
    Integration by Law." *West European Politics* 37, no. 6 (2014): 1314–35.
– "Through the European Looking Glass: Citizenship Tests in the USA,
    Australia, and Canada." *Citizenship Studies* 17, no. 1 (2013): 1–15.
– "Transformation of Citizenship: Status, Rights, Identity." *Citizenship
    Studies* 11, no. 1 (2007): 37–48.
Jurkova, Sinela. "The Role of Ethno-Cultural Organizations in Immigrant
    Integration: A Case Study of the Bulgarian Society in Western Canada."
    Canadian Ethnic Studies 46, no. 1 (2014): 23–44.
Karim, Karim. *Changing Perceptions of Islamic Authority among Muslims
    in Canada, the United States and the United Kingdom.* Montreal:
    Institute for Research on Public Policy, 2009.
Katzenstein, Peter. "Conclusion: National Security in a Changing World."
    In *The Culture of National Security: Norms and Identity in World
    Politics*, edited by Peter Katzenstein, 498–538. New York: Columbia
    University Press, 1996.
Kazemipur, Abdolmohammad. *Social Capital and Diversity: Some Lessons
    from Canada.* Bern: Peter Lang, 2009.
Kazemipur, Abdolmohammad, and Shiva Halli. *The New Poverty in
    Canada: Ethnic Groups and Ghetto Neighbourhoods.* Toronto:
    Thompson Educational Publishing, 2000.

Keenan, Edward. "When Stephen Harper Refers to 'Barbaric Culture,' He Means Islam." *Toronto Star*, 5 October 2015. Accessed 8 January 2016. https://www.thestar.com/news/canada/2015/10/05/when-stephen-harper-refers-to-barbaric-culture-he-means-islam-an-anti-muslim-alarm-thats-ugly-and-effective-because-it-gets-votes-edward-keenan.html

Kelly, George. "Who Needs a Theory of Citizenship?" *Daedalus* 108, no. 4 (1979): 21–36.

Keohane, Robert, and Jospeh Nye. *Power and Interdependence: World Politics in Transition*. Boston: Little, Brown, 1977.

Keung, Nicholas. "Parliament's Lack of Diversity Goes beyond Race, Gender: Study." *Toronto Star*, 2 January 2015. Accessed 15 July 2015. http://www.thestar.com/news/canada/2015/01/02/parliaments_lack_of_diversity_goes_beyond_race_gender_study.html

Khan, Sheema. "The Ontario Sharia Debate: Transformational Accommodation, Multiculturalism and Muslim Identity." In *Belonging? Diversity, Recognition and Shared Citizenship in Canada*, edited by Keith Banting, Thomas J. Courchene, and F. Leslie Seidle, 475–85. Montreal: Institute for Research on Public Policy, 2007.

Klausen, Jytte, Selene Campion, Nathan Needle, Giang Nguyen, and Rosanne Libretti. "Toward a Behavioral Model of 'Homegrown' Radicalization Trajectories." *Studies in Conflict and Terrorism* 39, no. 1 (2016): 67–83.

Knight, W. Andy. "Conceptualizing Transnational Community Formation: Migrants, Sojourners and Diasporas in a Globalized Era." *Canadian Studies in Population* 29, no. 1 (2002): 1–30.

Knight, W. Andy, Ingrid Johnston, Lan Chan-Marples, and John McCoy. *Immigrant and Refugee Youth in Alberta: Challenge and Resilience*. Edmonton: Ricoh Canada, 2012.

Knight, W. Andy, and John McCoy. "International Law and the Recruitment of a Child Soldier: Omar Khadr and Family Ties." In *Omar Khadr, Oh Canada*, edited by Janice Williamson, 285–304. Montreal: McGill-Queen's University Press, 2012.

Koring, Paul. "Guantanamo Bay: The Canadian Detainee." *Globe and Mail*, 26 October 2010.

Korteweg, Anna. "The Sharia Debate in Ontario: Gender, Islam, and Representations of Muslim Women's Agency." *Gender and Society* 22, no. 4 (2008): 343–454.

Kostakopoulou, Dora. "Matters of Control: Integration Tests, Naturalisation Reform and Probationary Citizenship in the United

Kingdom." *Journal of Ethnic and Migration Studies* 36, no. 5 (2010): 829–84.

Krause, Keith, and Michael C. Williams. "Broadening the Agenda of Security Studies: Politics and Methods." *Mershon International Studies Review* 40, no. 2 (1996): 229–54.

Kymlicka, Will. "Canadian Multiculturalism in Historical and Comparative Perspective." In *Canadian Multiculturalism: Dreams, Realities, Expectations*, edited by Mathew Zachariah, Allan Sheppard, and Leona Barratt, 1–8. Edmonton: Canadian Multicultural Education Foundation, 2004.

– "Comment on Meer and Modood." *Journal of Intercultural Studies* 33, no. 2 (2012): 211–6.

– "Ethnocultural Diversity in a Liberal State: Making Sense of Canadian Model(s)." In *Belonging? Diversity, Recognition and Shared Citizenship in Canada,* edited by Keith Banting, Thomas J. Courchene, and F. Leslie Seidle, 39–68. Montreal: Institute for Research on Public Policy, 2007.

– *Finding Our Way: Rethinking Ethnocultural Relations in Canada.* Toronto: Oxford University Press, 1998.

– *Multicultural Citizenship.* Oxford: Clarendon Press, 1995.

– "Testing the Liberal Multiculturalist Hypothesis: Normative Theories and Social Science Evidence." *Canadian Journal of Political Science* 43, no. 2 (2010): 257–71.

Lasswell, Harold. *Politics: Who Gets What, When, How.* Cleveland: Meridian, 1958.

Leech, Beth. "Asking Questions: Techniques for Semistructured Interviews." *PS: Political Science and Politics* 35, no. 4 (2002): 665–8.

– "Interview Methods in Political Science." *PS: Political Science and Politics* 35, no. 4 (2002): 663–4.

Lentin, Alana. *Racism and Ethnic Discrimination.* New York: Rosen Publishing, 2011.

Lentin, Alana, and Gavan Titley. *The Crises of Multiculturalism: Racism in a Neoliberal Age.* London: Zed Books, 2011.

Lepinard, Eleonore. "From Immigrants to Muslims: Shifting Categories of the French Model."Iin *Identity Politics in the Public Realm: Bringing Institutions Back In,* edited by Avigail Eisenberg and Will Kymlicka, 190–214. Vancouver: UBC Press, 2011.

Levesque, Stephane. "Rethinking Citizenship Education in Canada." In *Beyond National Dreams: Essays on Canadian Citizenship and Nationalism,* edited by Andrew Nurse and Raymond Blake, 131–54. Markham: Fitzhenry and Whiteside, 2009.

Levey, Geoffrey, and Tariq Modood. *Secularism, Religion and Multicultural Citizenship*. Cambridge: Cambridge University Press, 2009.

Lewis, Bernard. *What Went Wrong? The Clash between Islam and Modernity in the Middle East*. New York: Perennial, 2002.

Ley, David. "Does Transnationalism Trump Immigrant Integration? Evidence from Canada's links with East Asia." *Journal of Ethnic and Migration Studies* 39, no. 6 (2013): 921–38.

Li, Peter. *Destination Canada: Immigration Debates and Issues*. Toronto: Oxford University Press, 2003.

Mac an Ghaill, Martin. *Contemporary Racisms and Ethnicities: Social and Cultural Transformations*. Buckingham, UK: Open University Press, 1999.

Macklem, Patrick, Ronald Daniels, and Kent Roach. *The Security of Freedom: Essays on Canada's Anti-Terrorism Bill*. Toronto: University of Toronto Press, 2001.

Maclure, Jocelyn. "Reasonable Accommodation and the Subjective Conception of Freedom of Conscience and Religion." In *Identity Politics in the Public Realm: Bringing Institutions Back In*, edited by Avigail Eisenberg and Will Kymlicka, 260–80. Vancouver: UBC Press, 2011.

Mahdavi, Mojtaba Mahdavi, and W. Andy Knight. "Towards 'the Dignity of Difference'? Neither 'End of History' nor 'Clash of Civilizations." In *Towards the Dignity of Difference? Neither "End of History" nor "Clash of Civilizations,"* edited by Mojtaba Mahdavi and W. Andy Knight, 1–24. Burlington, UK: Ashgate, 2012.

Mahoney, Jim, and Ian Bailey. "New Immigration Guide Issues Stern Warnings against 'Barbaric' Practices." *Globe and Mail*, 2 April 2013. Accessed 15 May 2013. http://www.theglobeandmail.com/news/politics/new-immigration-guide-issues-stern-warnings-against-barbaric-practices/article10671286/

Makin, Kirk. "Witness May be Required to Remove Niqab while Testifying: Top Court." *Globe and Mail*, 20 December 2012. Accessed 10 May 2013 http://www.theglobeandmail.com/news/national/witness-may-be-required-to-remove-niqab-while-testifying-top-court/article6588243/?page=all

Malik, Kenan. "Assimilation's Failure, Terrorism's Rise." *New York Times*, 6 July 2011. Accessed 1 May 2012. http://www.nytimes.com/2011/07/07/opinion/07malik.html?pagewanted=all

McCharles, Tonda. "Canada's Role in Men's Torture Indirect, Inquiry Report Says." *Toronto Star*, 21 October 2008. Accessed 20 May 2013.

http://www.thestar.com/news/canada/2008/10/21/canadas_role_in_
mens_torture_indirect_inquiry_report_says.html

- "csɪs Used Bill c-51 Powers Several Times to Disrupt Suspected
  Terrorists, Senate Hears." *Toronto Star*, 7 March 2016. Accessed 3 April
  2016.http://www.thestar.com/news/canada/2016/03/07/csis-used-bill-c-51-
  powers-several-times-to-disrupt-suspected-terrorists-senate-hears.html

McCoy, John. "Our Values Sacrificed in Name of Security." *Edmonton
  Journal*, 5 March 2013.

McCoy, John, and David Jones. "Anti-Muslim Hatred Stirring in Alberta
  Is, Sadly, Nothing New." *Globe and Mail*, 3 February 2017.

McCoy, John, and W. Andy Knight. "An Attack on Multiculturalism." *The
  Mark*, 14 October 2011.

- "Europe's 'Xenoracism' Spawned Norway Horror." *Edmonton Journal*,
  28 July 2011.

- "National Identity Overhauled." *Edmonton Journal*, 5 October 2011.

- "Refugee Crisis Stirs the Ghosts of Fascism Past." *Edmonton Journal*,
  6 March 2016.

- "Twisted Motives in Europe." *Edmonton Journal*, 24 March 2012.

McDonough, Sheila, and Homa Hoodfar. "Muslims in Canada: From
  Ethnic Groups to Religious Community." In *Religion and Ethnicity in
  Canada*, edited by Paul Bramadat and David Seljak, 133–53. Toronto:
  University of Toronto Press, 2009.

McKay, Ian, and Jamie Swift. *Warrior Nation: Rebranding Canada in an
  Age of Anxiety*. Toronto: Between the Lines, 2012.

McLaren, Angus. "Stemming the Flood of Defective Aliens." In *The
  History of Immigration and Racism in Canada*, edited by Barrington
  Walker, 189–204. Toronto: Canadian Scholars' Press, 2008.

McRoberts, Kenneth. *Misconceiving Canada*. Don Mills, oɴ: Oxford
  University Press, 1997.

Memmi, Albert. *Racism*, translated by Steve Martinot. Minneapolis:
  University of Minnesota Press, 2000.

Miles, Robert. *Racism after "Race Relations."* London: Routledge, 1993.

Miles, Robert, and Malcolm Brown. *Racism*. London: Routledge, 2005.

Milewski, Terry. "Canada Accused of 'Complicity' in Torture in uɴ
  Report." *cʙc News*, 1 June 2012. Accessed 20 May 2013. http://www.
  cbc.ca/news/politics/story/2012/06/01/pol-un-report-torture-canada-
  milewski.html

Millar, Jeff. "An Interdiscursive Analysis of Language and Immigrant
  Integration Policy Discourse in Canada." *Critical Discourse Studies* 10,
  no. 1 (2013): 18–31.

Mills, Charles. "Critical Race Theory: A Reply to Mike Cole." *Ethnicities* 9 (2009): 270–81.

Milot, Micheline. "Modus Co-Vivendi: Religious Diversity in Canada." In *International Migration and the Governance of Religious Diversity*, edited by Paul Bramadat and Matthias Koenig, 105–30. Montreal: McGill-Queen's University Press, 2009.

Modood, Tariq. "Difference, Cultural Racism and Anti-Racism." In *Debating Cultural Hybridity: Multi-Cultural Identities and the Politics of Anti-Racism*, edited by Pnina Werbner, 154–72. London: Zed Books, 1997.

– *Multiculturalism*. Cambridge: Polity, 2007.

Moghissi, Haideh, Saeed Rahnema, and Mark Goodman. *Diaspora by Design: Muslim Immigrants in Canada and Beyond*. Toronto: University of Toronto Press, 2009.

Montpetit, Jonathan. "Will Interculturalism Replace Multiculturalism?" *Toronto Star*, 6 March 2011. Accessed 15 October 2013. http://www.thestar.com/news/canada/2011/03/06/will_interculturalism_replace_multiculturalism.html

Murphy, Christopher. "'Securitizing' Canadian Policing: A New Policing Paradigm for the Post 9/11 Security State?" *Canadian Journal of Sociology* 32, no. 4 (2007): 449–75.

Nesbitt-Larking, Paul. "Canadian Muslims: Political Discourses in Tension." *British Journal of Canadian Studies* 20, no. 1 (2007): 1–24.

Oleinik, Anton. "Mixing Quantitative and Qualitative Content Analysis: Triangulation at Work." *Quality and Quantity* 45, no. 4 (2011): 859–73.

Omi, Michael, and Howard Winant. *Racial Formation in the United States: From the 1960s to the 1990s*. New York: Routledge, 1994.

Park, Augustine. "Child Soldiers and Distributive Justice: Addressing the Limits of Law." *Crime, Law and Social Change* 53, no. 4 (2010): 329–48.

Parry, Tom. "Liberals Move to Overhaul Rules on Revoking, Granting Citizenship." *CBC News*, 25 February 2016. Accessed 27 February 2016. http://www.cbc.ca/news/politics/john-mccallum-citizenship-act-repeal-bill-1.3463471

Payton, Laura. "Ethnic Riding Targeting Key to Conservatives' 2011 Victory." *CBC News*, 23 October 23 2012. Accessed 20 May 2013. http://www.cbc.ca/news/politics/story/2012/10/22/pol-election-conservative-ethnic-riding-targeting.html

Pendakur, Krishna, and Ravi Pendakur. "The Colour of Money: Earnings Differentials among Ethnic Groups in Canada." *Canadian Journal of Economics* 31, no. 3 (1997): 518–48.

Perry, Barbara, and Ryan Scrivens. "Uneasy Alliances: A Look at the Right-Wing Extremist Movement in Canada." *Studies in Conflict and Terrorism* 39, no. 9 (2016): 819–41.

Peters, Guy. *Comparative Politics: Theory and Methods*. Basingstoke: Palgrave MacMillan, 1998.

Pew Research Center. "Muslims in Europe: Economic Worries Top Concerns about Religious and Cultural Identity." Global Attitudes Project. Washington, DC: Pew Research Center, 6 July 2006. Accessed 15 May 2012. http://www.pewglobal.org/2006/07/06/muslims-in-europe-economic-worries-top-concerns-about-religious-and-cultural-identity/

Picot, Garnett, and Feng Hou. "Preparing for Success in Canada and the United States: The Determinants of Educational Attainment Among the Children of Immigrants." Ottawa: Statistics Canada, Social Analysis Division, 2011. Accessed 20 October 2013. http://www.statcan.gc.ca/pub/11f0019m/2011332/part-partie1-eng.htm

Pipes, Daniel. "Trump: Ban Islamists, Not Muslims." *Washington Post*, 11 December 2015. Accessed 22 November 2017. https://www.washingtontimes.com/news/2015/dec/11/daniel-pipes-trump-ban-islamists-not-muslims/

Pitcher, Ben. *The Politics of Multiculturalism: Race and Racism in Contemporary Britain*. Houndmills, UK: Palgrave Macmillan, 2009.

Portes, Alejandro. "Migration and Social Change: Some Conceptual Reflections." *Journal of Ethnic and Migration Studies*, 36, no. 10 (2010): 1537–63.

Prime Minister of Canada. "Prime Minister Releases Letter of Apology to Maher Arar and his Family and Announces Completion of Mediation Process." 26 January 2007. Accessed 20 May 2013. https://www.canada.ca/en/news/archive/2007/01/prime-minister-releases-letter-apology-maher-arar-his-family-announces-completion-mediation-process.html

Privy Council. *Report of the Events Relating to Maher Arar*. Ottawa: Public Works and Government Services Canada, Integrated Services Branch, Publishing and Depository Services, 2006.

Public Safety Canada. "Building Resilience against Terrorism: Canada's Counter-terrorism Strategy," Ottawa: Public Safety Canada, 2013. Accessed 14 July 2015. https://www.publicsafety.gc.ca/cnt/rsrcs/pblctns/rslnc-gnst-trrrsm/index-eng.aspx

Rahnema, Saeedm. "Contradictions of Dissolving the Diasporas." *Journal of Community and Applied Social Psychology* 18, no. 4 (2008): 351–62.

Ramadan, Tariq. *What I Believe*. Oxford: Oxford University Press, 2010.

Reitz, Jeffery. "Assessing Multiculturalism as Behavioural Theory." In *Multiculturalism and Social Cohesion: Potentials and Challenges of Diversity*, edited by Jeffrey Reitz, Raymond Breton, Karen Dion, and Kenneth Dion, 1–47. New York: Springer, 2009.

– "Canada: Immigration and Nation-Building in the Transition to a Knowledge Economy." In *Controlling Immigration: A Global Perspective*, edited by Wayne Cornelius, Philip Martin, and James Hollifield, 97–133. Stanford: Stanford University Press, 2004.

– "Multiculturalism Policies and Popular Multiculturalism in the Development of Canadian Immigration." In *The Multiculturalism Question: Debating Identity in 21st Century Canada*, edited by Jack Jedwab, 107–26. Kingston and Montreal: McGill-Queen's University Press, 2014.

Reitz, Jeffery, and Rupa Banerjee. "Racial Inequality, Social Cohesion and Policy Issues." In *Belonging? Diversity, Recognition and Shared Citizenship in Canada*, edited by Keith Banting, Thomas Courchene, and F. Leslie Seidle, 489–546. Montreal: Institute for Research on Public Policy, 2007.

Reitz, Jeffrey, Rupa Banerjee, Mai Phan, and Jordan Thompson. "Race, Religion, and the Social Integration of New Immigrant Minorities in Canada." *International Migration Review* 43, no. 4 (2009): 695–726.

Rich, Meghan. "It Depends on How You Define Integrated: Neighborhood Boundaries and Racial Integration in a Baltimore Neighborhood." *Sociological Forum* 24, no. 4 (2009): 828–53.

Richmond, Anthony. "Immigration and Pluralism in Canada." *International Migration Review* 4, no. 1 (1969): 5–24.

Robertson, Dylan. "Never a Tougher Time for Muslim Youth, Local Leaders Say." *Calgary Herald*, 25 March 2015. Accessed 2 April 2016. http://calgaryherald.com/news/local-news/never-a-tougher-time-for-muslim-youth-local-leaders-say

Roe, Paul. *Ethnic Violence and the Societal Security Dilemma*. New York: Routledge, 2007.

Royal Commission on Bilingualism and Biculturalism. *Book IV, The Cultural Contribution of the Other Ethnic Groups*. Ottawa: Government of Canada, 1970.

Ruane, Janet. *Essentials of Research Methods: A Guide to Social Science Research*. Oxford: Blackwell, 2005.

Ryan, Phil. *Multicultiphobia*. Toronto: University of Toronto Press, 2010.

Said, Edward. *Covering Islam: How the Media and the Experts Determine How We See the Rest of the World*. New York: Vintage Books, 1997.

– *Culture and Imperialism*. New York: Vintage Books, 1993.

– *Orientalism*. New York: Vintage Books, 1979.

– *Reflections on Exile and Other Essays*. Cambridge: Harvard University Press, 2000.

Sajid, Abduljalil. "Islamophobia: A New Word for an Old Fear." *Palestine-Israel Journal of Politics, Economics and Culture*, 20, no. 2–3 (2005): 31–40.

Samuel, John, and Kogalur Basavarajappa. "The Visible Minority Population in Canada: A Review of Numbers, Growth and Labour Force Issues." *Canadian Studies in Population* 33, no. 2 (2006): 241–69.

Satzewich, Vic. *Racism in Canada*. Don Mills, ON: Oxford University Press, 2011.

Schiffauer, Werner. "Before the Law: Priorities and Contradictions in the Dialogue between the German State and Muslims in Germany." *European Journal on Criminal Policy and Research* 18, no. 4 (2012): 361–83.

Sciutto, Jim. *Against Us: The New Face of America's Enemies in the Muslim World*. New York: Harmony Books, 2008.

Scott, Eugene, and Ariane de Vogue. "Trump Says He's Calling It a 'Travel Ban'." *CNN*, 5 June 2017. Accessed 8 September 2017. http://www.cnn.com/2017/06/05/politics/trump-travel-ban-courts/index.html

Sefa Dei, George. "Speaking Race: Silence, Salience and the Politics of Anti-Racist Scholarship." In *Race & Racism in 21st-Century Canada: Continuity, Complexity and Change*, edited by Sean Hier and Singh Bolaria, 53–65. Peterborough: Broadview Press, 2007.

Seidle, F. Leslie, and Christian Joppke. "Introduction." In *Immigrant Integration in Federal Countries*, edited by Christain Joppke and F. Leslie Seidle, 3–22. Montreal: McGill-Queen's University Press, 2012.

Seljak, David, Joanne Rennick, Andrea Schmidt, Kathryn Da Silva, and Paul Bramadat. "The Challenge of Religious Intolerance and Discrimination in Canada." In *Selected Research Summaries 2006–2008*. Ottawa: Citizenship and Immigration Canada, 2008.

Shih, Margret, Diana Sanchez, Courtney Bonam, and Courtney Peck. "The Social Construction of Race: Biracial Identity and Vulnerability to Stereotypes." *Cultural Diversity and Ethnic Minority Psychology* 13, no. 2 (2007): 122–33.

Siddiqui, Haroon. "Sharia Is Gone but Fear and Hostility Remain."
     Toronto Star, 15 September 2005.
Siddiqui, Haroon. "Canada's Flawed National Census." *Toronto Star*,
     9 May 2013. Accessed 15 May 2013. http://www.thestar.com/opinion/
     commentary/2013/05/09/canadas_flawed_national_census_siddiqui.
     html
Silber, Mitchell, and Arvin Bhatt. *Radicalisation in the West: The
     Homegrown Threat*. New York: New York City Police Department,
     2007.
Sivanandan, Ambalavaner. "Poverty Is the New Black." *Race and Class* 43,
     no. 2 (2006): 1–5.
– "Race, Terror and Civil Society." *Race and Class* 47, no. 3 (2006): 1–8.
Soroka, Stuart, John Helliwell, and Richard Johnston. "Measuring and
     Modelling Interpersonal Trust." In *Social Capital, Diversity, and the
     Welfare State*, edited by Fiona M. Kay and Richard Johnston, 92–132.
     Vancouver: UBC Press, 2007.
Spalek, Basia. "Community Engagement for Counterterrorism in Britain:
     An Exploration of the Role of 'Connectors' in Countering *Takfiri
     Jihadist* Terrorism." *Studies in Conflict and Terrorism* 37, no. 10 (2014):
     825–41.
Spalek, Basia, and Mary O'Rawe. "Researching Counterterrorism: A
     Critical Perspective from the Field in the Light of Allegations and
     Findings of Covert Activities by Undercover Police Officers," *Critical
     Studies on Terrorism* 7, no. 1: 150–64.
Spencer, Robert. *Stealth Jihad: How Radical Islam is Subverting America
     without Guns or Bombs*. Washington, DC: Regnery Publishing, 2008.
Spickard, Paul. "The Illogic of American Racial Categories." In *Racially
     Mixed People in America*, edited by Maria Root, 12–23. Newbury Park:
     Sage Publications, 1992.
Stasiulis, Daiva, and Abigail Bakan. "Marginalized and Dissident Non-
     Citizens: Foreign Domestic Workers." In *The History of Immigration
     and Racism in Canada*, edited by Barrington Walker, 264–78. Toronto:
     Canadian Scholars' Press, 2008.
Sugunasiri, Suwanda. *Towards Multicultural Growth: A Look at Canada
     from Classical Racism to Neomulticulturalism*. Toronto: Village
     Publishing House, 2001.
Swimelar, Safia. "Education in Post-War Bosnia: The Nexus of Societal
     Security, Identity and Nationalism." *Ethnopolitics* 12, no. 2 (2013):
     161–82.

Taguieff, Pierre-Andre. *The Force of Prejudice*: *On Racism and Its Doubles*. Minneapolis: University of Minnesota Press, 2001.

Taureck, Rita. "Securitization Theory and Securitization Studies." *Journal of International Relations and Development* 9, no. 1 (2006): 53–61.

Tayob, Abdulkader, "Muslim Responses to Integration Demands in the Netherlands since 9/11." *Human Architecture: Journal of the Sociology of Self-Knowledge* 5, no. 1 (2006): 73–90.

Tolley, Erin, John Biles, Meyer Burnstein, James Frideres, and Rob Vineberg. "Introduction: Newcomers and Minorities across Canada." In *Integration and Inclusion of Newcomers and Minorities across Canada*, edited by John Biles, Meyer Burnstien, James Frideres, Erin Tolley, and Robert Vineberg, 1–16. Montreal: McGill-Queen's University Press, 2011.

Travis, Alan. "Hundreds of Young People Have Received Anti-radicalisation Support." *Guardian*, 26 March 2013. Accessed 30 March 2016. http://www.theguardian.com/uk/2013/mar/26/hundreds-people-anti-radicalisation-support

Trumper, Ricardo, and Lloyd Wong. "Canada's Guest Workers: Racialized, Gendered, and Flexible." In *Race and Racism in 21st-Century Canada*, edited by Sean Heir and B. Singh Bolaria, 153–91. Toronto: University of Toronto Press, 2007.

Van Munster, Rens. *Securitizing Immigration: The Politics of Risk in the EU*. Basingstoke, UK: Palgrave Macmillan, 2009.

Vasta, Ellie. "Do We Need Social Cohesion in the 21st Century? Multiple Languages of Belonging in the Metropolis." *Journal of Intercultural Studies* 34, no. 2 (2013): 196–213.

Vermeulen, Hans, and Rinus Penninx. "Introduction."In *Immigrant Integration: The Dutch Case*, edited by Hands Vermeulen and Rinus Penninx, 1–35. Amsterdam: Het Spinhuis, 2000.

Vidino, Lorenzo. "Islamism and the West: Europe as a Battlefield." *Totalitarian Movements and Political Religions* 10, no. 2 (2009): 165–76.

Waever, Ole. "Securitization and Desecuritization." In *On Security*, edited by Ronnie Lipshutz, 46–86. New York: Colombia University Press, 1995.

Walford, Geoffrey. "Classification and Framing of Interviews in Ethnographic Interviewing." *Ethnography and Education* 2, no. 2 (2007): 147–8.

Walker, Barrington. *The History of Immigration and Racism in Canada*, edited by Barrington Walker. Toronto: Canadian Scholars' Press, 2008.

Walks, Alan, and Larry Bourne. "Ghettos in Canada's Cities? Racial Segregation, Ethnic Enclaves and Poverty Concentration in Canadian Urban Areas." *Canadian Geographer* 50, no. 3 (2006): 273–97.

Werbner, Pnina. *Imagined Diasporas among Manchester Muslims*. Oxford: James Currey, 2002.

Wilcox, Shelley. "Culture, National Identity, and Admission to Citizenship." *Social Theory and Practice* 30, no. 4 (2004): 559–82.

Wilkinson, Lori. "Introduction: Developing and Testing a Generalizable Model of Immigrant Integration." *Canadian Ethnic Studies* 45, no. 3 (2013): 1–7.

Williamson, Janice. "Introduction: The Story So Far." In *Omar Khadr, Oh Canada,* edited by Janice Williamson, 3–50. Montreal: McGill-Queen's University Press, 2012.

Wong, Lloyd. "Transnationalism, Active Citizenship, and Belonging in Canada." *International Journal* 63, no. 1 (2007/2008): 79–100.

Wong, Lloyd, and Annette Tézli. "Measuring Social, Cultural, and Civic Integration in Canada: The Creation of an Index and Some Applications." *Canadian Ethnic Studies* 45, no. 3 (2013): 9–37.

Woods, Michael. "Doctors, Lawyers to Challenge Conservative Refugee Health-Care Cuts." *Ottawa Citizen*, 24 February 2013. Accessed 15 May 2013. http://www.ottawacitizen.com/news/national/Doctors+lawyers+challenge+Conservative+refugee+health+care/8009523/story.html

Wortley, Scot, and Tanner Julian. "Data, Denials, and Confusion: The Racial Profiling Debate in Toronto." *Canadian Journal of Criminology and Criminal Justice* 45, no. 3 (2003): 367–89.

Yuval-Davis, Nira Kalpana Kannabiran, and Ulrike Vieten. "Introduction." In *The Situated Politics of Belonging*, edited by Nira Yuval-Davis, Kalpana Kannabiran, and Ulrike Vieten, 1–16. London: Sage, 2006.

Zedner, Lucia. "Too Much Security." *International Journal of Sociology of Law* 3, no. 3 (2003): 155–84.

Index